I CAME OUT OF
THE EIGHTEENTH CENTURY

SOUTHERN CLASSICS SERIES
Mark M. Smith, Series Editor

I CAME OUT OF
THE EIGHTEENTH
CENTURY

JOHN ANDREW RICE

New Introduction by Mark Bauerlein
New Afterword by William Craig Rice

The University of South Carolina Press

Published in Cooperation with the Institute for
Southern Studies of the University of South Carolina

© 1942 by Harper and Brothers
New material © 2014 University of South Carolina

Cloth edition published by Harper and Brothers, 1942
Paperback edition published by the University of South Carolina Press, 2014
Columbia, South Carolina 29208

www.sc.edu/uscpress

Manufactured in the United States of America

23 22 21 20 19 18 17 16 15 14   10 9 8 7 6 5 4 3 2 1

Library of Congress Cataloging-in-Publication Data
can be foundat http://catalog.loc.gov/.

This book was printed on a recycled paper with
30 percentpostconsumer waste content.

Publication of the Southern Classics series is made possible in part by
the generous support of the Watson-Brown Foundation.

CONTENTS

Gordon Coogler, author of "Purely Original Verse"—these and other characters.

This is in sharp contrast to the first chapter, for it tells how people lived on a plantation that was poverty-stricken and run down, and ruled by another matriarchy, of aunts, who clung to a tenuous tradition of gentility even while they worked in the cotton fields. The dominance of Charleston and Charlestonian prejudices in the Low Country. Relics from the time when the plantation had been a self-contained economic unit, and ways of doing things that had not changed in two hundred years, as well as ways of thinking. An account of the boyhood and rearing of the author's father, Rev. John A. Rice, and of his doctor father before him, and an aunt by marriage who refused to be a lady.

First acquaintance with the "New South," which was the Old South falling to pieces. The beginning of the new aristocracy, the sheets-and-pillow-case aristocracy, and the downfall of the old. The Methodist Church, a curious mixture of despotism, oligarchy, and democracy, and some account of the resulting difficulties of the author's father, who had recently returned from the University of Chicago, tainted with the "Higher Criticism" that would soon bring him into conflict with Bishop Warren Candler, brother of Coca-Cola Candler. The Negro in the city, game for every unscrupulous white man. The rise of the Middle Class in the South.

The oldest boys' school in the South, among whose graduates were more Rhodes Scholars than of any school in the world. Sawney Webb, one of the founders, disciplinarian and Confederate soldier, who, with his brother John Webb, built the school to where it had no rival in the South and then almost destroyed it when he was called a "great man." John Webb, scholar, who gave the boys the finish that made them conspicuous in college but who was too modest to have allowed anyone to call him great. What it takes to be a teacher.

The story of three years at Rollins College in Florida under Hamilton Holt, former editor of "The Independent." Creating a college by publicity, and the consequence. The Professorship of Books, the only one in the world, and of "Evil," and Fishing and Hunting. A liberal college in an illiberal town, with the inevitable conflict, when the college had to decide not to be liberal. The author's dismissal, followed by the dismissal of others, and an investigation by the American Association of University Professors. What a college chapel can do to a college. The fantastic story of a trial.

The founding of a new college in the midst of the depression. A short account of the ways of educational foundations. Carnegie and Rockefeller had a wonderful idea, but no idea can be carried out by butlers. The story of six years that ended in failure. What it means to live in a pure democracy, with little or no money. Life among the artists, who were pretenders to art. Queer visitors, and some not queer, John Dewey, Albert Bames, Walter Locke. The search for the meaning of integrity. How not to start a college. How every college finally becomes European, hence unfitted to train Americans. Why the author left Black Mountain. Becoming a writer.

SERIES EDITOR'S PREFACE

Mark Bauerlein's trenchant introduction and William Craig Rice's edifying afterword to John Andrew Rice's, *I Came Out of the Eighteenth Century*, help us properly understand the life and times of an unusually keen mind. Republished in its entirety for the first time since its suppression in the 1940s, the memoir tells the story of Rice's early and middle years (from the mid-1890s to the mid-1930s). It also tells us about the South. In 1933, Rice helped establish Black Mountain College in an effort to introduce a progressive form of higher education in North Carolina. Rice was a candid man, a teller of cold truths, irking university chancellors and challenging readers alike. And, as William Craig Rice shows, it cost him. But his candor benefits us. John Andrew Rice spoke his mind with wit and acid and, in the process, left us some invaluable insights, always keen and sharp, about the South, religion, sin, education, racial injustice, slavery, poverty, southern whites, and the nature of southern politics. It is a powerful and enduring piece of southern nonfiction and is a welcome addition to the Southern Classics Series.

MARK M. SMITH

INTRODUCTION

The Witness and Wisdom of John Andrew Rice

Mark Bauerlein

Those of us who believe that a clear understanding of the past is essential to an honest, rational present are particularly fond of small facts that explode stereotypes about American history that people maintain for reasons other than knowledge. When the subject is the American South, subject as it is to simplistic and sentimental beliefs, certain records have a corrective value, each of the following, for instance:

- Today we think that the Civil War settled the nation's greatest crisis, Grant and Sherman routing the opposition, but for decades afterwards, "wherever men gathered, the Confederate veteran was present to tell how the South had been—not defeated, never that—bilked, cheated, tricked out of victory, overwhelmed. . . . 'If we'd just 'a had one more company, we'd 'a licked 'em.'"

- The idea that states have a distinctive character is quaint in our hyper-mobile society, but throughout the nineteenth century, before the New South arrived, southern states had acknowledged social identities. For example, Virginia and South Carolina were considered the only states in which gentlemen resided. The other states remained "colonial"; North Carolina was a backwater of mountain folk, Georgia was a place to which one "under suspicion of crime" fled, Alabama had "not seen enough of aristocracy to see through it," Florida did not count because it "can hardly be called a state," and Louisiana remained a "half-caste" outlier.

- We are a fairly hygienic people, with tobacco-free zones, but 120 years ago the South "was a spitting world." All working class and many middle class men chewed tobacco, and "no public place was without its receptacle." As for other options, "cigars were smoked mostly for convenience, when spitting must be restrained, or for relaxation; cigarettes were left to dudes." Women had their own habits, such as the "snuff box and dipping stick."

- Black and white boys knew their places but cooperated when they could, for instance, when whites had to don stiff new shoes after a barefoot summer: "My cousins allowed Negro boys to break theirs in and limp for a week afterward in return for one Sunday of glory."

- And this from a women's college, revealing an unexpected idol of the young: "One day I noticed a girl standing by a magnolia tree and looking with sad eyes at an inscription she had just cut in the bark . . . then I looked and saw that she had carved, 'Ruskin is dead.'"

These examples come from John Andrew Rice's edifying memoir, here republished in its complete form for the first time after its suppression in the 1940s. (See William Craig Rice's afterword for how the book's life was cut short.) The story contains enough of these instructive realities alone to justify its appearance in 2014, with the circumstances of Rice's early and middle life (roughly, 1895 to 1935) presented in one startling and illuminating vignette after another. Some of the scenes evoke shock, such as one which unfolds outside a religious camp meeting with its fringe accompaniment of "furtive dispensers of corn liquor": "I remember a farmer boy who lay on the ground in a drunken stupor while his father lashed him with an ox whip five feet long. The old man whirled the whip around his head and snarled with every stroke, 'I'll teach you not to be a sinner.'" Or, for example, this mode of maintaining order in the 1890s schoolhouse: the teacher assigned exercises to be completed in silence, then piled peach tree switches in the corner, and "by midmorning the whipping began, in the palm for the smallest, across the back for the rest, boys and girls alike."

Other scenes fill us with disgust, such as the white businessmen in Montgomery who sold goods to illiterate black residents on the payment plan, the payments never ending and the sewing machines and dishes never delivered; or the New Orleans doctor who tells Rice that if all blacks were moved to the cities, tuberculosis and syphilis would eradicate them, adding, "that's what we ought to do."

Still others astonish merely by their cosmic difference from our own time, for instance, the acute class consciousness in spite of degraded conditions. As Rice put it, "in the South Carolina of my childhood there were few or no rich, only the well-born—and they took no risk of contamination." Or consider the placement of churches, not media, social groups, or schools, at the center of youth culture, as Rice noted, "Singing School was the nearest thing to secular entertainment that we knew, and it was held in the church."

The facts of his testimony have an instructive as well as diverting impact, and we trust the witness. In a 1936 *Harper's Magazine* profile of Black Mountain College, the famous experiment in progressive higher education that Rice founded with colleagues in 1933, writer Louis Adamic described him as "intelligent, well-informed, fantastically honest and candid." That qualifier "fantastically" raises Rice's candor to essential status, and in his chronicle we sense a devilish habit of imprudence behind the discerning observations. Others find his truth-telling nothing more than sass (when he was young) and provocation (when he was older). After his mother died and thirteen-year-old John was sent to live with his aunts, Rice's father remarried, and as the couple's visit approached, John's aunts enjoyed warning him, "now you'll catch it, just you wait; she won't take any of your back talk." In his career in academia, his truth-telling irritated others, his cold judgment meeting prickly egos and turf-protectors, prompting the chancellor at the University of Nebraska, where Rice taught Greek and Latin in the 1920s, to advise him one day, "why don't you keep your mouth shut, Rice? If you would just keep it shut for, say, six months or a year, I could raise your salary. You know I can't do it now, the way you talk." (The chapter on Chancellor Sam Avery is the keenest portrait of the academic bureaucrat I have ever read.) A few years later, Hamilton Holt, the president of Rollins College who eventually fired Rice on allegations of incompetence and moral failings, including corrupting the young (an investigation by the American Association of University Professors exonerated him), asked, "Rice, why do people hate you so?"

Rice's response merits full quotation, for it rings accurate in its diagnosis of the weird psycho-dynamic that can ensnare colleagues, and at the same time it confesses Rice's own uncharitable analytical pose: "I have often wondered, and I think I know the answer. They know that, if I had the making of a world, they would not be in it. They take that thought as a desire on my part to destroy them. I don't, as a matter of fact, want to destroy anybody, but I suppose the very thought is a kind of destruction, and I can't blame them for hating."

This is an indicative expression. Perceptive and concise, the remark includes a note of self-recrimination, but will not retreat one inch from the godly decision not to let certain fellows exist. One does not know whether to smile or wince, especially as such a drastic imagining is offered in so calmly suppositional a fashion, but in either case we incline to believe Rice. His wit can cut deeply, as in this aside on a fellow professor: "He had come out of Yale dissatisfied—often said, 'I never learned anything at Yale,' a statement that had more than the one meaning he gave to it." But one suspects that Rice's targets more or less deserve it. He is as impartial and trenchant with intimates as he is with coworkers, saying of his father, himself a prominent Methodist minister and college president, that "he was admired as a man of action, but it would have been more accurate to call him a man of motion." Cotton Ed Smith served in the U.S. Senate for six terms (1909–44), a beacon of white supremacy and cotton interests, but Rice remembered him as Uncle Ellie, lovable and raucous, whose political success ruined him—"They [South Carolina voters] cheerfully helped him corrupt a brilliant mind and turn a gay and charming nature to devious ends."

When we consider how far gossip and display have overrun our culture, such moral verdicts act as a tonic, especially when Rice adds to them his psychological shrewdness. An aunt had desecrated her family by eloping with a small farmer "who could offer only affection and a good living," and the snobbish Rice family shunned her. Young John saw her only a few times, but his evaluation of the marriage reveals a sober and uncommon wisdom: "When I first saw them, some ten years later, he knew that he had stolen more woe than joy; his wife had used up all her courage in one act and now felt the weight of her guilt increasing with the years." He admired his father for his honesty and courage, especially in his unpleasant dealings with church overseers, but in this observation Rice recognized how easily principle becomes mingled with personality: "Always eager and usually willing to see the truth, he now became an unhappy martyr to his own clarity."

Rice explained broader social relations with equal clarity, his eye turning smoothly from home and family to the bizarre conditions of Southern politics and economics circa 1900. At one point, he inserted a summary of the "mutual hatred and contempt" between "po' white trash" and the African Americans beside whom they labored and neatly captures their toxic mix of insecurity and privation. Rice wrote: "The Negroes hated the poor whites because of their mean, cowardly cruelty and despised them for their social inferiority in the white world. The poor whites hated the Negroes because they were a constant menace in the struggle for a living and despised them because they were black. Many a white man in the South fights off consciousness of his spiritual degradation and holds on to some little sense of superiority by reminding himself that, after all, his skin is white." That description contains more psychological insight than most of what we read today about racism, with Rice's dispassionate idiom, with its absence of resentment and guilt, enabling him to render whites and blacks in fuller acknowledgment of their higher—and lower—humanity. Rice didn't spare the victims, either, and stated a few paragraphs later: "Slow of speech and action, they, and their children, and their children's children, clung to the rights and privileges of slavery and shunned the burden imposed by their new freedom."

To speak of slaves as enjoying "privileges," of course, offends current sentiments, and sometimes Rice's observations of African Americans, including the word "Negro" (preferred at the time), strike us as condescending. In every instance, though, he deplored the white supremacy of the time and places his criticism of ex-slaves and their children squarely in the light of social conditions created by whites. Indeed, Rice was known as a liberal, so much that a cofounder of the NAACP, President Holt, hired him to teach at Rollins College with the line, "I think it's about time I had a liberal on my faculty." Keep in mind, though, the difference between liberalism today and liberalism back then, the latter signifying more a willingness to question the authority of prevailing norms and institutions such as innate white superiority and the Methodist Church, than it did aggressive endorsement of contrary ones. Negro enfranchisement, atheism, and the like cast one as a radical, while Rice was a "gradualist" on the issue of integration, though irreligious remarks cost him dearly in professional life. Rice's liberalism sprang from a mind freed of prejudice, which led not to an attitude of nonjudgmental tolerance and an insistence on equality, but to a more rigorous and just discrimination.

One hundred years later, we lack the evidence to determine the accuracy of his perceptions, leaving the value of this voice from the past to rest upon his credibility. If we cannot test the truth of a witness' statements, as a rule, we have to rely on our judgment of his character and wisdom. Happily for us, Rice provided ample marks of his outlook ranging from capsule inferences drawn from direct experience to broad sallies on the human comedy. One could even collect them into a commonplace book for handy consultation:

"Poverty is the seedbed of piety."

"From them I learned what awful things silence can say."

"When it comes to people, clarity unwed to charity can be an evil thing."

"A man may remember his childhood with pleasure, but where is one who does not wince at the memory of his adolescence?"

"There is no way to describe existence: it can only be felt."

"Every man carries around inside himself two pictures, patterns, ideas, one of the human being as he is, one as he ought to be."

"You cannot change middle-aged men: they have to change themselves, and middle-aged teachers cannot change themselves."

"A man is a good teacher if he is a better something else."

"People think they want something new and different, think they want freedom, but what they really want is old things changed enough to make them feel comfortable."

"The young, the real young, have not yet discovered that they have a stake in not seeing the truth."

There are many more, and I quote them at length to impart the quality of Rice's *ethos*. A writer who tenders big opinions runs a great risk, for it only takes one false impression, one untimely ruling, to undermine the others and shake a reader's faith, but I have read Rice's memoir twice and found not a single dubious conclusion. Disagreeable ones, yes, and others one could challenge, but none that are wrong-headed, that make us wonder whether he registered things clearly. In his own life, to be sure, Rice made mistakes, showed poor judgment, and disappointed others, but he brought his unsparing eye upon himself as consistently as he did upon everyone else, which is another component of reliability.

Such maxims complete the tri-part justification for the republication of *I Came Out of the Eighteenth Century*. It combines crafty storytelling, historical witness, and ethical wisdom, and it should take a prominent place in the lineage of nonfiction Southern writing from Frederick Douglass to Zora Neale Hurston and Eudora Welty. Not least amongst its instruction is the overall trajectory of Rice's life, which he charted as a "spirit of opposition" whose "technique" improved as the years passed, estranging him from colleagues and straining friendships, but sustaining the precious capacity to see people and things plainly. It is, I believe, a disappearing talent precisely because of the personal costs an honest appraiser suffers, perhaps rightly so, and we should retain the example of minds and voices such as Rice's as an illuminating and difficult moral alternative to the present.

I CAME OUT OF
THE EIGHTEENTH CENTURY

CHAPTER I

Grandmother Smith's Plantation

EVERY DAY IN SUMMER AND ON WARM DAYS IN THE WINTER MY grandmother sat in her chair at the end of the long front piazza and smoked her clay pipe—a thing, I have since been told, a lady never did. But a lady did.

She did, in fact, whatever she pleased and no one had the hardihood to question. She was little and old and dried up, and attention to looks stopped at cleanliness; a stranger would not have guessed, to see her sitting there, that so much power could be lodged in so little space. The split-bottom chair was her movable throne, placed to catch the warmth of the sun; here she sat quietly puffing her pipe, meditating upon the rights and privileges and duties of a matriarch. She wore her crown as a busy queen must, on the back of her head: a generous coil to which her fine gray hair was drawn back straight from the forehead. Her steel-rimmed spectacles, impatiently pushed up on top of her head, rode out a precarious existence winking in the sun, to be used only on occasion, like false teeth and hats and corsets.

This was before the days when old women thought they could stay young, when they let themselves go in unstayed ease. There was a deep fold where bosom and stomach met, cut deeper by her apron string, a pleasant place for a small boy to warm his hands on a chilly day and useful for holding thimble, scissors, spools of thread—not needles; needles were worn high on the left shoulder, trailing from

1

their eyes lengths of black and brown and white. Her head had settled down between her shoulders and her chin was not very far from her nose. But there was no laxness anywhere. She was whole, and the full expression of her wholeness could be seen in her face, where the tiny muscles around the mouth and between eyes and ears held the flat surfaces of forehead and cheeks together in an active harmony. No part of her face ever spoke alone.

When she sat humped in her chair, her crown riding low on the back of her neck and the pipe going good, we knew that we could come to her with our troubles and our joys, all of us, children and grown-ups, black and white, and receive from her what can be got from only the very old and very good, a sort of fusion of love and justice, a thing so rare as to be without a name. Wisdom is perhaps the nearest word, though lacking in warmth.

But she could be stern. Her eyes grew sharp and pointed, as sharp and pointed as the words that came clipped from her thin and sensitive lips. A blundering male was most often the victim. She never forgot that women live in a man-made world, and she had a way with men; not, however, the way to which they were pleasantly accustomed. She had long put away everything that was female, even everything that was feminine, retaining in the armory of her old age only the intellectual trickery that is peculiar to women, a strange irrational logic that leaves men gasping and helpless.

She was gentle with women—with her three daughters-in-law, who were always being a little startled at the unruly household in which they found themselves, and with others who lived on and about the place. In general, she chose the gentler way, despising the coward precept, "divide and rule."

It was a wild kingdom when her children came for a visit, always at Christmastime and in the summer. It took skill to hold together a family of three sons and their wives, a daughter and her husband, and seventeen grandchildren, among them three orphans, ranging in age from infancy to middle youth.

The depot at Lynchburg, South Carolina, was the most exciting place in the world. I cannot remember the beginning of the journey with my mother from our temporary dwelling-place in Darlington or Kingstree or Columbia; I remember only my arrival at Lynchburg, grimy and cindery and happy. I was terrified at the snorting engine belching black woodsmoke and the lordly baggage-smasher dropping trunks from a dizzy height. My fears were matched only by the joy of greeting old Uncle Wash—coachman, blacksmith, carpenter, general handy man—and the horses again, and the lofty carriage. The step was still too high for a small boy's legs to reach, tinging with ignominy the delight of being lifted high to the driver's seat. Not that I was allowed to drive, not yet; only to sit at the left of the old man and hand him reins and whip and drink in the smells of horse and leather and Negro.

We drove over the bumpy road between fields of corn and cotton with an occasional cool cavern of pine-woods. All the while I was impatiently tugging and straining with every step of the horses to get to the end of my journey, only to be distracted to where I was by the freshly shined-up harness or the horses being different from last time, or a new whip. Happily a horsefly zoomed up and settled on the sweaty flank of a horse, to be whisked away with a skillful flick of the whip's lash. Meanwhile there was talk, questions from me to Uncle Wash as to how many puppies there were, and kittens, and calves—a thousand things, tumbling out of me so fast that the old man could hardly get an answer in edgewise.

As I twisted and turned I glanced back at my mother from time to time to see if she was happy too. She always was. Care had slipped away and she was calm and quiet, so serene that the very absence of her troubled look troubled me. She had never got used to the unrooted life of her preacher husband, who, according to a rule of the Methodist Church in South Carolina, in all the South, could not stay in one charge more than four years at one stretch; never got used, in fact, to being a preacher's wife. She took any pretext to get away and go back home. This was the reason we were always first to arrive, she and I, and later, as her family grew, my younger and youngest brothers. But this I was to learn when I was older. In these earliest years, unhappiness in others struck me a glancing blow.

We turned off from the main road into a grove of hickory trees whose roots pushed themselves out into the winding road and made the last part of the journey most precarious, as the carriage swayed from side to side and was almost turning over. When we finally came to a halt before the pillared porch my grandmother stood at the top of the steps waiting for us, to be reached through a swarm of delighted dogs, tremendous pointers and setters, whose cold muzzles left sticky patches on my face and hands. It was a mighty task to climb the gigantic steps, knee bumping chin, but to be managed unassisted. At last my face was hidden in the folds of my grandmother's apron and the top of my head pushed into her warm stomach. I was home, the only home I ever knew.

A double paneled door with fanlight above opened into the wide hall, a breeze-way in summer, in winter a chilly interval, except on Christmas day, when it was warmed by oil stoves and the long table stretched its full length. On either side of this door were narrow windows on whose panes had been pasted transparent paper designs to make them look like stained glass—only they never did, they always looked wet—and it was a delight to look through them at the many-colored trees outside.

Through this door and down the long hall Gran'ma led me, her favorite grandchild—my small hand holding on to her warm, dry fingers—just beyond the parlor to her room on the left. Here every Christmastime, promptly on my arrival, she gave me absolute proof of her love. There grew on the place a single fig tree almost Biblical in its parsimony of fruit, yet always bearing enough to make one glass of preserves. This was mine, to be eaten in aloof gluttony before the rest should come. When this ritual was over and I had eaten them all and licked the inside of the glass as far down as my tongue could reach, I set out to explore again the great plantation world.

First I went straight through the back door and along the covered runway that led to the kitchen, to greet the cook—Winifred was her name, Winnie for short—to be admired and measured and fed, and to be put through a catechism whose purpose, as I now see, was to keep me in the best tradition of the family. In the priesthood of service Winnie stood at the top, as her slave mother before her had stood, quick to detect and suppress any tendency toward change in her underlings or in the family. She was a complete conservative. What had been was to be, and life must be cut to a known pattern. As a rule I did not object —children seldom do—but sometimes I thought her prudence went too far. She boasted that for eighteen years she had not washed her head; didn't hold with head-washing, a dangerous experiment apt to bring on colds or worse. For eighteen years—it was always eighteen years (she, in common with other conservatives, had the knack of stopping time dead in his tracks)—for eighteen years she had not had a cold nor so much as a sniffle. She was also expert in the rearing of children, for had she not brought twenty-one into the world and were not seven of them still living?

The kitchen had originally been farther away from the house, when this was built in the latter part of the eighteenth century, but with the passing of slavery and the decrease in the size of households these sprawling plantation establishments had begun to pull themselves together. The old kitchen was now used as a storehouse, where, along with unimportant things, great barrels of cane syrup lay in rows, gradually to be emptied during the year, from early fall on through the following summer. When all the syrup had been drawn from a barrel, the top was knocked in and at the bottom lay a thick deposit of grainy brown sugar, rich and gooey, better than any candy, and filling.

But on this first day the house must be gone over, any alterations discovered and appraised. (A piece of furniture moved from one room to another could be disturbing.) . . . To the right of the back door was the children's playroom; to the left the dining room with a couple of bedrooms on the same side. From the hall a stairway led to the upstairs, where the layout was the same, wide hall with three bedrooms on each side. In the middle one on the left I was born, I have been told, in 1888. A big chest had stood in this upstairs hall unopened within the memory of any one then living. Later, a deed to the property was found in it, made out to a great-great-grandfather and signed by George the Third of England.

Off the front end of the upstairs hall a balcony projected over the piazza, from where I looked way down to the pediments of the four square pillars—off one of which, when I was very small indeed, I had fallen and broken my arm—and out through the pillars over the tops of the hickory trees.

The branches were now bare and the ground covered thick with brown leaves, underneath which lay the cream-colored nuts. With the swift leap of a child's imagination I was knee-deep among the leaves. The pleasantest way to gather the nuts was to wade through the leaves until you felt them bump against your toes. The best way to crack them was, not to lay them flat and smash them, but to hold them narrow side up and hit them where the shell was thinnest. In this way the halves came out all of a piece. The best implement for picking out the meat was a hairpin. The best place to find a hairpin was in grandmother's room—and safest, for she was nearsighted and scorned glasses except when she was reading or sewing. The quickest way downstairs, if no grownups were around, was by the banisters, worn slick by the crotches of one's forefathers. A swift descent landed one just in front of the parlor.

On this first day the parlor must be inspected, on others avoided, dismal as it was alike in aspect and association. Here were to be found all the family mementos, albums, enlarged photographs, an oil portrait or two, the family Bible (an excellent place to keep Octagon soap coupons)—everything that was unused or useless. It was exactly like the parlor of any of my numerous relatives, except for two things. From a whatnot in a dark corner of the room gleamed a silver cup and saucer, a memorable Christmas gift from my Uncle Coke, the bishop, to his mother. More wonderful still was a family tree made of hair, in a deep glass case, itself a wonder. The trunk of the tree was gray, the hair of some greatest-grandfather and his wife, and from this sprang many branches, topped off each with the bright yellow curl of a child. Mine was not there, for the tree was old when I was young.

Here in the parlor the family gathered on gloomy and disturbing occasions, funerals, weddings, christenings, and the reception of important unwelcome visitors, each occurrence an affliction of equal pain to children; but none so painful as the room's strangest use, for it was the seat of correction. Here we were always led for admonition or worse; but it was a question as to which was really worse, to be turned over a knee and feel the sting of a peach-tree switch and have the business shortly over with, or to sit on a horsehair sofa and suffer martyrdom down below from the stabbing hair ends while listening to a lecture on the development of character.

If in the house there were no innovations of such importance as to require justification, I set out on the long journey to the lot, the Southern name for barnyard, which lay a few hundred yards back of the main house. I might get there at last, if I could drag myself past the carriage house. This was a museum of vehicular travel in America, for here were preserved all the coaches, carriages, and buggies that the family had ever owned. That is, all except one. The most antique coach had collapsed some years before and the body been set out in the weather. Its red leather cushions were rotted, the horsehair bulged out through holes, the velvet straps were falling to pieces, and the paint was almost gone, but to young imagination it was still magnificent. In it we rode over wide western plains and fought off Indians, and in the mountains on narrow trails many a highwayman lost his life trying to capture it. From its windows were dragged bleeding victims of train wrecks. This was on fair days. If it was rainy, the carriage house became the place of slaughter. But sometimes my cousins were slaying and dying elsewhere and I curled up on a seat in the dark cool with a book. Nearby was the smokehouse, smelling of salt and brown hickory smoke, with hams and sides of bacon and links of sausages hanging from the crosspieces, and great tubs of lard ranged against the wall. If the ham in present use lay upon the chopping block, and no one else was there, I cut myself a slice and ate it raw.

It being unsafe to call on the dogs with a piece of ham in my hand, I went behind the smokehouse into the nearby garden, a world of private delight, surrounded by a high paling fence made of split slabs of hickory and oak. Against the winter sky the bare fruit trees etched themselves; I could tell them at a glance, but now I was looking for something more to eat, or rather, chew. There were turnips and the cool hearts of cabbage and collards with their broad green leaves, but these could be left for a slimmer day. There was something better waiting for me, hiding in its dark nest.

In the late fall, before the first frost, the chewing stock of sugar-cane stalks was gathered and piled in a great heap to the south of the smokehouse, where the sun would strike, and over them laid a thick matting of pine straw, on top of this a layer of earth—"dirt," we always said—and the whole mound well sodded. This was their winter bed. Close to the ground a hole was left, stuffed with straw to keep out the cold. I squatted, pushed aside the straw, felt with experienced hand for a large butt, and pulled out a stalk about five feet long, dark purple and jointed like a bamboo pole, which I balanced over my shoulder and took along until I should find someone to peel it for me, meanwhile laying it down now and then when it got too heavy.

In the far corner of the garden sat the privy, very far indeed from the house for a small boy in a hurry, but so placed for an obvious reason: scents travel far on a warm day. But I think there was another reason, seen in the countryman's contempt for the central plumbing of the degenerate city dweller. I think putting the privy so far away had something to do with the training of character. Else how explain the fact that they are still so placed in the colleges of Oxford? Oxford, when I knew it, was eighteenth century, and so was South Carolina, and the eighteenth century had a puritan hang-over. At any rate, far off in the corner of the garden sat the privy, a quiet place to take a book and read. (The mail order catalogue had not yet begun to corrupt the reading habits of the nation with its disjointed and dilettantish offerings.) It was a trifle smelly, but the scent was always the same, and children, like peasants, do not mind bad smells.

Through a crack in the fence I could see beyond the intervening cotton patch into another world. Around their quarters Negro children played, darting into sight and out among the ancient oaks, or sitting underneath the cabins, coaxing from their nests with whirling twigs the doodlebugs—little grey insects that made their home in the dust. The cabins stood high up off the ground, to keep them cool in summer and dry in winter. The oldest were built of pine logs chinked with clay, but often the clay had fallen out and on a cold winter's night the passerby could see ribbons of light broken by chair and Negro legs crowded close around the fire. When the logs of one had rotted and the roof of white-oak shingles could not be patched again, another took its place, built this time of different materials and in a different way, breaking into the row and standing out at first harsh in its newness. Two-by-fours and rough-dressed pine were cheap and nails could now be bought at the general store, no longer hammered out by hand but machine-made. But with age these cabins began to take on an unexpected beauty, as sun and rain painted them grey, mottled with the yellow of pine knots and streaked with brick red and black from resin and rusting nails.

The quarters stretched in a thin line squeezed between grove behind and cotton field in front. Down in the bottoms, where land was not so precious, the corn was grown, to be ground into meal at the water mill or fed to hogs and cattle; but here in the uplands the fields came edging close, for cotton was the cash crop and every square foot counted. The bare stalks stood now in spiny rows; in summer the fields would be a choppy sea of leaves, hiding beneath their shade dewberries, rabbit-tobacco, a dry grey weed on which we learned to smoke, and an occasional stray watermelon vine. Each field had its name, Upper Patch, Lower Patch, and half a dozen more. The House Patch lay behind the Negro quarters.

Here in the narrow space the men and women lay or sat in spots of sun, and talked and dozed—this was the slack time of the year and they could be as lazy as they pleased—the men in groups, the women in twos, one with another's head in her lap. Expert fingers searched among the stiff black wiry hairs for lice and nits, and cracked the finds between skillful thumbnails. Some of the women moved slowly between cabin and woodpile and washpot, calling to one another, scolding the children, and breaking into piercing cackles. I was tempted by the sounds, but I must first see my best and oldest friend, whose cabin was apart from the rest.

Uncle Melt, short for Milton, lived alone, for his wife Thisbe had died a year or so before. He was very feeble now; he had got his freedom nearly thirty years before and had called himself old even then. When I had climbed the steep steps I saw him sitting over by a tiny window, one of the two that lighted the single room, next to the broad hearth, in the "chimbly corner." As soon as he saw me he struggled up from his chair, leaning on his smooth hickory stick—I was white folks and he knew his place—and took my hand in his, told me I had grown a lot since last summer and was a fine-looking boy and a good boy, as he always knew I would be. Then, as if greatly surprised, he said, "Goodness gracious, where d'yu git dat stalk o' sugar cane? It sho' is a big old stalk. Where d'yu git it? You ain't stole it, is yu?" and he laughed. "No, Uncle Melt," I said, "you know I didn't steal it. I just got it out of the bed. Grandma always lets me. She always has," I said with a little uncertainty. "Sho', honey. I was jes' pokin' fun," and he drew me to him and pulled my curls. "Will you peel it for me?" I asked, but he shook his head and answered, "No, chil', I's 'fraid my peelin' days is over. My han' trimbles so I cain' hol' de knife. But yu wait. Dat triflin' little nigger Ginny'll be along in a minute to git my dinner. Yu wait. She'll peel it."

I sat down on a footstool by the wide hearth where his dinner was cooking, corn pone in the iron spider and sweet potatoes in the ashes, and we talked, the inconsequential talk of the very old and the very young. He never told me stories, nor sang, but he asked me questions and listened to the answers, and to my delight from time to time picked up with his bare fingers a live coal from the ashes and set it atop the bowl of his corncob pipe.

Ginny didn't come. "It must be nearly time for the dinner bell," I said. Uncle Melt shuffled to the door with me and inspected the shadows that the trees cast on the ground and cocked a measuring eye up at the sun. "It sho' is, it's almost noon."

From the top step I could see the big house looming immense between the mighty tree trunks, and beyond garden and smokehouse and carriage house the cotton fields stretched to the end of the world.

Growing up to a grownup's world is a trouble. When the doorknob is level with one's head, it strains young limbs to compass distances that mean nothing to one's elders; everything is built for them. When the child grows older and begins to explore beyond house and yard, it still is a trouble, for all the wonder. ("How far," a small cousin once asked, "is a little piece up the road?") But he manages it somehow, gradually and imperceptibly, and comes finally to accept his elders' sense of space, safe thereafter from the shock of an expanding world.

Not always. Old Sam Vaughan, who was a neighbor of my other grandmother in Colleton County, a low-country man and therefore dead against change, had never been more than five miles away; but he was finally persuaded by his sheepish family to travel the nineteen miles to Varnville, the county seat. When he got there he mounted the depot platform and, looking toward the horizon, said, "If the world's as big on the other side of Varnville as it is in this, it's a durn big place." It is, but we get used to it.

With time it is different. The young are immortal, for death has no meaning to them, and what have the immortals to do with time? They live in the blessed present. Yesterday is a long way off or right now, and tomorrow is only a teasing word. We have an inner clock when we are young that puts us to sleep, however reluctant we may be, wakes us up in the morning, and tells us when to eat—even the gods knock off for ambrosia—but these are part of the flow of life, taken with hardly a sense of pause. It must have been so with all, old and young, in the childhood of the race. Certainly it was so with me and my cousins, and the Negroes.

The clock is the destroyer of man's peaceful life within nature's time, which varies with the seasons, and from day to day. The farmer who objects to daylight saving as a violation of God's time is making a last vestigial stand for his right to live in nature. At the end of the last century the clock had not yet set up its tyranny in my grandmother's realm. We ate when the sun said it was time to eat, no matter what the clock said; Winnie saw to that. We consulted the clock when we had to meet or catch a train, the clock's strongest ally in clamping down on the human race and holding it in a fixed and rigid rhythm.

Trains had to move by the clock, though train operators were slow to learn that this was so. Four or five minutes this way or that makes a difference on a single-track railway, as writers of melodrama of that day knew, and the kitchen clock finally disappeared from the engineer's cab. But it took country dwellers longer to learn to watch the clock when they had to make a journey by train. It was seldom there when the schedule said it would be, but occasionally it was, and they were amazed and angry when they missed it. The Negroes sang:

Never see de like since I bin bo'n;
De people keep a-comin' an' de train done gone.

Confusion increases when time and space get mixed, when long and short begin to do double duty. From the parlor to the kitchen was in yards, feet, inches the same distance as from the kitchen to the parlor, and, if traversed at the same pace, the clock would have recorded that it took the same time exactly. But who will say they were the same with a cookie at one end and a switching at the other? To my cousins' question as to "a little piece up the road" the answer was "just a few minutes." But in those few minutes there might have been a thousand moments, or none, or a single moment that held within it all of life.

Calendar time is still more meaningless. What does it mean to be seven years old—or fifty, for that matter? Life moves through an inner chronology of experience, and every new experience is a moment in time. This moment may be fastened down later if at all—the calendar never catches up with the present—as year, month, day, by its relation to some other date, itself fixed in the same insignificant way. To say that a thing happened in one's seventh year is to say little or nothing. The history of a man is threaded on his inner chronology, his own unique private calendar. Each moment finds its place near or far from his center of being, coloring by its nearness and reinterpreting what is and what has gone before, and enlightening the future. Some moments come and go, others stay, defying the celestial clock. Those stay that are nearest what he is, his essential nature; and among them may be one

that includes them all, that is them all, and makes him at home, or a
stranger in the world.

On the covered runway between house and kitchen I met my Uncle
Ellie. After an indignant blustering refusal he peeled my sugar cane.
Beginning at the butt end he cut through the stalk below the first joint
and, with a quick flick of the knife, slit off the purple outer skin, then
quartered the pithy center and severed it this side the second joint.
I put a section into my mouth and began to chew, letting the mild
sweet sticky juice run down my throat. Then the dinner bell rang.

II

Elison Durant Smith, my Uncle Ellie, was a persuasive model of irresponsibility. Under my grandmother's eye he managed the farm, restless and restive then as afterwards under any authority. His life
revolved spasmodically around two centers, game birds and cotton.
He gave serious attention to nothing else, not even to the most beautiful bride I have ever seen, whom I for my part worshiped as only a
young lover can. Out of one preoccupation came a minute knowledge
of edible birds, out of the other a political career.

The farmer in the South was poor and growing poorer; as he worked
harder and planted more and more cotton the price went lower and
lower. He had no defense against the industrial East, which was drawing off most of the wealth of the country under the protection of high
tariffs and a benevolent government, in which he had no share. The
South came out of reconstruction in some hope, only to be most of the
time nationally disfranchised. Obliged to sell on a world market, the
cotton farmer found himself the possessor of a useless monopoly. He
was an uninspired martyr, at once pleased to keep up the war with the
Yankees and anxious for a savior.

Uncle Ellie offered himself. He proposed that they make cotton
scarce and raise the price by reducing acreage, anticipating the New

Deal by many years. There was one sour note on his trumpet of salvation: reduction of acreage had to be voluntary, for Southerners still thought they believed in states' rights, in those far-off days. But he made up for this by the shrillness of his blowing. Nothing came of the scheme, as cynics foretold, for every joiner planted more than he had the year before in the hope that others would be more honest than himself. That is, nothing came of it for the farmer; to me, as I sat at the table and listened to the debate that raged among my elders, there came a faint beginning doubt as to whether I lived in a moral world; my uncle, now known as "Cotton Ed," climbed untroubled to the Senate of the United States.

He was an evangelical politician. The world-saving strain that ran through the family was used by him for his own ends, and the vocabulary was ready to hand. At some point in every speech the Lord's will got mixed up with the boys in grey storming an impregnable height, the purity of Southern womanhood, Yankees, the glorious past and the still more glorious future, including the white man's sacred right to lynch. It was all very vague and inspiring. When the thin air of oratory had him and the audience gasping for breath, he descended to an irrelevant Negro story and his hearers yelped and spat with delight. Sometimes he became serious, but they would not have it. A voice called from the crowd, "Cut that out and tell us a story." They cheerfully helped him corrupt a brilliant mind and turn a gay and charming nature to devious ends.

He never fooled his mother. She loved him as mothers love their wayward sons, but she knew him, had always known him. Sometimes a revealing story bobbed up out of the past. When her children were small and she had to run the place under the slight handicap of a living husband, the cotton cloth used by the family was still spun and woven and dyed on the place. It was out of the last step in this process that her first public and prophetic judgment of her youngest son had come. One day her children came clamoring to her, frightened at something he had told them and hoping they were right in having called it a whopper. "It ain't so, is it, Ma? Tell him it ain't so." "Well," she said, "you know Ellie always sets his colors with lye." In his subsequent political career some of his ill-wishers were willing to acquit his mother of exaggeration.

Yet he might have been a great man, if he had only repudiated something, if he had followed his nature and quite escaped the stamp of Southern Puritanism. He never did. He half turned his back on the church, then as now the most powerful regressive force in South Carolina. In the days of prohibition, when the state was drenched with raw shine, he called it a "land flowing with milk and honey." He mouthed "white supremacy," when he knew that white-trash supremacy was ruining the state. Tears came to his eyes as his voice throbbed of Southern womanhood and the sanctity of marriage, when he knew all the time that the state was cursed with the sacrament of bigamy. He flattered and cajoled those whom he despised, a thing the thorough aristocrat would never do.

He never had the courage completely to accept or reject anything. He was half pious and half profane, half good and half bad, half honest, half everything, half slave and half free. And yet, in spite of his un-centered nature, perhaps rather because of it, I loved him very much, seeing in him something prophetic, getting a dim foreknowledge of my own struggle to find a center.

He knew every trick by which children, and grownups, could be teased, and how to coin a nickname or touch a weakness. My mother once made me throw away an already completely sucked orange, immediately, and I whined, "She wouldn't even let me lick it." I heard it for years, intoned, sung, chanted. But we children followed him around all the time, asking for it—and the dogs, for he knew how to tease them too.

He hitched up the buggy. We gathered around and chorused, "Where you goin'?" He became more intent on the harness. "Where you goin'?" we shouted. Not a word from him. We chanted, "Where you goin', where you goin', where you goin'?" "To Dienomo," he said. This enraged us. "Aw shucks, Uncle Ellie, where you goin'? Where?" "I told you," he said. "Didn't you hear me? To Dienomo." We danced around, ecstatic with curiosity and hope, for he might relent and take some of us with him. But he climbed up into the buggy, and, as he picked up the reins, lifted his voice in familiar song, known to every Methodist:

y-y

a-

wa-a

I'm goin' a

To di-i-ie

no

mo-

o-re

"Dienomo" meant "none of your business."

Sometimes, instead of driving away, he sat thoughtful for a moment, as if he had forgotten something important, climbed down again with a deep frown on his face, passed us without a glance, and went back into the house. This was maddening. Often, for he was without pity, he returned and drove away singing his hateful song; sometimes he came back with a gun over his shoulder—this for the dogs—and sometimes, sometimes, with a bundle of fishing poles under his arm.

His brother the bishop, my Uncle Coke, was different. He was all of a piece. I think my grandmother never looked at her eldest without astonishment that she should be the mother of such a son. He was tall and bearded like Christ and in his nature like Christ in Christ's milder moments. Every gesture of his hands, every word he spoke, was part of a greater harmony. He was always just, always calm and kindly, never pompous nor patronizing, as the approved good are apt to become: really a saint, a born saint, for he never knew how to be anything else. He was a walking law of love with no conception of the law of hate, shaming people into momentary acceptance by the simplicity of his belief. To listen to him preach was like getting quietly drunk. He led his hearers by easy stages into an unreal world of effortless peace, drugging them gradually into unconsciousness by the melody that was himself. They went home to eat their big Sunday dinners in dazed silence and remain befuddled until Monday morning, when they woke up and went about their business.

The politicians in the Methodist Church, among whom were most of those in positions of importance, not knowing what to do with such slippery goodness, and, since they were Christians by definition, being constrained from telling his admirers what they really thought of him, elected him bishop and thereafter let him alone and stayed out of his way as far as they could. They were often upset by his guileless appointment of good men—my father among them—to charges they wanted for themselves or their friends. Their hatred of him was almost un-Christian, equaled only by the admiration of his disciples. The legend of this glandular Christian still persists. I have met people whose eyes filled with tears at his name, and who, befogged by memory, assumed to my discomfort that I had inherited collaterally his unsalted virtues. I did not dislike him; I was numb in the presence of his perfection; but I had a queasy misgiving of the article of my grandmother's creed that said whatever he did was right, for even the good may blunder. She steadily refused to admit what she knew to be true, a bad example for the young. In Uncle Ellie this deliberate blindness of his mother roused blasphemous disgust.

The bishop's wife, Aunt Kate, did her best work from Monday through Saturday. Like many preachers' wives, and most intelligent Southern women, she had no respect for the church; but, after all, her husband was a bishop, and she made the best of it. While he was being good, she was seeing to it that goodness did not go unrewarded. She was shrewd and ambitious, for him and for her seven children, most of whom, particularly her sons, disappointed her by inheriting an overplus of her husband's virtues—one unworldly member of a family was enough. She was too kind to despise the poor, but she loathed poverty and providently preferred as her associates those whom Hamilton had called the "rich and well-born." She had an eye for investments, social and economic, and when her husband died in his early fifties she had accumulated enough in the way of connections and money, supplemented by her pension, to put all her children through college and send them out into the world tagged with magic letters—one of them even got a Ph.D. She had the American belief in education, as end and means; had educated herself, in fact, after her marriage. She often sat by a child's cot, heavy book in hand, reading to catch up with her learned husband, and when she was called away she tucked the book under the mattress for safekeeping until she could hurry back.

Years later when I saw her again in Florida, where I had gone to perform the experiment of trying to be teacher in Rollins College—the experiment resulted in an explosion—she was still avidly reading, now over seventy years of age. She had acquired a mellow, half-cynical wisdom, with which she was now pushing her grandchildren to greater affluence. I always liked her very much.

Every Christmas, as the day approached which was to herald the bishop and his family, who were the last to arrive because they lived far away in Virginia, we were all a little subdued, but Uncle Ellie was like a bird dog on the first day of hunting, nervous and skittish, wondering how the sport would be this year. Quiet and solemnity settled down over the household as we awaited the advent of the man of God. He stepped gracious and serene from the carriage and ascended the front steps to greet his mother and bestow upon her this year's gift.

This was the moment Uncle Ellie had been waiting for, craning and impatient to see what it was, to what uses it could be twisted. One year it was a "fascinator," a knitted scarf that fashionable ladies wore over their heads. As long as the bishop's visit lasted, Uncle Ellie would never let her be without it, always solicitous lest she catch cold, knowing perfectly well how she hated anything on her head. Another time the gift was a wicker sewing basket, which her attentive youngest son fetched from her room and set beside her as she sat smoking on the porch. In the bishop's presence he praised his generosity, hinting that it must have cost great sums to buy such things. How could he do it on a preacher's salary, even a bishop's salary? There were references to munificence of former years: the silver-backed comb and brush; the gold thimble, which, though it had unfortunately been lost, was, he supposed, not irreplaceable, if one had the price; and the silver cup and saucer always. He never allowed her to forget the one time she had tried to use it, and burnt her lips. Thus in the bishop's presence. When he got his mother alone, the attack was direct and he never let up.

It was still pleasanter when the discomfort of others could be added to hers. He, and Winnie the cook, and everybody who drank coffee, never forgot the new-fangled drip-pot that came one year. All through vacation it was used, every time only after a tussle with the cook— coffee was meant to be boiled, she said—and at every meal extolled by my grandmother, looking this side and that, but never at the other end of the table where a pair of glittering eyes were trying to catch hers. Sometimes he joined in with the ambiguous "I never tasted such coffee in my life," or "Do you think it's the roasting that makes the difference, or is it all due to the pot?" or he sent a message to the cook asking how on earth she made such coffee. Meanwhile Winnie was doing what she could to bring disgrace on the pot, but each time swearing that she had done exactly what she had been told to do. "Tain' my fault," she said to my grandmother afterward in the kitchen, "I don jes' whut yu said to do. I put de coffee in here and de water in dere, an' tain' my fault ef t'wan fit to drink. I don't wanta mess wid it nohow," but she had to mess with it, as long as the bishop was there.

When he was gone and the new pot had reached its permanent resting place on the top shelf in the kitchen, and the cook and the old-fashioned pot had been restored to grace, the storm broke in the open. I could never tell exactly what was being talked about, the pot, the bishop, or the coffee, or all three at once, but there was no doubt about the effect on my grandmother, who ducked and dodged and sometimes cringed at the stream of scornful invective that flowed from the other end of the table. But she never said a word.

More amusing to the young was the bishop's Christmas present of another year, an automatic fan to keep the flies off the dinner table. This was before the days of screened houses, and flies were plentiful and hungry. Usually a little Negro boy stood at the end of the dining room and manipulated a contraption that hung from the ceiling, made of newspapers cut in strips, tacked to crosspieces of wood and worked by a set of pulleys. But sometimes he was absent, officially on account of illness duly attested by as many witnesses from his family as were thought likely to lend a touch of verisimilitude. On these occasions the duty fell on one of us, the unfortunate young, and the debate that raged among the grandchildren as to who should be, should not be, had been, had not been the victim, was quite as bad as the flies.

The new machine was to do away with all this bother. From a heavy base that contained a ratchet-spring arrangement, which was to make it whirl, an iron rod projected upward and to this were fastened horizontally two cloth wings. These were to shoo the flies. Christmas day was appointed for its first use, at dinner. We all gathered early, none earlier than Uncle Ellie. My grandmother showed some misgivings, I thought, for she had neglected to try it out first, but she sat bravely at the head of the table, with the bishop on her right, looking down the long table at her children and their children, seventeen of them, but not at her youngest, poised at the far end. I, the chosen one, the favorite, was told to turn the switch and—well, to this day, as I write, I can feel the surge of consternation, joy, shame, laughter, tears, chagrin, hatred of the ogre at the foot of the table and companionable love for him, and love for my grandmother, and hatred of her too; but for the bishop, hatred, pure and simple. The wings barely moved.

My Uncle Charlie stood halfway in years and nature between the bishop and the brother who was afterwards to become the senator, with unused virtues that neither had. Following the example of his elder brother and tradition—my grandfather on this side the family had been a lay preacher, that is, a layman ordained to preach, a thing not uncommon in sparsely settled parts of the country in the middle of the nineteenth century—Uncle Charlie had early given himself to Christ. But not entirely, not completely, and very rashly. There was in him a fierce passionate nature impatient of the restraints of piety, even of civilization.

Hands that longed for plow or axe or hoe to connect him with the earth were clumsy for Bible and benediction. A mind that moved intuitively in the world of nature halted and stumbled and was confused among the subtleties of theological disputation. Farmer turned preacher, a loss to civilization and no gain to the Kingdom of God, he blundered through life hurting and being hurt, trying to be a good Christian, trying to find out what a good Christian was, and never being able to understand. He had gone through college and theological seminary, a medium credit to the family according to the records, learning by rote mathematics, Latin, Greek, Pauline theology and theories and arguments about the Virgin Birth, salvation by Grace, the atonement, remission of sins, the nature of the Trinity, the fatherhood of God and the brotherhood of man, without the slightest notion of what any of it meant. When he stood in the pulpit he was a ventriloquist's dummy. The words he had learned flowed through him and left the man he was untouched.

He was always angry, with himself and with the world, especially when he was with his two clever brothers, alienated from both by his lack of their kind of brains but pulled toward the one by the paganism that was in him and toward the other by his desire for peace. He never found peace, and when his untamed soul could bear it no longer he broke out in a rage that was nearly madness. Afterwards awful guilt enclosed him and he slunk about the place intolerable alike to himself and us. Sometimes he could not endure his shame, and there was always speculation among the family as to whether he would stay out the full time of the holidays. We never knew when he would suddenly depart, trailing behind him a desperate wife and children.

We also never knew what would set him off. Once he thoughtlessly suggested on Christmas Eve that the men should hang up their socks beside the children's stockings in the parlor, to see what Santa Claus would do for them. The next morning he found in his sock, put there, of course, by his younger brother, a quid of chewed tobacco and the barn key. This was a double insult. Quids, when they had been thoroughly chewed and there was no more juice left in them, were saved as smoking tobacco and given—I record this with shame, acquired considerably later—to Uncle Melt. The key was a subtle, but not too subtle hint that Uncle Charlie go out to the barn and feed the horses, and, a turn that no one else had thought of, conjured up out of an enraged spirit, that he do a little work to pay for his board. As he packed up to go, pushing his helpless and dismayed family this way and that, he returned again and again to the charge, deploring his poverty, the more galling in that others, from whom he might have expected a little sympathy, lived like princes on the "fat of the land" while he scratched and scraped to make a living for his wife and tender babes—one, at least, of whom was tough as nails. We stood aghast as he exploded from the house and hurled his wife and tender babes, by no means tenderly, into the waiting carriage. He had to drive only four miles to the depot at Lynchburg and would have to wait there six hours for a train, but anger has no sense of time. We stood awkward, silent, looking down at the floor and up at the sky, but not at one another. When we went into the house, we found, in a long row on the parlor mantelpiece, all the presents that had been given his family on that Christmas morning.

But children loved him, and the bird dogs loved, and feared him, for he was as keen after a bird as they, and when they failed to retrieve they understood his threatening rage. I have seen him stand over a quivering, whimpering dog damning him in gorgeous Biblical language, the finest medium of abuse ever invented—and ten minutes later he and the dog would be congratulating each other on a magnificent shot. When I went with him I was as eager as the dogs, but cautious, for I had learned what I must do when the dogs pointed. I fell flat on my face. As the covey rose the hunter saw only the whirring partridge, and nothing in between. Into the killing of little birds he poured all his lusty uncentered life, easing the pain of frustration and disappointment.

One night I was prowling around upstairs when I should have been in bed—the life my elders lived apart from us was a gnawing mystery— and, passing by his room, saw him kneeling by the bed with his arm about his wife's shoulders. The next day, with unusual boldness, I asked her for an explanation. She told me that they said their prayers this way because, when Uncle Charlie prayed alone, he often went to sleep on his knees. "Now," she said, "when I feel his arm slipping down, I can wake him up. He doesn't catch cold any more." The service of the Lord is not easy for a divided soul.

III

Uncle Charlie had an only son just my age. When the two of us were very young, I have been told, our parents compared us point by point and I came off the loser, for Pinckney's head was much larger than mine. His father gloated, but as the child grew older his head became huge, out of all proportion to his thin body. Then they found that he could not walk, could barely move his spindling legs. He was paralyzed from the waist down, a hopeless cripple with an enormous head, bril-

liant and useless. I think my uncle felt the wound most deeply when
he went hunting and had to leave his son behind, alienated from him
in this his fullest joy, a son whose genius of mind had already put a
gulf between them.

Pinckney was the first to lead me into the world of recorded imagination. Since he could not move about as the rest of us did, he had a huge
pile of books on the floor—we had to live on the floor because it was
difficult for him to get into his wheel chair. We read them all, Henty,
Alger, Scott, Marryat, weird books of travel, almanacs, an occasional
catalogue, Stevenson, McGuffey's readers, all of them, Dickens, even
the Bible, reverently. In later years I did not feel free to ruin my eyes
by reading twelve glorious hours on end, lying propped against the
wall in a bad light.

The children's room was just off the runway, a few steps from the
back door, insuring the hall against too much tracked-in mud, and our
elders in some measure against noises peculiar to the young. In the
room was one piece of furniture, a big four-poster bed, but it was full,
of us and the things we brought in, and the animals. There were cats,
and kittens in peril of being squeezed to death in loving hands; small
turtles and snails, marking their glistening pattern on the floor; frogs
in all stages of growth, from strings of eggs to tadpoles and on to
mighty monsters, a terror to the very young and a danger to us all, for
we knew it was of their nature to cause warts. June bugs tied to strings
zoomed about, bashing themselves against the wall and landing in the
hair of little girls, accidentally. There were home-made cages for
squirrels, and an occasional young wild rabbit, but these always got
away; and disappointing chameleons, for they never turned anything
but green or brown, try them as we would. There were bird dogs in
plenty, waddling pups and hardy perennials, among them the rheumy
old hero Pompey whose reputation as a mighty hunter grew with his
senescence and whose death was to send a flame of sorrow throughout
the family connections, grief such as follows few great men.

Usually we played out of doors. Then, if the adventure was very important and its scene was near enough the house, we took our crippled cousin Pinckney along, bumping him down the steps and hauling him up into his wheel chair, all the while receiving from him directions and admonitions delivered in erudite circumlocution, a gift we all admired and none envied for even I couldn't go big words. The only person on the place who emulated him was a young Negro given to language and, probably therefore, with a leaning toward the saving of souls. Evidently he was not uniformly successful, to judge from the peals of laughter that came from my cousin as he rocked the wheel chair in his mirth, rolling his great head from side to side. But wherein the error lay, we did not know and did not care, for we had taken no learning as our province.

One of the favorite places to play on a rainy day was the shed in which the cotton seed were stored, in the hope that then seemed vain that they might some day be useful. It was huge, filled with valleys and mighty mountains of seed. We climbed and slid and fought battles, and got cotton seeds up our noses and in our ears, and breathed lint and were generally and severally uncomfortable, but in a world of our own. (This was forty-five years ago and Progressive Education had not yet reared its benignant head.) Children were still allowed, and encouraged, to keep to themselves and mind their own business, to be "seen and not heard," and preferably not even seen, provided they kept out of mischief—as amiable nuisances, in fact. We ate at a separate table, except on festival occasions, and had, therefore, a polity of our own, governed by and governing ourselves. Except when the fight got too hot we never appealed to our elders, and even then the plaintiff lost caste, for he was convicted thereby of seeking justice. I was later to see that here began in me the conflict between human and personal relations, the deep suspicion of ulterior motive in the imposition of "rules" for the conduct of life, resentment of the pattern that was slowly but firmly being pressed down on me.

And yet I had already accepted without question—that was to come much later—some of the figures in the pattern. I can remember clearly one that I recognized first among the cotton seed. The cousin whom I was to marry—I have not seen her since I was thirteen; I think her name was Isabel—whom I adored with complete blindness, was leaning over digging a hole, exposing to view her precious bottom. Another cousin, male and brutal, saw, not what I saw, but a target, and, picking up a shingle, gave it a resounding wham. From this moment dates my acceptance of the belief that was once enclosed in the words "sanctity of womanhood." Try as I will, and I have tried very hard, I have never been able to rid myself of the belief, of a something deeper than belief, that women are superior to men, that men are pretty common and cheap stuff compared to them. I am unable to argue the matter. When I am exposed and attacked, more often by women than men, I am helpless. I sit dumb and angry beneath the shower of scorn, dumb because I cannot explain, angry at being made an outcast from decent society, but I emerge unwashed of my sin.

I know as well as anyone what a shoddy thing Southern chivalry is, what an insult to women, how it has been used by politician and ecclesiastic to keep the world in the hands of men, and by women to sneak from men some of their power, coiling and slithering around with their perpetual charm, to what rotten ends it can be put in the war between black and white. But all the same, I believe that these are perversions of something that is good, just as Southern Methodism, and not only Methodism, is a perversion of Christianity.

It is a strange mixture, this chivalry. Within it men live, not only bigamous lives, but actually two separate and distinct lives. And yet some decent women have been able, within it, to find for themselves a wider expression for what they need than Northern women have got out of their sham equality. Its very vocabulary betrays its inner discord, partly Biblical, partly sheer poetic license, partly imitation Sir Walter Scott. To this day, in the low country, you can hear heralds in jousting tournaments mouthing about queens and kings, fair ladies and gallant knights, love and beauty, doughty deeds, and all the rest.

We boys were all the glorious heroes of chivalry, and the girls played their parts, too, but with increasing reluctance, for they were already beginning to see that their hope of survival lay in keeping their intellects clear. (Let no one suppose that Southern women, when they are being feminine, are unaware of what they are doing. They can turn the juice on, and off, with perfect control.) But we knew, and herein we differed from the men, that we were play-acting; yet all the time we were unconsciously tempering and testing and perfecting a weapon that we were later to use in defending ourselves against reality.

In another area of our life, our relation with the Negro children, we were learning to live in two worlds. As playmates they were our equals, and it is for this reason, I think, that I find it difficult to distinguish in memory between them and my cousins. And not only our equals, but growing up as we were always never being but becoming, they changed so rapidly that they will not stay put in time. But when night came, and we went to the house and they to their cabins, we drew apart into different and incompatible worlds.

Sometimes these two worlds came into sharp and painful conflict, and all that I was cried out against the separation. At one time there was much talk of migration back to Africa, a scheme hatched by some rascal to mulct the Negroes, and the debate between the children and the cook raged violently. But we were always defeated, not by her words, for we were her match in speech, but by her fierce longing for a place that she could call home, which reduced us to hurt and angry silence, hurt because she was willing to leave us, angry because deep inside we knew that she was right.

Another time we were apart was on late summer afternoons, but on these occasions with anticipations of pleasure such as to draw the sting. When we saw the watermelon wagon coming up from the spring house, we dropped into oblivion Sir Arthur and his whole round table, herds of buffalo, Sitting Bull and Ivanhoe, scalps and tomahawks, spears and shields, Noah and his ark. We raced one another to the tables under the great oak at the back of the house, but here we divided, the Negro children to sit at the table by the smokehouse, we at the longer table in the yard. A mighty battle ensued, greater than the one we had just abandoned, as we pushed and shoved to get a place near the head of the table, for it was here that Uncle Ellie cut the melons. We sat and rocked on our haunches with impatience while our elders with maddening leisure strolled to the benches farther down. At last the first melon was brought and we craned over the tables as the knife touched its wet glistening skin, waiting and hoping for the sharp splitting sound that would tell us it was ripe. This, however, was only a minor ordeal, for, after the two halves were exposed, my uncle had to decide whether it was good enough for us to eat, and he worked us up to a frenzy of hunger and exasperation as he turned it this way and that, hemmed and hawed and hesitated, completely unaware of our presence and greatly surprised when we finally broke out in a roar. If the melon passed the test, he cut the halves into quarters and we began to dig in, that is, four of us did. The agony was repeated until each had his first go. With the first quarter the pangs of hunger were beginning to be relieved, and thereafter we began to be attentive to the method of his judgment. To this day anyone who sat at that table can tell a good watermelon at a thump and a glance. If the melon did not pass his scrutiny, it was passed on to the Negro table. If they were able to endure, they in turn passed it back to the wagon to be fed to the hogs, for they knew that by and by the good ones would begin to come their way, when we had filled our stomachs to complete distention (sometimes a whole wagonload of melons would be cut in one afternoon) and sat belching at ease.

Presently we began to flip the wet seeds from between thumb and forefinger, carelessly and tentatively at first, then, if our elders did not stop us, trying for direct hits. If even this did not rouse them from their lethargy, if no "Stop that this very minute" came from their end of the table, we essayed and sometimes succeeded in carrying on the greatest sport of all, for there is no better weapon or missile than a watermelon rind. The trouble is that after a watermelon fight you have to take a bath, and at this time of day it was too late to go swimming. We were beginning to learn to take the bitter with the sweet.

There was the bitter and the sweet of curls. Every boy in those days had to wear them, for this was the end of the nineteenth century and the dying age dripped away in the liquid putrescence of little Lord Fauntleroy. Sundays were a horror with velvet suits and lace collars and inspected cleanliness, but every day began in tears as my impatient and abstracted mother combed and curled away. Yet there was sweetness mingled with it, for a child will endure much to have the attention of his mother, and my mother was not overattentive to her children as a rule, given rather to sudden bursts of affection after long periods of vague unhappiness. Often she would stand at a window, apparently, to the casual observer, completely absorbed in what she was looking at outside, but in reality her gaze was turned toward some strange and inexplicable trouble. All the same, the curls were a nuisance and I looked longingly forward to my eighth birthday and promised release, when I should no longer have to envy my nine-year-old cousins their manly looks. Finally the great day came, and after I had inspected and appraised the various gifts I climbed gaily into the high chair and felt the longed-for towel being wrapped around my shoulders. My cousins stood in a circle, all eager to take part in my transition from baby- to boyhood. My grandmother alone added a note of vague discomfort as she sat in her split-bottom chair at the corner of the porch twisting her tobacco bag in strange distraction. But all else was joy as my mother raised the scissors and snipped off the first curl. Then, when I saw it lying on the floor, I let out a wail of despair. For the first time in my life I was meeting the shock of sudden change.

The next day I had become accustomed to the feeling of unwonted lightness and all my pain was pushed back into forgetfulness as I stood before the looking glass and slicked and slicked my hair back to look as near as I could make it like my cousin Gaston's.

He was an alien, this cousin Gaston, in the boisterous world of my grandmother's, one of the three orphans left by Aunt Fanny. Outside the circle of our life he swung in an orbit all his own, detached and dreaming, wandering from the piano and back to the piano, to strike a single chord or sit hours on end playing to himself, snatches of this and that recognizable piece interspersed between long intervals of strange personal music. When the fit was on him I would slip behind the piano and let the music flow through me until I no longer knew where or what I was. Here was another language, and, when he had finally stopped and walked away without looking at me, I drifted about the place trying to accustom myself again to the harshness of speech and other meaningless noise; for, compared to music, all other noises were trivial and thin, tied forever to things and pictures of things, seldom breaking away into the realm of pure meaning. At the time, of course, I did not put it to myself this way, I did not put it to myself in any way at all; I simply lived in the music, whole and complete, and comfortably alone. Even now I feel guilty of paradox and only the old habit of putting everything into words is my excuse for trying to reduce this first experience of music to their brittle cacophony.

This feeling of music must have been going on in Gaston all the time, and sensitizing him not only to itself but to the world outside, for he visibly shrank when he knew that others were thinking about him. Not that they did very often, but once a year he and his two sisters became the subject of loud and insistent debate. They were orphans. My mother's sister had been caught in the tide of missionary evangelism that swept over a guilty world toward the end of the nineteenth century, and had followed a futile young husband out to Brazil, where

he was shortly afterwards to find in death final release from responsibility, leaving her with three tokens a year apart in age. She had returned to her mother's home, lived a few years, and died. Her three
children were the family's charge, and, while any member of the family
would cheerfully have assumed the burden if there had been no one
else to do so, no one would be put upon by the rest, not even the
bishop, under the vicarious eye of his wife. By unspoken agreement
consideration of "what to do with Fanny's children" was put off until
after Christmas day. It began in a slow tempo, with quiet observations
as to how the children looked since they had last been seen, how they
were getting on in their school work, whether they seemed happy, what
they were going to do when they grew up. But, although they really
meant their interest, this was merely tuning up. The real thing was
yet to come, the debating, the scoring of points, the introduction of
feminine irrelevancies, the complete forgetting of the children as human
beings. And it was a public debate, carried on anytime, anywhere, at
meals and between meals, with an occasional yawning silence as they
realized that the subjects of their wrangling were listening. I used to
wonder why my grandmother sat long without speaking, patient and
slightly bored, for it came up every year and nothing new was ever
said, nor did I ever cease to be surprised at the way it came to an end.
But as I look back on it now, I see her wisdom in letting her passionate
family talk themselves out.

Uncle Ellie was characteristically the first to tire of philanthropy and
bring matters down to earth with a query: who was to pay, and how
much. At this the bishop and Uncle Charlie shifted uneasily in their
chairs; and my father, who sat an unwilling participant, averse to
being drawn in for several reasons. He never allowed himself or them
to forget that he was an outsider from the low country, where if you
were not the best you were nothing. He was afraid of my mother's
sharp tongue and Uncle Ellie's violence, and—I record with reluctance
—alarmed at the prospect of having to help with money.

The principal expressed antagonism was between my mother and Uncle Ellie, although underneath it all they were allies, secretly gunning for the bishop. But he always acted as the peacemaker, blandly unaware. His wife knew they were after him, and why. He was as yet the only brilliant success in the family, an offense hardly to be endured.

Uncle Charlie was miserable, for he was wretchedly poor and his crippled son was burden enough for any man to bear. So tethered, he tried to keep silent, but he dearly loved a fight and sometimes he threw discretion away and plunged in, with dread and foreknowledge of the blow that was to knock him out.

Finally, when even the small children began to feel they could not stand any more of the row, my grandmother spoke, and all was peace. Sometimes, usually, it was a single sentence, but it contained all justice; it was, in fact, what everyone had known all the time it would be. The sun came out, the birds sang, and all of us went happily about our business. All except Gaston. He wandered about like a stranger, completely cut off and alone, for the debate had been more than words to him. Even I, who loved him best, stayed away from him.

IV

If Winnie the cook had known of heraldry, she might have demanded as her crest a double-headed eagle, like that of another monarch whom she has followed into oblivion, for she ruled two kingdoms, one of them not easy to define and harder still to justify. She was head of the house Negroes, the aristocracy of her race, and also the chief social arbiter of our world. From her and those under her immediate sway I got my feeling of superiority, the tentative approach to aristocracy. She and they saw to it that we children should be and remain uncontaminated by contact with "po' white trash."

Among the dependents on the plantation, a small world, but large enough to inculcate its prejudices everywhere in the South, were the landless whites, descendants of landless whites, tenants and farm hands, who called for the nicest discrimination in their handling. They lived in a half-world between the landowners, the gentle and almost gentle, and the Negroes, by whose side they were often obliged to work in the fields. Between them and the Negroes burned mutual hatred and contempt. The Negroes hated the poor whites because of their mean, cowardly cruelty and despised them for their social inferiority in the white world. The poor whites hated the Negroes because they were a constant menace in the struggle for a living and despised them because they were black. Many a white man in the South fights off consciousness of his spiritual degradation, holds on to some little sense of superiority, by reminding himself that, after all, his skin is white.

In the middle and upper classes—I never learned to use these handy and misleading importations until later; "quality" was inclusive—every child acquired from the Negro servants an inner sense, a touchstone, a delicate instrument of measurement, an added faculty that was to plague and bless him all his life. I did not need, never needed, to be told; there was direct, immediate knowledge of another's social status. I learned to see people not as compounds, the bane of the psychologist, but as fusions, wholes, complete entities. The removal of a single blemish would not change the result. In fact, the aristocrat could do exactly the same thing as his opposite and remain the aristocrat. The distinction lay deeper than the world of action, somewhere in the world of being. But I had to learn for the most part from my elders the responsibility that went with one's status in this confused world.

Irresponsibility, easeful death-in-life, made its lazy bid. All the Negroes on the place—field hands, who sat contented at the bottom of the social scale, and house servants—were descendants of slaves. A few still lived who had moved from one world to another when they were already old and accustomed to their lot. Slow of speech and action, they, and their children, and their children's children, clung to the rights and privileges of slavery and shunned the burden imposed by their new freedom. They stumbled about laughing in the half darkness, slyly choosing whatever was to their advantage in their old life or their new. If treated as slaves, they became instantly, sometimes aggressively, free; if as free, they retreated into slavery. The question was, where they could find the greater comfort, more ease in Zion. Not all of them, of course, not Winnie and her kind; but this was the pattern.

The sanctions of slavery were gone—no one on the plantation was allowed to punish them, however great the provocation—and no effective new sanctions had come to take their place, for they did not want much money, the white man's sanction. I can remember the time when, if they were paid at the rate of fifty cents a day, they worked six days; if a dollar a day, they worked three. All they wanted was three dollars a week. (I record this without disapprobation. On the contrary, I think they showed sense.) They were sometimes dismissed, but that was no great hardship, because most of their wants were satisfied much as they had been under slavery. They had shelter—eviction was unknown on my grandmother's place—and if food got scarce they could beg or borrow (the same thing) corn from their more opulent fellows, and there were rabbits and 'coons and 'possum—they all had dogs. They might resort to theft—chickens were a real temptation—but this more obscure form of borrowing was rare, not exactly within the code. (With firewood it was different. The morning after the first cold snap of the winter the pile of wood in the back yard had invariably disappeared. Sometimes Uncle Ellie was exasperated to the point of outburst even against the venerable: "In the name of all that's good and holy, Uncle Melt, why don't you cut your own wood, while the weather's warm?" "Providence will provide," replied the tolerant old man.) They might even go so far as to take a job on another plantation, an extreme expression of disapproval of the treatment they had received, but this was frowned upon by their families and neighbors as being a breach of loyalty. After all, if the white folks didn't know any better, they at least did.

Living close-packed in their cabins, one family in a single room, knowledge was transmitted easily from generation to generation. There was little that my Negro playmates did not know in certain areas of life, and willingly impart to me and my cousins, employing good Anglo-Saxon monosyllables. (At that time I knew no word that covered all these matters, except sin. Twenty-five years later, when I was teaching in the University of Nebraska, nice people had a different word. The Dean of Men used to say, "We have no immorality here," by which he meant that, in so far as he could avoid knowing, there were no illegitimate babies.)

Their whole life was an easy community. A Negro was seldom seen alone. If he was, he was asleep. They swarmed in and out of each others' cabins, went to church in groups, worked when they could together—at corn shucking, cane grinding, cotton chopping, hoeing, hog killing—whenever they were paid by the day. Even during cotton-picking time, when each was paid according to the amount he brought in at night, they bunched together in the late afternoon in one part of the field and sang.

One evening at supper Uncle Ellie said, "Cotton picking tomorrow," and instant excitement spread among the children, for this meant wealth for all. Furious argument and calculation went on about the table, so many pounds a day at half a cent a pound—we were paid at the same rate as the Negroes—so many more days until school began and we had to go home, so much for a bicycle, so much for a pony, so much for anything a boy or girl longed for, wild spending. I alone sat in troubled silence. Finally I had the courage to ask, raising my voice above the clamor, "What field are you going to start in?" "What'd you say?" said my uncle. "What field?" I shouted. He knew, from the look on my face that the question was important. "What'd you say?" he asked again, cupping his hand to his ear. "What field?" I screamed, silencing the others into curiosity. "Oh," he said, scratching his chin, "what field? Now let me see if I can remember. I think, yes, I think [drawing it out] I think we will begin with the—er—Upper Patch." I could have slain him in spite of my relief.

My watermelon lay in the middle of the House Patch. It sometimes happened that a stray watermelon seed found itself in a row of cotton, and escaping the chopping hoe of a Negro or the scrape of the passing plow, sent out its vines after the cotton had been laid by and grew in safety but with little sun under the broad grey-green dusty leaves of the cotton plants. I had discovered this one in my wanderings and every day, sometimes several times a day, I went to look at it and feel and thump it. It was safe for a while.

The next morning after breakfast—the Negroes had been in the field since daybreak, but we needed our sleep—each of us gathered together the equipment needed by a professional cotton picker: a straw hat, to avoid sunstroke, for it would get very hot in midafternoon of this long and arduous day; a crokus sack, called elsewhere a gunny sack, with a shoulder strap fastened to the open end, broad and flat so as not to cut into the shoulder when the weight became excessive; and a sheet about five feet square made of sacking, to be laid at the edge of the patch and filled from the picking sacks as the day drew toward its close. This was all, but it took some time to get it together, for our elders were not so eager as we, betraying an annoying skepticism.

When we finally got to the scene of operations the broad leaves of the cotton plants were already beginning to wilt with the heat, for it was now about nine o'clock. The Negroes were scattered about, picking alone or in pairs, each following an individual rhythm, which would be kept up until late afternoon, about an hour before sundown, when all of them would gather in one part of the field and pick together, and something new and strange would happen.

Meanwhile we children attended to the important business of choosing our rows, with bickering, each of us looking for one where the open bolls grew thick. It requires care to pick cotton with young and tender fingers, for each section of the boll, when it is open, has a sharp spine. (The Negroes did not have to worry. Their hands were as callous and tough as their heels, about the consistency of a mule's hoof. When they were gathered around a fire on a cold night one would call to another, "Git off dat coal, nigger, your heel's a-burnin'," and snort with glee.)

Each section of the boll yields a drift of snowy cotton about the length and thickness of a forefinger, and there are four or five sections to a boll. A skillful hand takes the cluster at one pull, but a child must work more slowly. Even so, at the end of fifteen minutes we all had pricked our fingers, within half an hour the heat of the sun was unendurable and the weight of the sack with its two or three pounds of cotton began to drag on our shoulders, and it was time to empty. The meager yield was almost lost in the wide expanse of the sheet. It was time to go to the house and get a drink of water. Then, after several drinks, we began to think of neglected tasks, things we had solemnly promised our mothers to do, resolutions suddenly remembered: to feed the cats, to help water the stock, to make our own beds—the words we used were "to spread the bed"—tidy the room, any room, do a bit of reading every day and become learned like our crippled cousin, a thousand things more important than picking cotton and amassing wealth. The disintegration of character had begun and within an hour was complete. And yet, although character was gone and with it hope of pony, bicycle, and all other unattainables, there was something left, some compensation for the loss. Imagination put forth new shoots. It was not enough to sit and dream of what might have been, if something else had only been. I had to do something. I could not remain unconscious of my plight, and was driven, in my flight from duty, to new explorations, to things so serious and absorbing that they could make me forget, a habit that I did not lose in later years.

All that day I stayed where I could not see the cotton field, but toward evening when the sun had gone down I crept out to the shed to see the first weighing-in of the year, to watch the hands coming in with their mountainous bundles on their shoulders, and to hear their raucous laughter of delight or chagrin as the bundles were swung up on the clanking scales and their weights called out by my uncle. And also to watch the weighing of my own eight or ten pounds, and receive my pay.

A week later the pickers were getting near the House Patch and the time had come to gather my melon, ripe or not; but it was ripe, of that I was persuaded—it thumped with a deep enough thud, I said to myself, and the stem was twisted and brown, as it should be. I went to the kitchen and, engaging Winnie in a lively conversation as to the origin of her race, whether she was descended in fact from Ham, the son of Noah, or from some later strain, I slipped a large knife out of the kitchen drawer and hid it in my trouser leg, a slight hindrance to walking and a danger to limb and life, but safe from sight. I went with it to where I had put the melon that morning, in the deep ditch that ran from the spring, for this day I would not eat melon with the rest but would gorge alone. The dark green skin was beady wet and cool to the touch, darker against the grass on which it lay. I pressed the knife edge firmly into the rind and listened for the sharp crack, which did not come, and, as I cut deeper into the resisting flesh, tears came to my eyes, for I knew what I should find, what I did find when the two halves lay exposed. Inside was a sickly yellow green.

I hid the knife under an alder bush and climbed out of the ditch, on the far side from the house, for I did not want to see my cousins now. As I stood there, uncertain what to do, from out of the west, where the setting sun was touching with its lower rim the flowering tops of the cotton plants, there came, as if from the sun itself, the sound of the field hands singing. I hurried towards them and as I got near I found them working close together, part of the day's ritual, and saw their bodies moving within the song, feet and shoulders marking the beat, while each pair of hands darted in and out weaving their individual patterns of intricate rhythm. It was as though the hands matched in their motion the soaring voices of the women, voices that moved above the song of the men like willful violins, and yet returned again and again to the central theme, free and unfree, caught within the net of sound.

I stood listening, and felt myself being drawn into communion with the singers, but not complete, for somehow something of me stayed outside. I was a white child; and I was beginning to think; and, beginning to think, I was being drawn, so slowly that I did not see it then, outside the whole plantation world.

CHAPTER II

Columbia

COLUMBIA IN 1892 WAS AN AWKWARD OVERGROWN VILLAGE, LIKE A country boy come to town all dressed up on a Saturday night. The red clay roads from the countryside flowed into it and became by definition streets, kept straight by the bordering sidewalks and lot lines, and only a little less muddy or dusty in their new setting. The residences along these streets were, except the newest, farm and plantation houses squeezed into spaces too small for them, and the State House in the central square was only an enlarged courthouse such as might be seen in any county seat. There were trees everywhere, in rows and out of rows; paling fences continuing as wrought iron or not at all; clipped lawns next door to plain weeds; hitching posts with and without carriage blocks; brick pavements suddenly becoming footpaths as muddy as the middle of the street. The business section never knew where it began or where it ended, and the slatternly shops betrayed their origin, the crossroads store.

Since that time cement and electricity have brought change, mill and factory have moved in, and Columbia has become a city—or so an inhabitant will tell a listener—but in its essential nature it is still a village, like most other cities in the South, where the center of life has always been farm and plantation and the town eccentric. Herein, as in most other ways, the South is different from New England, which started with the town and in which the cities spill over into the country round about. Excepting a few old seaports, such as Charleston and New Orleans, there are no authentic cities in the South. Everywhere else the farm, although it is losing the battle, hangs nagging on the outskirts of the city, hinting that she is no better than she should be.

The main entrance to the town was the depot, and here was something new, something that marked the town as different from the country and the country depots at Lynchburg and Darlington and Varnville: two doors to two waiting rooms and on these two doors arresting signs, "White" and "Colored." Here in cold impersonal language was a statement of belief in the caste system, the barrier of pigmentation. The architecture was something new too, the like of which I was not to see again until I came upon the Harvard Memorial.

We had descended from the dusty cindery train into a crowd of bawling barking frightening hack drivers, one of whom seized us and hustled us into an ancient vehicle that had once been a gentleman's carriage and come down in the world. Later I was to learn that clean and shiny carriages were never let for hire; these were reserved for the well-born and for funerals. Negroes paid fifteen cents or more a week for life that they might have one or more carriages follow them to the grave. Death and the aristocracy were entitled to the best, perhaps because they are so much alike.

We drove through the business section, a block or so of fly-specked shops and stores that reflected dry heat from their false fronts of tin pressed to look like stone, and tin cornices painted to look like something other than they were, such as had aroused disgust in Louis Sullivan a few years before and started a revolution in American architecture. But no one who lived in South Carolina had ever heard of him; he lived in the twentieth century, and besides he was a Yankee. Carpenter and tinsmith had supplanted architect and artist in the state, where the only reminder of earlier days was the column—every South Carolinian still thinks no house is complete without its columns, the bigger the better—and there were no models or memories of business places except the country store. On one side of the street a racket store, ancestor of the five-and-ten, faced a dry-goods store on the other, where an indigent female cousin was one day to take a job and thereby cause a scandal in the family. Dent's butcher shop, with unscreened door, welcomed customers and admitted flies. A little farther on a livery stable, with an entrance high and wide enough to let a coach pass, served as breeding place for the flies—the Southerner lived in a world of flies—and poured out on the passer-by its peculiar composite smell of horse and sweaty harness and the ammonia of fresh manure. Next door was a blacksmith shop with other smells, of charcoal and red-hot iron and burning hoof. The wares of the general store spilled out onto the sidewalk, plows painted a brilliant red, split-bottom chairs, sacks of sweet potatoes and pinders—known in the low country as goobers or groun'-nuts, elsewhere as peanuts—and armfuls of sugar cane leaning against the front. There was even a shoe store—specialization was beginning—its windows covered with festoons, loops and rows of shoes, the way the British still display them in the cheapest shops. Somewhere near was a printing shop entitled to grateful recollection, for from here was published to an astonished world *Purely Original Verse,* a slender volume with which the bemused J. Gordon Coogler was making a bid for fame and getting notoriety. These and other things I was to find when I should go exploring.

In the middle of the square sat the wonder of Columbia, the State House, surrounded by statues and monuments bearing commemorative inscriptions in swollen rhetoric. On its walls were reverently preserved the scars chipped out in the War between the States by the cannon of Sherman, who shocked the world by saying, "War is hell." Nearby was the Episcopal graveyard, green with creeping myrtle and grey with the tombs of aristocratic heroes. Most of their unburied descendants had their houses on the main street that led away from the State House toward the girls' college, where my father was soon to be president and I to broaden the field of my education. Meanwhile we were to live in the parsonage, beyond which, towards the edge of town, the homes of the poor began, increasing in decrepitude until they became the shacks in which the Negroes lived.

Sherman had put meaning into his words by burning Columbia on his march to the sea, leaving only a trace here and there of what it once had been, an occasional mansion standing in a grove of magnolias that almost hid its white columns with their glazed leaves. Many houses showed that they had been erected in haste; some were new, in the style afterwards known as "gingerbread" but at that time thought wonderful. Scroll saw and wood lathe were chewing their way through American taste, assisted in their revolution by machine-made nails. House fronts were a riot of pillars, carved and turned with all the rings that an ingenious carpenter could conjure out of the wood, and every corner was choked with scrollwork even more fanciful. Over all was laid by preference an oily coat of sickly brown. The parsonage, as I recall, was just such a house, but I cannot trust my memory when it comes to parsonages; in the perspective of time they all look alike because they are alike.

All my young life, except when I was at my Grandmother Smith's, I was surrounded by hostile furniture. In every parsonage there was a collection of oddments placed on permanent loan by good church people. Instead of sending to woodpile or attic the things they no longer wanted, they sent them to the parsonage and thought they were performing a Christian act. Whenever former owners came to call, they looked carefully to see how their pieces were being treated, and if my mother had the grace to grant them the seclusion proper to their age, explanations were awaited. So it was wiser to put up with them and deal with them gently. Rockers that could not be rocked without peril to one's life; chairs from which the backs exploded, and splay-legged tables; temperamental springless beds whose slats slipped out in the middle of the night and hit the floor with a crack like a pistol shot;

worn-out rugs and chipped china ware; white lace curtains that felt dusty to the touch; lamps with cracked shades, and pots and pans that leaked: these were parsonage property. I learned to ask before I touched a thing, "Is this parsonage?" and came to think that everything in the world belonged to the parsonage. When a new baby brother was shown me, I have been told, I begged to be allowed to hold him, but the nurse said, "No, you might drop him." I asked, "Is he a parsonage baby?"

We had no furniture of our own in the early years, for, having to move at least once in every four years by a rule of the church, usually oftener, to ship household goods by freight was an act of faith beyond even a Christian minister. The railroads were not yet the humble petitioners we now know, and the freight handler led as gay and carefree a life as the baggage-smasher, whose skill was attested by our twisted and battered tin trunks.

When the bureau drawers had been aired of some of their smells and dangerous furniture stored in the attic along with the trunks, when leaky pots and pans had been thrown away and the cook persuaded to put up with the second-hand stove, we settled down to receive visitors, to be quizzed and appraised by curious members of the church. My mother's face grew hard and drawn at the indignity, and my father had to call on all the Christian love that was in him to keep his temper under control while they were still present. (When they had left, we got the backwash.) Yet his was the greater ordeal, for on the following Sunday he would have to preach his first sermon to his new congregation, and have his soul subjected to the scrutiny that had been obliged to stop at the clothes and manners of his family. But at such times he could be magnificent. In the small affairs of life he was himself often small, but when the chance came to attest the faith that was in him he never doubted himself nor his cause, and the man that he was subdued his hearers to awe. The rest of us, however, lived our lives on a lower level and were overcome by the irritations of parsonage life.

We were open to invasion. Church members felt free to come in at any time on any mission or pretext, and to criticize or condemn the actions of the preacher's family, and ask shameless questions. Why were we not at church last Sunday; when was the new baby expected; didn't my mother think she set a bad example in letting me play ball on Sunday (I had been discovered throwing rocks—"chunk" was the word we used—at the back fence)—these and a thousand others. We were their creatures and they let us know it. If they wanted to be sure to find my father, they came at meal times. Occasionally it was for help in real trouble, sometimes for periodical spiritual comfort, sometimes just for a chat. Often we sat in explosive silence, letting the food dry up on the stove or get cold on the table, while some habitual penitent dished up his sins to a hungry pastor.

This living without privacy was a thing my mother never got used to, and moving from one public exposure to another aggravated her unhappiness. She had been born and reared on the plantation near Lynchburg and had lived there continuously, with an interval of schooling, until she was married. Surrounded by familiar things and faces, she had been used to peace and quiet, accentuated by family storms. My father had met and loved and married her quickly, and whirled her into this other life. She had thought love would be enough; when I first knew her, it was no longer, and I do not remember her without her troubled look. In a picture taken in her early thirties, not long before she died, the look is there, for all her loveliness. She was always longing for a permanent living place—"some place," she said, "I can call home." She never found it. Time and again she burst forth with "I'd rather die than move again," and I took her feeling, as I took most of her feelings, as my own. My father's "Well, Anna, you knew when you married a preacher that you'd have to move" seemed as unreasonable to me as it did to her. He did not understand, for since boyhood he had been intent on escaping from the poverty, economic and spiritual, of the home from which he came.

In my mother's family there was no scratching poverty, no poverty at all. They were not rich, even as wealth was measured in the South, but there was always enough money to buy necessities, and some luxuries. Of the civilizing links with the past, and the future, they had few: no music, no pictures, some neglected pieces of good furniture; but there were books—not many, nothing like the collection of Governor William Byrd of Virginia, but good according to the standards of the day before: history, biography, some Greek and Latin, which none of my elders, educated in the Classics, could read, and a few pious volumes. There was even a set of Audubon, the only bird guide of that time, huge elephant volumes that had to be looked at on the floor. Years later, when it had become a rarity, I asked what had happened to it; I was told that Uncle Ellie, when he moved out of the house after his mother's death, had left it there, and the children of the tenants, used to playing with paper dolls, had cut out the pretty birds.

We moved from the parsonage in Darlington to the parsonage in Columbia when I was about four years old. The only private life I ever had in childhood was on my Grandmother Smith's plantation, a little world but complete, where everyone knew and kept his place. The land saw to that. The city was an upstart in the South, on its way to becoming middle class; the plantation had its roots in history. All its dwellers, from my grandmother to the youngest plow hand, depended ultimately upon the land, something solid and enduring. Ownership might shift and landlords come and go, but the land was everlasting and in the end was ruler. This gave to life a kind of impersonal quality. Such injustice as there was had the sanction of time, and time can make wrong seem right and even good. The city was different. Here the land had lost its life-giving nature, sustaining, not people, but houses and grass and weeds, a thing to walk upon while earning one's living off one's fellows, an indignity to which the Southerner has not yet become accustomed. No one knew quite where he stood or where he would be standing tomorrow. Good will of the land was supplanted by good will of man as the source of life, and men lived in a dependency on strangers, a new thing to a countryman. City life was confusing to a small boy, who kept the country habit of greeting all he met—"mawnin" before noon, "evenin" afterward—and wondered how it could be that he did not know their names. "Who was that?" I often asked and found my companion's ignorance very puzzling.

Columbia was the "call" my father had been waiting for. (Men were "called" to preach, and every move thereafter was a "call," however contrived.) In the unspoken part of the prayers of every ambitious young preacher in South Carolina there was somewhere the petition, "Lord, call me to Columbia," for it was the center of the state, source of renown and quotation, sometimes the last rung in the climb to the bench of bishops or equivalent ecclesiastical preferment. The only newspaper read widely by the living was published there—the rest read the Charleston *News and Courier* then as now—and the editor of the Columbia *State* was trying the experiment of looking somewhat toward the future. (In all fairness it must be recorded that he finally got shot.) Meanwhile, to be mentioned favorably in the *State* was a desideratum, even in the day that did not know the word "publicity." Here also each year the politicians gathered in and around the legislature and, when the session was over, took back to their home towns news of promising young preachers, for everyone, except the confirmed unregenerate, went to church; and Columbia was a substation of the aristocracy, who, until the coming of Ben Tillman, had ruled the state and were now offering up the aristocracy's equivalent of prayer that he would shortly be gathered to his low-class fathers.

II

One of my earliest memories was of my father's black beard. Part of the mystery of his nature was for me in the full brush that half filled the space between ear and eye and flowed downward to conceal the muscles around the mouth that tell of thought and feeling. Behind this mask the eyes alone, set deep beneath heavy brows, were left as his betrayers; but eyes are more cautious than mouth, much less committal. Sorrow and anger glaze them with the same tears, and even laughter; but laughter too can be angry and scornful. My father's laughter was seldom gay and free; it was one of the weapons with which he struck people, though at rare times it could be gentle. So I had no full clue to his nature and moods. Nor did his voice help much, for it was the voice of a preacher, which, like the voice of an actor, is used for effect, squeezed to strain the last teardrop out of a syllable. His vocabulary, like that of other Southerners whose only serious reading had been the Bible, was a mixture drawn from the King James Version and the cotton patch—it took him a long time to conquer "ain't." But there is not only a theological vocabulary, there is a theological speech-tune. His "O Lord," when he was trying to find something he had mislaid, might have come out of a prayer, and when he was ill, which seldom happened, a request for a glass of water was the pitiful plea of a martyr deserted by God and man. Once he had a tooth out, and Job, if he had heard him, would have torn up his manuscript.

Beard, cold blue eyes, the thrust of harsh laughter, the backward jerk of his head and the exploding cackle when he told a joke, large blunt-fingered hands that could be as caressing as my mother's and could also sting like a paling off the back fence, his tall heavy frame— all these found their place in memory somewhere, somehow. But memory is set in no pattern of time, for memory has little or no relation to time: memory has relation to memory. Fix a point in memory and the arrangement of events begins, backward and forward and around that point. The inner quality of experience is the determinant of nearness or farness. Time is stranger to experience. Time is linear, while experience is three- or many-dimensional, capable of running with or against or across the line of time. My Uncle Coke, I am told, was over fifty when he was made bishop. That is what time says. I say otherwise. I say he was always bishop, from my first knowing of him, when he was, according to the reckoning of time, not yet forty and I was a very small boy. His life was threaded on the line of time, and in time, as we say, he became bishop; but to me, once made bishop he had always been bishop. I had known and felt him, experienced him, as bishop all along; what happened was that, at a certain point on the line of time, I got a word for it, for the quality that was in him, the quality of my experience of him that I had already felt. Now, as I look back along the line of time, his being bishop, his bishophood, is what memory seizes on, and in relation to that fixed point in memory everything must take its place. Whether a thing happened ten years ago or forty makes no difference. Memory may make the happening of ten years ago farther away from what we are than that of forty years ago, for what we are is what we were, changed and added to, but still what we were.

The illuminating moment, the fixed point in memory, may be for one the advent of death, for another of love, or of some other dreaded thing, or even of something that to others would seem trivial; but all these moments have this in common: it is then that we are alone, and being alone, struggle hardest not to be. It is then that we feel our reluctant dependence on others, on other life, and yet are helpless in isolation. We drown in loneliness and fight our way to the surface time and again, to the surface which is love and hate, rebellion and submission, fear and longing for others. Suspended between the twin heavens of love of self and love of others and the twin hells of hate of self and hate of others, we come alive; we are alive, and this is when life begins, or begins again. Everything that happens in the thing called time is like or unlike this moment, near or far from its center. With Uncle Coke the fixed point, the moment, was the sudden look of sadness; with my father, it was my discovery of his lips. (I have no notion how old I was. It makes no difference.) He lifted the cup of coffee with a hand that trembled slightly—he was always quick and nervous in his movements—and then I saw and see his full sensuous lips reach lovingly toward the perilous drink, for it must always be boiling hot. The mask of beard fell; eyes, muscles, lips, all became one, and frightened me at the moment of revelation. I never forgot and never forget the face that came from behind the beard and told the history of a life that was and was to be.

He wore a beard from no dire psychotic twist, but because it was the fashion of the day and nearly all young men wore them. The Civil War left one memento in a race of bearded men, for it was fought before the invention of the safety razor, when straight razors were not the light delicate instruments that one now may use, but heavy clumsy things, like battle-axes, unhandy on campaign. So men wore beards, usually full and fan-shaped, and let their hair grow long and flowing—heroes and the sons of heroes—just as, at the end of the last war, the soldiers came home with peeled faces and set the fashion of a head closely clipped all round. The lineal descendant of the First World War haircut is the present crew cut, affected in centers of learning; so the Civil War beard eventually became pointed, in the style of Van Dyck's Dutchmen. As time went on, my father's beard was cut to a point and stayed so for years, until grey hairs drove it from his face, leaving only a severely trimmed mustache.

Uncle Ellie and Uncle Coke also wore beards—Uncle Charlie a large handle-bar mustache, about the thickness of a breakfast roll and tapering to a point out beyond his cheeks. To all of them the mustache was a bother when it came to drinking; sometimes they used a special coffee cup devised by an inventive philanthropist. This cup had, on the inside of the brim, a sort of bridge, flat and about an inch wide and stretching from just below the handle to the other side of the brim. The place where the water would have run, if the bridge had been over a stream, was the outlet for the coffee. The method of use was to bring the cup to the lips and let the coffee pour into the mouth through the opening, taking care that it should not flow over the top. We children watched hopefully to see if it would, and sometimes vigilance was rewarded, to our restrained delight. When an ordinary unbridged cup was used, or soup was being drunk, there was nothing for it but to use the mustache as a strainer. This was not such a disadvantage if the soup was clear, but with thick soup or buttermilk, which they all liked very much, it was otherwise. The lower lip was thrust upward, clamping firmly the wet fibers, and with a hard suck most of the residue was removed. When a man grew old and his mustache was white, there was a brown stain as far up as the high-coffee mark. (The beard was usually also stained, but that was from tobacco juice.) Some old and careless men waited until the end of the meal and cleansed the mustache with one mighty suck; young men, and the fastidious old, were constantly sucking and wiping their mouths, for even the special coffee cups left some moisture. Uncle Coke, willing to be in the forefront of his time, always used his cup; Uncle Charlie never; Uncle Ellie sometimes, in keeping with his inconstant nature. My father tried it once, but the boiling hot coffee heated the bridge too much even for his heat-loving lips.

He loved fierce heat, of food and fire. I have often seen him on a hot summer day stand over the kitchen stove, stretching over it his big hands, coming so close that one almost expected to hear the flesh sizzle. In the sitting room he would stand with his back to the open fire, almost touching the bed of coals. Even now I can smell the scorching wool. He never knew what he was doing, and sometimes jumped clear across the hearth at my mother's reproving voice. He loved hot water with the same fierceness. In his mother's house there were no bathtubs, only great wooden washtubs brought in on Saturday nights and set in front of the fire. It was a gigantic task, and almost spoiled our visit, to heat enough water to satisfy him. The rest of us were content with warm water, but for him it must be blazing hot. He squeezed his huge body down into the tub of scalding water and scooped it up over himself until the room was a cloud of steam. In his own home the zinc tub roared with the attack of the hot water faucet, and throughout the house there was the smell of cooking flesh.

He was as fierce with food. The soup was never too hot. While we sat blowing on our spoons he leaned over his plate and gulped it down and asked for more. Once a friend brought him a bottle of Tabasco from New Orleans and he was drunk with the double heat. The biscuits must come straight from the oven, the greasy Southern beans right out of the pot. The roast beef, the chicken or the turkey, came smoking to the table.

If things were not hot, they must be cold, never lukewarm. In midsummer, if the water was not cold enough to suit him, he would put blocks of ice into the bathtub, and, when it was melted to the right temperature, he plunged in and snorted and howled. Tea must be steaming, or cold as dawn.

There was never too much food. He often came home from church, where he had moved his congregation to tears, and attacked the heavy midday dinner with savage frightening hunger. I have sat in astonishment at the sight of him stoking his mouth with terrific speed, until I thought he would burst. Then, when what was left of the roast was barely sufficient for the help, and my mother had reminded him of that fact, he would sit with his eyes eating it still, and would chip off a bit here and there, or filch a morsel from the congealing blobs of grease.

There is no place like a dining table to discover the nature of a family. If good will is there, good will is everywhere—this holds especially for breakfast. With us, when my father was at home and if there were no visitors, or if they were familiars, nearly every meal was an adventure in irritation, the occasion for inquisition and such correction as could be applied with the tongue. Here within this small circle we felt the radiating power of the man, which, for its full employment, needed a great cause, not our little sins. We were pygmies eating with a giant. He knew no moderation, and was as hard in his demands on us as he was on himself. If our lapses were in their nature heinous or grew in the telling, he promised to implement his disapproval at some future time. Sunday's sins were a peculiar torture, for they were to be punished on Monday, if he remembered, for Sunday was the Lord's Day, dedicated to peace and harmony among all His creatures. How my father knew that the Lord had no objection to switchings on week-days, or failed to know that punishment begins when it is promised, was beyond my comprehension, to be put down as another item under the general heading, "The ways of providence are inscrutable" —and of one's elders. I could only stay out of his sight as much as possible and pray for forgetfulness; and for once prayer was earnest. Sometimes it was answered, and there is no pleasanter memory than going to bed on Monday night hugging to myself the secret joy of having sinned successfully.

Every meal except breakfast began with asking the blessing, got through shortly, unless some visitor tried to convince us of his piety by bombarding heaven with wordy petition. Worse than grace could ever be, however, was the institution of morning prayers, offered up before breakfast, just before breakfast, when the food was already on the table. There was a time within memory when they had been held earlier, under more leisurely auspices, but some careless, or careful, members of the family had gradually got into the habit of waiting until the ordeal was over before showing themselves. My mother was not without guilt, as I remember, a fault which was not mended by her excuse that she preferred to praise God on a full stomach. Faced with this insubordination, my father had decreed that all of us should be there on time, also fully dressed, before prayers should begin. As a rule this was no great hardship, for he tended to abbreviation under the new dispensation, especially on the morning of pancakes, while the whiff of country ham shortened the prayer to the compass of a blessing. But here again a transient divine might hammer away at length, while the food got cold and a small boy squinted at the gravy growing grey in the platter and swallowed faster and faster.

On Sunday the church, the ominous monster that hovered over and dipped down into our lives during the week, moved into the parsonage and took complete charge. It began with dressing for Sunday School and not spilling things on myself at breakfast and not saying things that would upset my father, who was nervous about the morning sermon. But it was no use; I usually did upset him, or was allowed so to believe. We lived some distance from the church and all had to be ready to go at once, as soon as the carriage came. If we were on time, Jack, coachman on this day, had managed to mislay some piece of harness, and we at length set out some minutes late, in a swirl of dust and un-Christian rage. Then there was the debate as to whether I should be sent home after Sunday School or stay on for church services, a debate that usually ended in indecision at the church door.

I sometimes stayed and slept. Southern food is the best in the world —and the worst. Whether at its best it is equal to the food of the gods is beyond conjecture, though we did have a dessert that we called ambrosia; but I know that their ambrosial slumber could not have been sweeter than the annihilating sleep that used to descend upon me in church. Once, late at night, when I was tossing on my cot and could not sleep, I sent for my father and asked him to get up on the mantel piece and preach me to sleep. I meant it as a compliment.

We never knew at what time we would eat Sunday dinner. After services the family waited anxiously in the back part of the church while my father stood at the chancel rail and received congratulations and gave hurried comfort. Sometimes, however, comfort would not be hurried. The one thing we looked for and dreaded was the person who stood halfway down the aisle and a few feet inside the bank of pews. When we saw this we knew we were in for it. She, or rarely he, would wait until every one else had gone and my father was on his way out; then she would strike. We began the pious equivalent of swearing, but with such people he was infinitely patient. I think he knew that in these moments he was really being a Christian. There was no pulpit nor dogma standing in the way; suffering and hope had an open road to him and he became gentle and quiet and let the strength flow out of him without doubt or fear. But I strolled around and kicked the pews and sat on the steps outside and waited and waited. After an hour of gracious listening he would send the suppliant away cleansed and happy. Then he hustled us into the carriage and charged homeward, for all the world as if we had been the cause of delay.

Before he could eat his dinner he had to take a bath and change his clothes, for he always came out of the pulpit, winter as well as summer, dripping wet with sweat—not perspiration; there was too much of it to be called by that polite name. In his early years of preaching he did not know how to control his voice and make of it the wonderful organ that it afterwards became. He began, as other evangelical preachers did, at something higher than conversational pitch, and as feeling soared upward his voice soared with it, until the rafters rattled in their joints. When he was in full flight he could be heard blocks away, as he roared and mopped and mopped and roared. His handkerchiefs came sopping wet out of his pockets and sometimes the back of his Prince Albert was a streak of darker black where the sweat came through. Herodotus tells of a king who complained to his wife because she had never told him of his halitotic condition. She replied that she had thought that was the nature of men. I thought that my father's was the nature of preachers, until a few years later, when he had become a college president and I could go wandering and sampling elsewhere, I found my way into a Presbyterian church and was amazed to see that a man could praise the Lord without a drop of sweat, or even perspiration.

We might of course have gone on home and had our dinner in peace; this was even suggested at times under extreme provocation. But it was never done. It was not in the code of the South. The man was, by a carefully nurtured fiction, head of the house, and everything must be done to keep him in comfort, and helplessness. This duty and right my mother never questioned. Whenever the cook or maid took an unexpected day off, she did the work without complaint. If my father had been left alone in the house for any length of time, he would have starved to death. He never in his life so much as boiled an egg or made a cup of coffee; he never built a fire nor "spread a bed," nor even answered the door bell. This was woman's work. My mother laid out his clothes for him in the morning and picked them up off the floor at night, put studs in his shirt and links in his cuffs—these were barrel-shaped and detachable—turned on his bath and saw that there were plenty of towels; did everything that might be expected of a competent valet. It never occurred to him that he might do these things for himself, nor to her. One day I came in and found him striding about the house in exasperation. On such occasions I usually backed away out of range, but this time, in a mood of distracted folly, I asked what was the matter. "I've got to go on a trip," he said. I had sense enough to know that I had gone far enough, but some devil prompted me to ask, "Why don't you go, then?" He glared at me as if I had gone utterly mad, and barked, "I'm waiting for your mother to come home and pack my grip"; then, as if to load me with deeper guilt, he added, "and I can't find my pass."

One of the pleasantest, and most dangerous, of our indoor sports was "finding father's pass." At that time every man of any importance was given annual passes over the railroads; not to have at least one was to confess social inconsequence. My father had a respectable collection. Whenever he was about to go on a journey, when my mother had packed his grip, brushed his hat, given him a clean handkerchief, and helped him into his coat, he suddenly discovered—this happened often enough to become the rule—that he did not have the particular pass that he needed. Then the frantic hunt began. He stood helpless in the middle of the room, fussing and fuming, while we searched over and under and through everything, with the occasional question, "Do you think you could have put it here?" and his impatient answer, "Of course not." Why the "of course" no one ever knew, for it turned up in the most unlikely, and likely, places. Sometimes, when our search had reached the screaming pitch, he took a hand himself, and this was what we dreaded, for when he got through pawing and raking things off desks and tables and emptying drawers into the middle of the floor, the house was a shambles. It was pleasantest if, after the whole place was torn up, he said, "O here it is," and fished it out of a pocket, with gesture and tone that implied that some one must have put it there when he wasn't looking. At last, when it had been found and he had jammed his hat on his head and rushed furiously away, we sat down and laughed; but with an eye to the door, for once upon a time he had come back to fetch something and had caught us at it. On one or two remembered occasions the pass was actually not found and he had been obliged to pay his fare, an injustice hardly to be borne.

Not all preachers' sons go to the dogs. It may be that they have had sufficient foretaste of that life; and it may be something else. To live in a parsonage is to be back-stage in the big show that is the church; to know how the scenery is braced and how unsubstantial it is, to stumble over discarded paint cans and props, to be a prop oneself; to wait in the wings for the applause out front and then to receive the exhausted actor and see him as an ordinary human being. But he is not quite ordinary. No man is ordinary who once elected to do good and be good. Time, that wears all things down, may reduce his life to irritation and despair, to make of him a mean and little thing; yet he never entirely accepts his fate, always there is left in him something of the person he wanted to become. My father never gave up, and in the end he won. Uncle Charlie became blind twenty years ago, and in the quiet darkness found peace at last. Others I have known went down to old age defeated, but on them all rests the benediction of a noble election.

III

Ordinarily the physical world is a blend of color and line and mass, each merging into the other, and noises indistinct in the same way; but when fear and anger arise things and noises tend to stand apart as distinct entities, to take on, as it were, one's own condition. One remembers with startling detail the surroundings of a moment of crisis, the corn stalks by the side of the road as one calculates the tip of the overturning car, the blue shirt on a man's body stopped in motion. Everything seems to draw apart into itself, to deny communion and stand out sharp and alone. One memory I have not lost is of a breakfast table, the glass, the china, the smell of coffee and hot biscuits, even the texture of the table cloth, and the sound of my father's voice, like that of a hostile stranger. He said to my mother, as casually as if it had just occurred to him, "Don't you think it would be a good idea for John Andrew"—he always called me by my full name—"to start school?" and she replied, in an equally familiar note, a "yes" that meant, "We've had this out; you take the responsibility." He turned to me and said, in a voice as light in touch as the clumsy paw of a bear, "Get your cap and let's go." I was outraged. Then I knew why my mother had tearfully and stubbornly dressed me in my best clothes that morning and indignantly combed my curls, meeting my questions with a grim silence.

Few men have a natural aptitude for fatherhood. They are awkward, a little shamefaced and resentful, and try to make up for their deficiencies by imitative bluff, by falling back on memories of their own fumbling fathers. My father was no exception. When genius fails, memory takes charge, and his memory of stern moments in his own childhood was brilliant. So, avoiding my mother's eye, he hauled me off to school.

Not that I objected to going to school; I had indeed been looking forward to it, for some of my playmates went and reported that it was satisfactory; no, it was the way it was done, the assumption that I should accept his decisions without question, however capricious they might seem. But with him there was something more than memory working, though I did not know or understand then; there was behind his attitude toward me a theory about the rearing of children. John Wesley, backed by the Old Testament, had said, "The will of a child must be broken," and Wesley and the Old Testament were for Methodists guidebooks to life. I got my cap, after an annoying search, and, reminding myself that when it came to father I had no rights, followed him laggingly down the street.

School was not unpleasant after the first day or so, for here I found more of my fellows than I had ever known before, and discipline was social rather than intellectual, no new thing to me. The schoolroom, where every morning about twenty-five of us gathered, had been in more opulent days the drawing room of the old mansion, and from the center of the ceiling hung a great chandelier that split the morning sunlight into a shower of color. Off this room was the conservatory, also in disrepair, that still contained a giant rubber tree, towering from a green tub over a single struggling orange and other potted plants. Another caged wonder was an ancient canary, now no longer capable of more than a feeble peep. I sat in my split-bottom chair and gazed seeing and unseeing at them all as the morning exercises began with a formal reading from the Bible in the singsong detachment peculiar to Episcopalian ritual. I was used to the hearty Methodist personal way and at first found confusing, but finally came to like, this abstracted treatment of the sacred word.

The lady who ran this private school for the more or less solvent gentry had a pedigree of unimpeachable antiquity, and looked every mile of it. She was little and fragile and rustled when she walked. For years thereafter my idea of the utmost in elegance was silk on silk, until an old-maid aunt poisoned me with the knowledge that even the best could be imitated: through a crack in the door I saw my relative pinning tissue paper to her semifinal covering, thereby producing the same kind of rustle. Meanwhile I listened for and admired my teacher uncontaminated by doubt. She was the first member of the aristocracy that I had ever seen close up and I was prepared to invest her with the virtues of her class. Dressed all in black set off by jade buttons, she wore around wrist and high collar a narrow strip of white lace. Her feet were tiny as a baby's, to judge from the pointed toes that showed at the bottom of her ruffled skirt as she sat erect in her straight chair. She never crossed her legs nor sat humped over like my grandmother; every movement and posture was grooved to some inner pattern, as was her speech, in some way fixed and final, admitting of no change. She was all past and no future. Tomorrow would be a duplicate of today, as today was the duplicate of a thousand yesterdays. I did not see her like again until I saw the dons of Oxford. At the time, of course, no such thoughts entered my head, only the materials of thought; but I was unconsciously in quest of a stable past, and the teacher seemed to be the sort of person I wanted to become. And yet I was not sure, for I always carried with me my grandmother, who was very much the present, ready at any moment to cut loose from the past, and not without ungrudging contempt for the aristocracy.

Another thing that worried me was the teacher's attitude toward money. My father, who was never discreet about such matters within the family, had been annoyed that she was not ready to assume that he, being a preacher, was entitled to a reduction in fees. She taught, she said, because she wanted to teach, and I believed her. Why then this haggling with a preacher? Sometimes too she would be called from the classroom and we could hear the altercation between her and the vegetable man floating in from the back door. I felt ashamed and I was sure at such times that I wanted to be exactly like my grandmother. Out of my unreflecting discomfort came in time the knowledge that one's sensitiveness to money is in direct relation to one's nearness to starvation or opulence. I have met few rich people who were not mean and stingy when it came to money. The teacher had once been wealthy and combined within herself the vices of poverty and wealth, the one real, the other recollected.

The school was my conscious introduction to parasitology. Among the pupils were some others who did not pay the full fee, children of professors and preachers—and professors never pay for education, nor preachers for anything, if they can help it. There was no outward difference in treatment of the charity scholars, only a subtle, almost imperceptible shade, but enough to let a sensitive child feel an inequality. But even this disappeared when teacher and child met over a task, for the lady was after all a lady.

She kept life leisurely and quiet, for she thought, as I did out of the wisdom of six years, that one need not be in a hurry about one's education. I learned a little arithmetic and tried to learn grammar, but found it as senseless as I do now. The examples of incorrect usage were all taken from the best authors. If they could make mistakes, why not I?

Best of all was reading and being read to, as we sat in a semicircle around our teacher and drank in the words of imagination, just as I sat on the floor in Lynchburg with my crippled cousin Pinckney and traveled over the known and unknown world. Being read to is a kind of directed daydreaming: the thread is there, we can catch hold and be drawn along, or we can turn loose and soar, and having tried our own wings for a while, return in time to get in step again with the steady march of the story. All of what is called reality is shut out; when it does come, whether pleasant or not, it breaks in with a shock. One day I was sitting close and holding tight to the thread, watching her lips and every movement, for good readers read all over, when out from behind her ear a louse crawled, down her neck, over the barrier of white lace, and onto her shoulder. I was struck with terror, not knowing what to do or think. I knew that poor whites were infested and I had often seen a Negro catch and crack a louse, but what did this mean? Meanwhile the louse explored her shoulder, crawled leisurely up her collar, over the lace, and into her hair again. Years later, when I could think calmly about the matter, I saw the lady and the louse as a symbol of the South.

IV

On the red rutted hills of South Carolina lived those to whom hope was only a word heard on Sunday, and from these scarred hills runnels of white and black and brown, "scum of the earth," we called them, trickled along the red roads into Columbia, there to live side by side with the formerly rich and presently well-born, and mix and mingle on the streets and in the stores and around the State House. The men wore blue jeans woven in New England from cotton they themselves had grown—the mills were just coming into the South—and walked barefoot or in sockless brogans. Some wore hats of plaited palmetto, but most of them wore, summer and winter, black felt hats rusty from sweat and dust, the badge of their class, the "Wool Hat Boys." Their respectable women were dressed in calico and on every head was a quilted bonnet.

The men chewed, the finicky and toothless slicing the quid from the plug with a pocket knife—no male was complete without his knife —the rest biting or gnawing it off with such teeth as they had. Of the biters there were two kinds: the clean, whose teeth went through the plug with the click of a precision instrument and left a pattern of perfect occlusion, and the ragged, whose eroded plugs were stringy evidence of missing teeth. While the chewer was talking, his quid, now a spongy and swollen wad, rested between upper jaw and cheek, making a bulge like a small boy's aching tooth and slightly impeding speech. Dead quids were picked up by Negroes and given a second chewing or stuffed for smoking into corncob pipes. When white men smoked pipes, they shredded the tobacco from the plugs with their knives, for prepared pipe tobacco was unknown. Cigars were smoked mostly for convenience, when spitting must be restrained, or for relaxation; cigarettes were left to dudes.

The women dipped. Snuff box and dipping stick were that day's equivalent of cigarette case and lighter. The snuff stick was a peeled twig, preferably from the sweet gum tree, shredded at one end to make a brush; the method of use was to wet the stick with spit, dip it into the box, and rub well the gums. One good dip made the dipper's spit reddish brown for hours afterwards. Women, except Negroes and the very old, seldom smoked pipes in public. Cigarettes for women were not banned; they were not even thought of. I never saw a woman smoke a cigarette until I was over twenty-one—twenty-three, to be exact, and in Germany.

Boys learned to chew at an early age, but long before chewing time we had begun to collect tobacco tags, tokens of plain or colored tin stuck on the plugs. While in other parts of this country boys of the same age were learning geography through collecting postage stamps, we were learning and debating the virtues of the various brands of chewing tobacco. Every boy knew which one he would some day chew, his choice being determined, as was fitting, largely by tradition. My family's favorite brand was "Brown Mule"; other families chewed "Jay Bird" or "Snaps." Meanwhile we practiced spitting, sometimes chewing coffee grounds in the cause of realism.

I was born into a spitting world. Everybody, except ladies and aspirants to that title, spat. No public place was without its receptacle. In hotels and local trains one still sees survivals of those days in the cuspidors—"spittoons" to us—squat and dumpy in the trains, tall and shining brass in hotel lobbies and legislative halls. (They cost the state two hundred and fifty dollars apiece during Reconstruction.) Most homes had them also—"bring paw his spittoon" was a familiar command—and in any case it was a wise precaution to have one handy, for the use of a spitting guest. Out of doors there was greater freedom for the sport and it was here that spitters liked to prove themselves expert in placing shots, and the traditional target was a knothole in a fence.

To recall the distance and accuracy of the skill of legendary heroes would put a strain upon credulity.

To the clean spitter there was more to spitting than getting rid of spittle; he pressed two fingers at right angles to his lips and ejected an amber pellet of the size and force of a twenty-two, and left no trace on beard or chin. But the sloven was more common, with wedges of deep brown at the corners of the mouth that looked, on the very old, like permanent scars, or with flares thinning to a lighter brown in white beards. Spitting was no indication of social status; only the elegance with which it was done marked the gentleman, who wiped his mouth with a handkerchief instead of the back of his hand.

Between the gentleman and the meanest of the poor white trash, the scum of the earth, the chief outward difference was in manners and dress, and not much difference in manners; and, for that matter, not always in dress, for the gentleman could be careless about the way he looked, if he was sure he was a gentleman. Often, however, he was a man of fashion and went about wearing Prince Albert or claw-hammer, with striped trousers or black, and black tie and shoes. These he himself could not see, once he had them on, for his martyred head was wedged between beaver hat and high starched collar and his chin held rigidly to the horizontal.

The most splendid of these ancient dandies was Dr. Tally, who wore a gold-headed cane in the medical tradition of the eighteenth century. The rest of his get-up was a concession to the nineteenth, but early Victorian. His long black coat was a stopping place for germs from three generations of the best people—there was no dry-cleaning, brushing had to do. To this conventional costume he added an unusual tonsorial touch, which was called, I think, "military": he parted his silver hair in the middle from forelock back over the crown and all the way down to the nape of his neck. He was Columbia's most admired physician, for what he lacked in medical knowledge he made up in pomposity, the only gift a man needs for success in the world.

The most loathed man in town was a livery-stable keeper—that was his title; in reality Negroes did all the keeping while Gus sat tilted back against the wall and chewed and spat and cussed and said whatever he pleased. He had traveled so far out of respectability as to come full circle and share this privilege with the most secure gentleman. At that time there were two places, livery stable and barber shop, where men gathered to learn the news and gossip of the day, and both were completely masculine in their range and point of view. Now there is no place where a man may go to pick up items of male interest, for both of these centers of learning are victims of progress, the one wiped out by the hurried garage, the other silenced by the radio. The livery stable was dedicated to more leisurely loafing, for there no white man did any work, least of all the proprietor Gus. Here was a fraternity in the real sense of the word: all men were brothers, and age was no bar; small boys were allowed to hang around and pick up whatever they could understand—the rest they could store away for future explication.

One day, during a hot political campaign, bets were laid that Gus could not, as he said he could, tell a Tillmanite from an Anti-Tillmanite at sight. Presently a well-dressed stranger came down the street and Gus said, "He's a Anti." When the stranger reached the crowd of loafers and was asked, "Are you for Tillman?" he replied indignantly, "Certainly not," and Gus collected his dollar. Another of the same looks gave the same answer and Gus collected another dollar. Then a brogaloned blue-jeaned unwashed customer came along; Gus put him down as a Tillmanite and won again. At last he grew so confident that when another man came in sight, unkempt and unshaven and dressed in a suit that had once been decent but was now spotted and caked with mud, Gus varied his question and said to him, "You're for Tillman, ain't you?" The man gave him a cur-dog look and said, "No, pardner, I ain't. The reason I look this way I bin drunk three days."

The livery stable was the hang-out of another figure that was to prove common in the South, the man "of good family" who had come down in the world and gone to the dogs. The one I first knew, in Columbia—others were waiting, in Montgomery, New Orleans, and elsewhere to fit themselves into the type—was middle-aged, paunchy, with shifty resentful eyes. He was never quite the equal of his fellow loafers nor yet their superior. He took with such good nature as he could their jibes at his good name—for he had no choice, this was now his world—but every once in a while he would separate himself from them and return for the moment to the world into which he had been born, bowing elaborately to ladies in a passing carriage who acknowledged his greeting in the cause of their class, or, moment of triumph, passing the time of day with Wade Hampton, the hero of the state, as the general, governor, senator, rode by on his horse. Just what was meant by "going to the dogs" I did not then know for sure. When the man of good family had left, key words were used, "women," "drink," "craps," but these had little or no meaning for me and I had to wait, sometimes years, for answers to my unspoken questions.

Saturday was the great show day for a small boy in Columbia. The town was full of buyers and sellers and loafers, and every one had time for unhurried explanations. Even the nimble free-lance cotton buyer took time out for a chat and sometimes let me hold in my hand the long auger with which he bored into the bales for samples, and I learned to say as glibly as he, "low middling," "middling," and "good middling," although I had no more notion what they meant than I had of Uncle Ellie's "spot cotton" and "futures." The broker's only other capital was a knowledge of cotton staple and a tricky tongue, with which he hoped to dupe the countryman. He would belittle the quality of the cotton, or try using big-sounding fractions in his offer, in the hope that five-sixteenths would seem like more than one-half, and it sometimes worked. But at times a farmer could be tough. I remember one who brought a bale to town when the market was low and the offer made to him very low indeed—for every buyer told the same story, that his was "storm cotton," full of sand and leaves, and would fetch next to nothing. He refused to sell, drove his wagon down to the Congaree, and dumped the bale into the brick-red stream. "I'll be durned," he said, "if I'll sell a bale of cotton for five dollars."

The pinder man, looking for all the world like Uncle Remus, waded through the crowd with a basket in his hand, calling softly, "biled pinders, biled pinders"—peanuts boiled when they were fresh out of the ground. . . . Men and women leaned and sat and squatted or walked with the leisure of one going nowhere; ate the good fried chicken they had brought with them and home-baked bread, made from yeast that sat in the chimney corner from one generation to the next; or, if they were flush, treated themselves to more esteemed food, a can of sardines with a sustained odor like nothing else on earth and a bag-full of crackers as dry as a Presbyterian blessing. . . . Throughout the crowd were Negroes, thickening with their peculiar smell the air already thick with dust, laughing and joking and boasting. One would reply to another, "Go on, nigger, you ain't strong 'til you gits hot."

To the hitching posts along the sidewalk were tethered every kind of cattle, oxen, cows, calves, pigs, and goats, of all degrees of fat and lean; and horses, from the sleek saddle horse to the bag of bones that would soon furnish the buzzards with disappointment. . . . Oxcarts with wailing wheels moved side by side with the spick-and-span turn-outs of the gentry, and of others. To my already practiced eye some of these others were not of the real gentry, they were merely forerunners of the shoddy rich that one finds now all over the South. But some could claim an ancient history, as I was one day to learn; at the time no one would tell me who they were, these gayly dressed ladies with bright red cheeks who rode always two to a carriage, turning their heads neither to right nor left, but using their eyes for all they were worth.

From the time I was six years old I went to school from Monday through Friday, but Saturday was when I learned the most. It was then that my whole world came together, and Columbia, now country

and village and city, the place and the people, with all their contra-
dictions and incongruities, entered and made a temporary truce inside
me. I was becoming a Southerner.

v

Columbia Female College, when my father became president in the
year 1894, was an asylum to which the daughters of good Methodists
were sent during the interval between childhood and marriage, pri-
marily for safekeeping. There was also something more than an off
chance that a young lady, under chaperonage more expert than parents
were able to maintain, short of locking her up, might pick up a husband, and a little education. Presbyterian College, a few blocks away,
offered the same services to members of that denomination. Except for
sectarian differences, imperceptible to themselves as well as others, the
inmates were alike, so much alike that a young man, on being introduced, inquired, with no intention of humor, "Are you a Presbyterian
girl or a Female girl?" She, equally oblivious to anything but meaning,
admitted that she was Presbyterian or Female and asked hopefully,
"Are you a South Carolina boy?"

South Carolina College, afterwards known as the University of South
Carolina—a change in name only—had been established by the state
years before anyone began to take seriously the education of women.
Here were to be found eligible young bachelors in plenty being
admonished by the authorities to remain or become gentlemen and to
make themselves into scholars, a task that is still imposed there as the
only aim worthy of a university. There was also in the town a theological seminary, but its young men, somewhat pale and awkward, were
not of the first choice.

Columbia was therefore not only a seat of learning but also the
principal matrimonial agency of the state, preferred by many to the
home-town church, the usual clearing-house, because it offered a safe
modicum of exogamy. My father met my mother there, Uncle Coke

met Aunt Kate there, and Uncle Ellie might have followed the convention too, if he had not performed the unusual feat of flunking at the end of his first year in South Carolina College and been obliged to rusticate at Wofford, a Methodist college in the upcountry.

Wofford soothed timid or disappointed parents with the assurance that their sons would return home not only gentlemen and scholars but, unlike the output of atheistical rivals such as South Carolina College and the Citadel, also Christians—a distinction, it must in fairness be said, not easy to detect in the graduates. The Citadel in Charleston, called by Ben Tillman the "dude factory," also received young gentlemen at the expense of the state and put them into uniform. Uncouth males went to Clemson; their future wives to Winthrop. Both of these had been founded by Tillman for what are now called the "underprivileged."

These institutions—cautiously noncommittal word—drew students from the whole state, a few even from Georgia and North Carolina; but it was valued knowledge, except at Clemson, that no North Carolinian was ever a gentleman, and there was a common saying, when someone had taken himself off under suspicious circumstances—a little matter of murder or such—that he had "gone to Georgia." Virginians would have been welcome in accordance with an article of the creed that there were no gentlemen nearer than Virginia, but the sons of that state had their own institution. (It was known in evangelical circles, however, that they drank.)

Thomas Jefferson had planned for his native state a system of education which he hoped, it may be supposed, would serve as model for others. As the first great democrat—destined to be the father of a strange menagerie—he believed that survival of the new order depended upon its future leaders and that these must be found early and educated for and in democracy. As the top of the structure he founded the University of Virginia. Here were to be gathered the best minds, sifted out from the less-endowed by a process of rigorous selection; there was to be no question as to previous social or economic status, only of intellectual fitness. The university was to be their final training ground. It had now, a century later, been taken over by the aristocracy as a playground for their sons. The dreamer had reckoned without his tough equals and their distrust of democracy, and also had evidently not known professors. South Carolina had no Thomas Jefferson, and the aristocracy had never committed themselves to such democratic nonsense. Had not John Locke, in writing the "Constitutions of the Carolinas," provided for a "not too numerous democracy"?

But the democracy was already numerous and busy founding colleges in the small towns throughout the state, for those who could not afford or were afraid to send their sons and daughters away from home. These colleges were for the most part centers of piety rather than learning—the saving of a soul was more important than enlightenment—established and stingily maintained by the evangelical sects. The Episcopalians were not interested in education and certainly not in salvation. Their sons might take advantage of South Carolina College or the Citadel for a little added luster; their daughters, content with the state of ignorance to which it had pleased God to call them, were kept at home tethered to the family tree until such time as they should be unleashed into matrimony, intellectually intact.

Not that I ever knew them, or their brothers. They swung in a circle outside and higher than mine. Nor did it matter much to me then—it mattered a lot to my father, who was very family-conscious—and I left the state before it could. Besides, the old aristocracy was becoming increasingly unimportant and the present sheets-and-pillow-case aristocracy had not yet come to take its place. The Civil War had destroyed the old order and Ben Tillman with his "Wool Hat Boys" had driven the best families from their vestigial political power.

Democracy was on the march; and directly ahead, coming closer every day, was the day of promise, the land of hope and glory, the twentieth century. It is impossible now to recapture, difficult even to recall, the awe with which the words were uttered. I can remember, however, how puzzling it was to a small boy struggling with arithmetic to get it into his head that nineteen hundred could be twentieth. We must be prepared, we were told, for the great event, and that meant to get education, more and more education. Just exactly what education was, no one knew. (Teachers College was not yet begotten.) But that made no difference; into school and everything that called itself a college the crowds poured. I got caught in the jam.

The building that was for me, among other uses, my dwelling place during the next six years, stood in half a block of land on the main street of the town. I had often seen its three stories towering beyond the high wooden fence that was intended to keep curious eyes out and in, for the girls must be protected against others' and their own weak selves. (But there were knotholes.) On this day in early autumn we went through the great sagging gate, my mother and father, my three-year-old and my year-old brother, and I, up the granite steps where leaves and the dust of summer still lay, and twisted the bell in the peeling door. Presently it was opened by the first white servant I had ever seen, a middle-aged woman whose every gesture deplored her low estate and yet truculently reminded us that she was after all our equal.

The wide entrance hall into which we were led was empty—the girls would not arrive until next week—and it was dismal. Doubt entered with me: this was not the palace I had imagined when my father had told me of the great house in which we were to live. There was a moment of hope when I caught sight of the banisters that ran zigzag from the cupola that topped the building; but only for a moment, for pillars stopped the railing at every turn.

The woman conducted us down a long hallway to the four rooms set aside for the new president and his family, rooms that were gloomy in the shade of the near-growing magnolia trees. They were exactly alike in size and shape and furnishings. From the ceiling depended a double-angled pipe, at the end of which stuck out the button of a gas jet. Except for this novelty our future home was not much different from the parsonage we had left behind forever. The furniture lacked the variety to which I had been accustomed, for it had all been operated on by the same scroll saw, but to me it was in nature essentially parsonage. I knew without being told that this was college property as the other had been parsonage property, and was not to be treated with familiarity. One look at my mother's face told me that this was no home.

I soon recovered. Out of sight of my elders I explored the immense building, trying the banisters anyway and finding them as disappointing as they had looked, racing down the long corridors and finding things, a piece of last year's candy, pencils, many strange leather things that looked like dried earthworms that my mother told me were curlpapers and I was to throw them away at once. I turned on the faucets in the zinc bathtubs, fearfully hopeful that they might overflow, tubs of a size that I was not to see again until nearly thirty years later, in Germany. (When I told my landlady that in America bathtubs were white porcelain, she said she didn't see how we could keep them clean.) Then I discovered, downstairs at the back, a covered runway leading to the kitchen and there a big slow-moving cook, who praised and scolded me and made me feel at home. The day before the girls arrived she let me punch holes in the ends of a dishpanful of eggs and blow them out the way we did birds' eggs in the country, not minding the quantity of saliva that went along; pointing out, when I showed some hygienic hesitation, that you couldn't tell it from the whites of the eggs.

Then the girls came, in tens, hundreds, thousands. To the cold eye of arithmetic there were, I think, not more than two hundred in all, but I had never seen so many, nor have I since; nor kissed so many, for half of them, or so it seemed, were my cousins, and cousins to whatever degree greeted one another with a kiss in South Carolina. With their arrival the dead building came to life. Hack drivers tossed trunks about, cautious parents entrusted their daughters to anyone who would listen, girls ran up and down stairs and chattered and shrieked and laughed, and some of them cried, the new ones. It was like a steamer an hour before sailing time. They fed each other on candy and cake and pinders, and I had my share, as long as I could stuff them away in stomach and pocket. They pulled my curls and teased me, asking how would I like to be their "fellow," and the bold ones made jokes that I did not understand.

When a last year's girl could pass another in the hall without stopping and my cousins felt no longer impelled to give, nor I obliged to receive, another kiss, we settled down to life in a girls' college. For my mother and me it was not greatly different from life in a parsonage, only in degree; for my father hardly at all. We were now entirely public characters; what little of family life there had been in the parsonage was gone. Four rooms that looked exactly like any other four rooms could be hardly called home, and we ate every meal with students and faculty in a big clattering dining room. Also, my father now became a complete stranger to me. At the college he was always in a hurry, rushing in and out of rooms and issuing orders over his shoulder, always in motion and loving it, for, as a Southerner said of Theodore Roosevelt, "his nat'ral gait was running away"; and often he was away for long stretches on the road. My diluted respect for college presidents in after years may have come from having found out, at the age of seven, that a college president is nothing but a high-toned drummer.

College was not exactly parsonage. My grandmother had already accustomed me to a woman's world, but nothing could prepare one for a world of women. Everything was keyed to their foibles, predilections, and desires, and there were no males present in person. I was like the American public school of thirty years later, drowned in a sea of femininity. There was one difference, however: every girl hoped, and all except the ugliest believed, that some day she would be married, the Lord being willing, and the sooner the better. This made the new world in which I found myself not only feminine, but, as I soon learned, also female. I think I was getting ready to prefer coeducation, which, for all that can be said against it—and there is plenty—at least does one thing, it curbs the imagination. The trouble with a woman's college is that there are too many men there, in closets, behind curtains, under the bed, and elsewhere.

South Carolina was beginning to stir in its eighteenth-century sleep and after a while would turn over and consider waking up. One of the disturbing noises was women's rights. No one quite knew what they were—some said "votes" and "careers"; there was even talk of divorce, but the good-natured South Carolinians recognized these for the jokes they were, like wearing bloomers and riding astride. There was one insistent note, however, at first faint and then very noisy: education. Women were ready to prove that they were intellectually as good as men—a meager ambition—and they had a right to education, just the same as men. They got it, just the same education the men were getting, education for leisure, which few of them would ever have. Ben Tillman was saying that farm girls were entitled to a practical education, but he was no gentleman and the graduates of his proposed state college would certainly not be ladies.

The fiction of the lady was strong in South Carolina, as hardy as the fiction of the gentleman, and fictions can be more tenacious than reality; both were making men and women cripples in the life they were to lead, and both were rooted in inequality. No civilization can set up with impunity one kind of life for women and another for men. The Athenians of the fifth century, in order that they might see life steadily and see it whole, locked the women up in the back room, only to produce a breed of effeminate men. The Southern gentleman set woman up on a pedestal and spent the rest of his life in the reasonable fear that she might fall off, which she was so ready to do that the pedestal became a cage. Contempt is infectious, whether phrased in the persuasive admonition of Pericles—to be of no repute, for, as he said, no good woman is ever mentioned—or in the equally insolent words of chivalry. The Southern man, idealizing life in a lazy woman, himself became lazy, without charm.

The cult of fitness had not yet struck the state. Exercise, if one got any at all, was incidental to something else, as when one shot partridges or ducks. Gentlemen who could afford to own horses sometimes went fox hunting, and a few ladies rode timidly along on sidesaddle; but hunting was without the finish and trappings that the English have given that sport. There were no red coats nor masters of hounds nor carefully nurtured packs—only hound dogs. In the low country, which was heavily wooded, horses had to be ridden for sport in limited spaces, on race track or tournament field, the field of honor. The honor consisted in spearing iron rings on the end of a sharp stick while riding rapidly. The rider, Knight of Walterboro, Knight of Lawson Pond, or such, who caught the largest number of rings on his lance was entitled to name some fair lady as queen. There was all the mummery of plumes and silk costume and Arthurian verbiage. This still goes on around Charleston, naturally, with an occasional modern innovation. In 1938 I saw a knight wielding a lance that had for guard a rubber plunger that plumbers use for a humbler purpose. No one smiled.

Occasionally a young man rode by the college on his bicycle, dressed in white and carrying a tennis racket in his hand; but these only served to mark him as a sissy, a theological student or some other unmale. Women, not ladies, were beginning to ride, too, but this was not only indelicate, it was dangerous; for, folk science said, bicycle riding by females imperiled the future of the race.

No lady ever got up a good sweat. Muscle and tan were stigmata of low origin; parasol, veil, and mittens were used to shut off the enemy sun, and trailing skirts made rapid movement impossible. Then there were corsets. Every young lady looked like an egg-timer and the goal was a twelve-inch waist. Feet were tiny and no girl child who might some day be a lady was allowed to go barefoot for fear her toes would spread. Every afternoon young ladies strolled, if they used their limbs at all—they had no legs—on the path that ran alongside the college fence, taking the air or the opportunity to pass notes through the knot-holes to their admirers on the other side. Plain-looking girls despised such traffic and walked, the plainer the faster. My father became their ally by ruthlessly removing the fence, and himself the target of con-servative Methodists, whom he had already outraged by changing the name of their institution to "Columbia College."

Aspirants to ladyship among the girls had their difficulties, for there was some doubt as to whether a member of an evangelical sect could ever reach that height; whether Southern puritanism, more painful than the Northern brand because it was capricious and unsure, could ever mix with gentility. Between the aristocratic ideal of doing nothing and the puritan fear of doing anything, life moved in a narrow groove for them.

Recreation in general was disapproved by piety. Life was real and life was earnest, as we were being reminded from the distant hub. The theater was classed with card playing and novel reading, and dancing was forbidden, except the kind called classical or interpretive, though what there was classical about it or what it interpreted the Lord only knew. Girls bloused out in bulging cheesecloth, with metal bands on their heads, moved slowly to slow music and looked completely un-female. "The Dance" was already hermaphroditic.

Not all the girls, however, wanted to be ladies, though they would hardly have put it that way. A new kind of woman was beginning to grow out of the dump heap of chivalry, women who preferred to use rather than conceal their clear intellects, who were hungry to know. The food offered was for the most part the same as was being set before the young men of their age in South Carolina College, a powder-dry curriculum: Latin and Greek for the improvement of their English, mathematics for their reason, a little science and some history. Art and music, and the appreciation of literature, were concessions to the feminine soul.

To some the teaching of literature did not obscure its meaning, but most of them were content to appreciate, and swoon. The place was cluttered with Tennyson's chaste heroines and Pre-Raphaelite maidens going into a decline. Some dived deeper, into Browning, and Pippa passed quite regularly. Keats was mentioned and quoted, and Shelley, whose "dome of many-colored glass" roused in me unquenched curiosity. One day I noticed a girl standing by a magnolia tree and looking with sad eyes at an inscription she had just cut in the bark. I reminded her, with vice-presidential firmness, that she wasn't allowed to hurt the trees; then I looked and saw that she had carved, "Ruskin is dead." "Who was Ruskin?" I asked. She replied, "You wouldn't know if I told you, you impudent brat."

The teachers were ill-paid in any coin, and unhappy; a few men, flaccid and ignorant, the rest women, most of whom were zealously unprofessional. The feminization of American education was not yet under way in the South, and, while a few were content, many of them would have been happier in the usual role of the old maid, general help in the family—where there was always the possibility of picking up a widower. They hated the girls as only disappointed women can. Some tried to mother the girls, only to deepen their hatred when their loving gestures were repulsed or the girls proved fickle; some coated themselves with ice and chilled the inhospitable air with frigid intellection; others gave spastic demonstration of the effect of beautiful literature. Once a year, on April Fool's Day, the girls openly showed their feeling in a spate of contempt. I shall never forget the contorted face of one of their victims, screaming out of the window for someone to come and open her door—"I'll report you," she said, "I'll report you" —nor the tears in the eyes of another when she opened an envelope and was struck in the face with a hideous picture of an old maid with hateful verses underneath.

At the time my vegetative mind was merely recording experience and storing it away in forgetfulness, but later, when I taught in a woman's college, it all came back to me. I had only to change one name for another and these teachers came to life again. Their sick eyes were the same.

Some of the teachers, of course, were loved, for they were teachers.

I became a college boy at the age of seven, suddenly jerked from childhood into an adolescent world. (All colleges are essentially adolescent. That is why they are uninteresting to adults—and get endowments from arrested alumni.) School was now endured by me with lofty patience and minor application; the tasks were easy, and my age-fellows, from whom I drew away to enlightened company, were not half so knowing as I—except in regard to certain matters, of course, as to which we pooled our misinformation. As soon as the leaving bell rang, I raced back to college, thirsty, if not for knowledge, at least for attention. I was unpleasantly precocious, if I can trust those who knew me then, sticking my nose into everything with tranquil insolence and relying upon the general fear of my father for immunity. When this did not work, I became a child again, and blubbered. But underneath my arrogance I was really very small and scared, and curious. I went to some of the teachers in my hope of learning, quite unprepared for the attitude I found, the assumption that no one really wanted to know what they had to teach, and I began to suspect that they had never wanted to learn anything themselves. And yet, in spite of this early preparation, I have never become inured to the shock of rediscovery that most teachers are mere jobholders.

I tackled music, hoping to become another Gaston. Professor Brockmeyer, who spoke with a German accent and wrote a capital B with a flourish, both novelties to me, received me with official interest and took me into a practice room, where there was an antique piano with keys the color of Uncle Melt's tobacco-stained teeth. He gave me a piece of paper with horizontal lines printed on it and elliptical notes that all looked alike. These also were something new, for I had never looked carefully at any music except hymn books with shape notes, such as were used in singing schools in the country. I was told to look at certain notes and hit certain places on the keyboard; then the professor went away and left me to become a musician. I tried it several afternoons and was about ready to give up and become something else, when he came into the room looking for a piece of music he had lost and found me in tears. I told him I was sure that was not the way my cousin Gaston had learned, and besides the piano sounded funny. "Funny!" he roared. "Funny! I don'd know whad you mean," and he shoved me off the stool and took my place. Then he pushed back his coat sleeves and assaulted the old piano, making it groan and squeak and spit strange noises under the fury of his attack. When he had finished with a savage blow that left him gasping, he turned to me and squeezed out, "Brahbs! You call dad funny?"

When I had learned from the music teacher how to make a capital B, I took up art. The fluttering teacher specialized in charcoal and water color; I tried both. I drew horned stags at bay, though I had never seen one, and castles, which of course I had known only from illustrations to "Ivanhoe," and bunches of grapes in midwinter, all invisible or invised. When memory and imagination lagged, she had us draw plaster casts of antique feet and other seemly parts of the human body, and once or twice we took as our model the curious creature that sat disconsolate on a pedestal in the corner, apparently as confused as we were, by the single leaf of bright new plaster that it wore, as to whether it was male or female. But one day a ribald student let out a snicker that sent her from the room, and him, if it was a him, to the corner, to stay there with brooding back turned toward us forevermore.

The use of water color was taught in the same general fashion: we always painted what was not there, and it was this pedagogical principle that finally caused me to give up art; not disappointment, for by this time—I was about eight—I had begun to regard all methods of teaching as belonging in the special classification of "Acts of God," untouched and untouchable by reason. I gave up art because it led me into temptation and I yielded.

The sin I committed was theft. Miss Vance told us to paint an iris. They were of course out of season, but I remembered exactly how the iris in Lynchburg looked. I quickly sketched one in and got ready to color it, when I found that I had only a bright blue left, my red was all used up, and I could not get the purple I wanted. The teacher saw I was in trouble and solved the difficulty instantly, to her own satisfaction. "Why!" she said gaily, "I think it would be nice to paint a bright blue iris, don't you? Try it." I painted it for her, bright blue and monstrous; but when class was dismissed in the late afternoon I hid in a nearby closet until everyone was gone, and then I sneaked back into the studio and stole some red from a neighbor's box, and made that iris a deep rich purple, the way it ought to be. But in the moment of elation terror struck into me, for I realized that I might be asked next day how it had turned purple over night. Inside I felt morally and aesthetically right, but I knew I could never bring myself to attempt public explanation, so I never went back.

A tentative approach to the French language became nothing more; life itself was irregular enough; I wanted something fixed. I found it in botany, but also, what most botanists do not yet know, that it was in the main name-calling, really the study of another language. Cowslip and Jimson weed, familiars of mine, issued from the thin lips of the thin young instructor confusingly translated into Latin. To him plant and flower were not to be looked at and smelled and felt, but grimly dissected and classified. I gave up; this was no better than school.

There was, however, unsystematic knowledge to be got through eye and ear, and nose. I developed an unerring nose for the contents of packages from home. Whenever mail man or express wagon came with them, I was on hand to inspect and whiff, and choose new friends from among their owners. As soon as a girl had taken hers upstairs, I followed and knocked on the door about the time I judged the lid would be off the box. Casually and with the look of one on nothing bent, I entered, and thereafter was a steady visitor until the box was empty; then I found another friend. Once or twice, early in my career, I got fooled; the package held clothing or some other inedible, and conversation was strained; but this was before I became perfect. Sometimes I went for an honest visit, and sat in a corner while the girls, two or a roomful, talked, taking my silence for inattention. In their homes they had become accustomed to having children around and under foot, and thought nothing of my presence; for in the South generally children, allowed and expected to live in a world of their own, were ignored as long as they did not presume to take part in the conversation of the grownups. Occasionally one's elders had a twinge of discretion and talk was stopped in mid-flow with "Little pitchers have big ears," and one had to guess the rest; but discretion was not the rule. The college girls could not know that I was a seasoned listener, an addict from experience. One day, about a year before we had come to the college, I was sitting on the floor in the parsonage, underneath the sewing machine, waiting for the signal from my mother to start the treadle and meanwhile letting the talk of the women, cousins and aunts and my mother, flow by half unnoticed, when suddenly she spoke openly of her unhappiness with my father. From that day I was never inattentive to my elders' talk.

The talk of the girls was narrow in its range, having to do usually with their being women, and edged with consciousness of men. Otherwise it was the talk of women generally, which is something of its own kind, obedient to its own law and no other, and as incommunicable as the taste of caviar or the smell of skunk. Words, the dull mattocks that men use to grub their way through thought, are to them the tools of artists, with which they paint and etch and chisel; logic, man's invention for tying himself in knots, is a pair of wings on which to get somewhere, or simply soar out of the reach of reason; reason itself, a beating of swords into plowshares and back again. There is only one law, the law of irrelevancy. It is no accident, I think, that America, where woman has had a measure of self-expression, has been the nursery of pragmatism.

Sometimes the girls let me take part in the conversation, inviting me with gentle teasing, how did it feel to be a man now that my curls were gone, who was my girl; but as a rule I was content to listen, and I let no day pass without a visit. Then my father discovered that I was growing up and declared upstairs out of bounds for me; thereafter I was to stay on the ground floor, where only we and members of the faculty lived. For a few days I considered obeying, but I found life on the lower level of grownups uninstructive and began to sneak upstairs, for which, when I got caught, I was soundly thrashed. I was not resentful, not very; this was justice, according to my father's lights, and also evidence that he was aware of my existence.

Sometimes I even welcomed punishment. There was one room whose tenants and visitors were different from the rest. One of the girls was large and full-bosomed, with the splayed feet of a farm girl and the skin of a scraped porker. When I read *Gulliver's Travels* I found her like again. The other was small and wiry and her hair stuck out like that of a freshly combed Negress. She came off no farm; she was the granddaughter of a South Carolina novelist, and never let it be forgotten. Cat and rattlesnake, scorpion and toad, they and others who gathered in their room spat and clawed and stung in a language I had never heard, but the words were curiously able to carry their own meaning. I sat and looked and listened with flushed face, and when I finally crept away I was relieved if my father caught me coming down the stairs.

Preparation for love started early and never let up. Psychologists from cold climates say there is a period of latency, between the age of five and the time of puberty, when the male and female in children goes to sleep. It was not so in South Carolina; we were kept awake. "Who's your fellow?" and "Who's your girl?" were conventional greetings to the young of all ages. One might make denial, but even if it was true, and it sometimes was, it was simpler to satisfy the curiosity of older people with invention rather than seem queer. In the home, girls were never unaware that some day they would be women, being early given such tasks around the house as they could perform, while boys were encouraged to be as helpless and domestically out of place as older males. In school separation began in classroom and on playground, girls on one side, boys on the other; by the time we were of an age to go to high school, it was complete. Outside the home generally, the situation was reversed: we were not only unequal, we were allowed to believe that we were unlike. Women were weak and frail and willing, men were dangerous. The common vocabulary carried these implications. "The purity of Southern womanhood" was an expression of hope rather than belief; "a woman's honor," which was understood to be in the keeping, not of herself, but of her nearest male relative, gave a hint of the shaky doubt within. One day my father came home perturbed and indignant, and said, indiscreetly in my presence, that he had just refused to perform the ceremony in a "shotgun wedding." I asked what that was, and he became silent in confusion; but from the way he looked at my mother I knew. We, boys and girls of all ages, needed to have put into words what we already knew; the air was charged. The cavalier tradition, the new freedom of the descendants of slaves, and the exigencies of the climate were our hereditary tutors.

In a hot climate a period of latency would jeopardize the future of the race; if no one beat the tom-tom, there might be no awakening. A lot of misplaced praise has been heaped upon the passionate male in the lands were the sun's ray strikes direct—the Latins even write books about their prowess. It is nonsense. The brave, in love as in war, never boast. The glimpse of a leg can set a Swede off to greater excesses than a strip-tease can arouse in a Southerner. (At least it was so before the installation of central heating, which changes the mores, and literature, of cold countries.)

Until I was about ten years old I had to rely upon the tradition of the gutter, but one day enlightenment came from authority. I was driving along in a buggy wedged in between a young man and the girl he was to marry, when I suddenly felt a mutual recognition between him and two women in a passing carriage. When I asked who they were he became confused and avoided the eyes of his girl. Later he explained to me, in detail. Regard for one's health, he said, demanded certain relaxation and the occupants of the carriage were the instruments provided by society. Fifteen, he told me, was the age to begin. While his girl was paying a call we sat outside waiting in the buggy and he instructed me. As the lesson proceeded my teacher glanced from time to time at my burning face and trembling hands and smiled with satisfaction.

There were moments of excitement in the college. One morning before breakfast time I heard a dreaded word shouted, rushed out into the yard in my nightshirt, and saw a roll of black smoke pouring out of a round window in the gable. Others came running, in all stages of pull-on. I was used to the early-morning look of members of my own family, but this undress parade was startling and disillusioning. The college beauties showed up worst of all, with wrappers incompletely concealing rumpled nightgowns—no pyjamas yet—and with their hair in curlpapers or simply stringy; and of these the blondes were the most cindery. An early-morning blonde is something not to forget. I remembered this morning of the fire on another morning years later in Oxford, at a "commem" ball, when the inevitable picture of the dancers was to be taken and the blonde beauty of the night before came out, reluctantly, I hope, into the truthful dawn.

Presently the fire engine came down the street at a good ten miles an hour, flanked by troops of small boys who, like the Cadmeans of old, had sprung full-bicycled from the earth. The horses were unhooked and led away, their singletrees dragging behind them, and the hose attached to the hydrant, with all the fumbling of ineptitude in a hurry. Fire fighting, like policing, engine driving, or any other public service, was still an amateur's game. At last steam was up in the boiler and the hose snaked out over the grass. Then the happy firemen proceeded to wet everything in sight except the fire, which leisurely gutted the attic and, when they finally got around to putting it out, left behind the dead smell peculiar to water-soaked burnt wood. The rest of us scurried about in Lilliputian terror, saving what we could from the firemen, wading along the corridors and in and out of rooms, rescuing something; something or other, anything. Zeal outdid judgment. I remember one slender girl tugging a big trunk down the dripping stairs, followed by a policeman who carried in his great hands a tiny vase. Some girls stood outside and let the whipping wind make sculptor's models of them, afraid, they said, to go into the burning building and exchange their garments for some clothes; others had to be kept out of the attic. It was a field day for a Freudian.

Uncle Willie was the resentfully innocent cause of another panic. My first memory of my uncle is of a timorous medical student about to become and remain a timorous doctor. He was the baby of his family, and always tied to babyhood in name and nature by his sisters, who poured over him the foolish adulation of old maids and widows. He had dawdled into the profession—chosen is too firm a word—through lack of will and imagination, in casual emulation of his father, who had bequeathed to him pride without ambition, and spent his life being pushed this way and that, with an occasional burst of obstinacy. Others did most of his thinking for him, and he was glad to let them. My father, impatient of his brother's lack of force, found in him a willing victim of his desire to direct the lives of his fellow man; he put him through college, put him through medical school, and put him into practice in Columbia. Uncle Willie drifted in and out of the college, his bald head gleaming in the sunlight and the gaslight, like a pup uncertain of his status—until smallpox broke out in the town. Then he had his brief moment of importance. The girls were lined up and vaccinated, not however as painlessly as it is now done, or with an eye to future comeliness. The young doctor, who had just received his license and apparently took the word rather literally, gouged holes as big as a quarter in their arms—no one was so indecent as to suggest that legs would be more seemly—and rubbed in the vaccine until it stung. A week later most of them were suffering as much as they would have from the disease itself, and all except a lucky few were in time prepared to match scars with their Confederate grandfathers.

He now shared the lot of all college doctors and was cursed deeply, until rumor let loose a wave of glee over the college: Dr. Willie had the smallpox. Then came consternation. He had caught it, in spite of vaccination; so might we, and have an orange flag stuck up on the college. By this time it was epidemic, and whole sections of the town, especially the meaner sections, were bright with these signals of quarantine. But after days of anxiety it was certain that we were safe and it was possible to settle down to quiet enjoyment of Uncle Willie's pickle.

His attitude was a mixture of resentments, against the disease itself, against the class of people who usually had it, and against the vaccine in which he had put his faith. The flag went up on his boardinghouse and he was immured in the best room, which, with its big window, had once been his pride. Here he now sat disconsolate, in full view of the passers-by; for, apparently unaware of his pimply looks, he could not resist the desire to sit at the window and watch for acquaintances and friends, to see who had the strength of character to walk by the infected house and who would cross the street and pass at that safe distance.

The latter he never forgave. In the obscure processes by which he arrived at an idea, or notion, willingness to expose oneself to the present risk got mixed up somehow with a test of affection. If his future wife had not bravely stayed on his side of the street when she came to wave and smile, I think his love would have died at once.

J. Gordon Coogler, self-made poet laureate of the state, came often to the college, wearing a white starched collar of an enviable tallness and a mustache with tips waxed to a needle sharpness. His pamphlets of verse he distributed to his admirers, who improvidently threw them away, not knowing that they would in time be listed as "rarissima." He also wrote in memory books, being careful however to keep copies of his best, to be included in his next collection. These were about love, for he was a great lover in his thin, emasculate way; but they were so much alike that they have become jumbled in memory, from which only one stands out, for a reason: a poem to a cousin, which began,

> That lily-white neck
> That bears not a speck,

and inspired Uncle Ellie to sing, with greater accuracy, of

> That sunburnt pole
> That bears but a mole.

No occasion or thing was safe, for he squirted verse like a leaky hose. Snow, which was not frequent in Columbia, got a firm grip on memory with

> The snow, the snow, the beautiful snow;
> The sparrow, the hawk, and even the crow
> Make their tracks in the beautiful snow.

Laughter and ridicule had no effect, for he was as brazen as Horace.

VI

Coogler sang,

> *Alas for the South, her books have grown fewer,*
> *She never was much given to literature;*

nor, if he had continued and forged another rhyme, to music. Hymns and "Hearts and Flowers" were the range, and of the hymns the old were being displaced by the new, the jangling shoddy noises of Moody and Sankey. It was the same with art. Delicate old miniatures and soft daguerreotypes, the best portraits the camera has ever made, were no match for the enlarged photograph that buckled out of its oval frame, with doll-pink cheeks and eyes of unheavenly blue. Old china gave way before hand-painted pieces with rims of abrasive gilt, and old lace to stuff with which, among other things, England was corrupting the taste of the world. Quilts and hand-woven coverlets were stored or thrown away, their place taken by machine-made counterpanes whose surface was as rough to the touch as a crude wood carving. Four-poster and spool bed were set out in the weather, shoved from the house by convoluted brass. Tradition usually treasured the wrong things. What could not be got rid of was covered. Floors of wide pine boards, aged by time to a deep brown, were hidden beneath carpets and druggets—another gift from England to a sentimental world—whose two-dimensional flower gardens were as rough as sandpaper to a small boy's bottom. Women were wrapped in layers of petticoats, and even tables were not allowed to show their legs. Sentimentality, which is shame and fear of sentiment, was the arbiter of taste, and of life itself. I was never told when my mother was going to have another baby; I guessed, but I did not know. Such a condition was never mentioned unless the pregnant woman happened to be unmarried, when not even sentimentality could cover the offense.

Of all the arts there was only one, the one art that comes to flower in a decaying civilization, and not till then: oratory, the poetry of death. Whatever of his future a young South Carolinian might foresee, he could be fairly sure that some day he would be making speeches. In other parts of the country a new form of intellectual perversion was coming into fashion and within twenty years a public debate would be a meeting, not of minds, but of card indexes, whose manipulators took one side or the other without conscience. It was otherwise in South Carolina; men spoke out of conviction, and the only source and authority needed were the Bible and the Civil War, both of which every child drank in, as we said, "with his mother's milk."

Two figures stood against the light and cast their shadows over the state, the canting preacher and the Confederate veteran. These were our teachers; and their language was the language of the Bible, the South's one book, out of which has grown as much bigotry and authenticated ignorance as its most literal interpreter could wish, and on most tongues was a dead thing. Occasionally it has come to life in a Tom Wolfe or a Paul Green, but as a rule it was merely vocabulary and speech-tune, drained of meaning. The church militant had taken its stand against the enemy, thought; the boys in grey won battles from the tops of cracker barrels and built the myth of invincibility, as innocent of reason as their spiritual comforters. (We did not lose the war. We were overwhelmed.) They lived in the past, as men do who can see no future, and were its suspicious watchdogs. On public occasions the audience must be well salted with Daughters of the Confederacy and the speaker approbated in what he was about to say by the presence of a preacher and at least one old soldier, else the cause was lost. The veteran might in private life and on another day be despicable, but now he was a sainted phantom from the past.

Heroes were to be found at every crossroad, but the greatest of them all was in Columbia. Wade Hampton, Confederate general, governor, senator, rode erect and undefeated on a big bay horse, bowing elaborately to ladies without removing his hat, and they reverently received his covered salute. The first time I saw this happen I was curious and hopeful; if a great man was permitted to dispense with convention, here was some incentive. But, I was told, he had lost the use of an arm in the service of his state, and it now hung lifeless from his shoulder. He had also lost a leg, which was imperfectly replaced by cork, and the unknowing were allowed to suppose that this meant a sacrifice too. It did, to sport, on a turkey hunt, and the sacrificial instrument had been the hind leg of a mule. No meeting of importance in Columbia was complete without this limping apotheosis of gallantry and glory. The poor, they say, are always with us. So are the heroes.

At the time I had no such feeling, in spite of the scornful envy of my kin. The truth is, I wanted deep down in me to be exactly like Wade Hampton, muttonchop whiskers and all; to ride down the street in the shade of the hackberry trees and bow to ladies—they would be young, of course—and have ordinary folks like me look up to me and call me sometimes general, sometimes governor, sometimes senator, but always hero, and preferably in a lost cause.

To me and my age-fellows Washington and Lafayette and all the other Revolutionary heroes stood outside time; they might just as well have been coeval with Moses, Columbus, William the Conqueror— Americans seldom have a sense of history—and as for Napoleon, who was inspiring others to be permanently infantile, he was not more than a name to us. But the Civil War was yesterday, Lee and Stonewall Jackson were familiars in the talk of our elders, and in Wade Hampton the past became the present, a present past that yet, for all our blowing, held humiliation. To the victor belongs forgetfulness, but the vanquished cannot forget. The angry truculence of Germany is intelligible to one born and reared in the South, which has also been a nursing ground for dictators, small and smaller.

Wade Hampton was the last of the ruling aristocrats, into whose hands John Locke had carefully placed the government of the Carolinas, even conjuring out of his eclectic brain fine titles for them,

"Landgrave," "Cacique," "Baron." This was going too far, and the disrespectful Carolinians laughed the words into oblivion; but the reality remained, and the period before the Civil War was the measure of his success. During that time not more than five governors had been Baptist or Methodist, stigmata of social inferiority; the rest had been Episcopalian or nothing, a difference indistinguishable to the eye of an evangelical. After the war, white people, when they were allowed to vote, resumed their old habit, until Ben Tillman spoke and said, "You don't have to vote for those damned aristocrats. You can choose me; I'm one of you," and democracy had been born in the state.

As I crawled over the floor in Darlington and grew big enough to bump my head on the dining table in Columbia, I of course knew none of these things; but I think "Tillmanite" and "Anti-Tillmanite"—the only kinds of people in the world—must have sunk into me very young and nourished, among other things, an inclination to dichotomy. Seeing everything as "either—or" makes life simple. Before I was ten years old I was a confirmed "Anti," who knew he wanted to be an aristocrat in a world composed of the best and the rest. My family, squinting from below, saw the virtues of the aristocracy less clearly than the vices—arrogance, lack of aspiration, insolent individualism, impatience of any authority save that of the senses. Their grace of life and suspiciously easy manners were evidence to eyes cocked for hypocrisy. Tales trickled down of doings no good Methodist could approve, and grew in the telling by envious tongues. But I longed to be lifted up into their careless world, to share their security and snobbery, to be an Episcopalian and not a Methodist.

Wade Hampton was the perfect example. Before the war he had been wealthy even by Yankee standards, owning upward of a thousand slaves on his plantations in South Carolina and in Mississippi, from which alone, as prying scholars were later to discover, he drew an income of a quarter of a million dollars a year. When I first saw him on his horse he was, in comparison, a poor man, but he looked rich to me. His lost wealth alone would not have made him a hero to his state, though it might have helped, for to many the dispossessed rich seem heroic; but he had other claims, for he was reckless in courage, on the field of battle, and in politics. Having risen to become a general, he had come home to a land ruled by carpetbaggers, stood it as long as he could, and then, as leader of the "redshirts," been elected the first native governor after Reconstruction. The means employed, I was gleefully told, were such as would now land a man in jail. Afterwards he was for some years in the United States Senate, until Ben Tillman ordered the legislature to throw him out. First he had fought the Yankees and lost; then he had fought the poor whites and lost. He was a great man.

While I was soaking up hatred that comes to its finest glow in factional politics, an ironic revolution was taking place: the "mudsill" of society was becoming the roof tree. Senator Hammond had defended the "peculiar institution," slavery, as well as a man could, comparing it to the mudsills that were commonly laid down by the crude builders of his day, great hewn logs placed in trenches as foundations. From that time, a few years before the Civil War, the metaphor, as is the way with analogies, became the reality, and to question slavery was to put oneself down as a doubter of the need of foundations for houses and invite scornful laughter from a listener. But the analogy was not pushed too far; it was conveniently forgotten that mudsills eventually rot and bring the house down. The orator in the Senate, having fixed the picture in the minds of his hearers, then reminded his colleagues that the North also had its mudsill in the factory hands, who only waited for a leader to tell them of their power. He was as foolishly unaware as the listening senators, for within his own state there was an equivalent class, Tillman's "Wool Hat Boys," who would one day take over and control the state; but it took forty years for his folly to be proved.

While Senator Hammond was making his last stand for the old

order—Southerners are never so happy as when making a last stand—
and charming his audience with Ciceronian periods, an eleven-year-old
boy in Edgefield County was nursing a swollen eye and, when the ball
fell from the socket and hung down on his cheek, enduring the pain
without flinch or whimper. In his reading, Lincolnian in its breadth,
he had run across the Spartan boy and he would be another. Years later
he told this to Judge Hammond, grandson of the Senator, and laughed
at himself. "Lord no," he said, "I ain't such a damn fool now. Even
a little bellyache starts me howling like hell for the women folks to
come and make a fuss over me." This was Ben Tillman, the villain of
my childhood, lovingly and hatefully called "Pitchfork Ben," for he
said, when running for the Senate, "Send me to Washington and I'll
pitchfork the guts out of Grover Cleveland," and the name had stuck
as a symbol of his native violence.

We were all, except the postmaster and mail carriers, Democrats,
which meant that there was no party, only factions, and factional politics are personal politics. The aristocracy had kept this fact veiled in
oratory, but Tillman knew, and in order to expose his opponents to
public view and castigation he invented a kind of circus: candidates
for state offices traveled about the state together, speaking from the
same platform and pommeling each other, often in the same words,
every day at a new place. Sometimes the followers of a favorite made
such a hubbub that his opponent's speech was drowned out; this was
counted a great success. People came from long distances, as distance
was counted then, to listen and laugh and eat and drink; white people,
not Negroes—Negroes were excluded, but often some of them stood
on the edge of the crowd and looked on and listened with quiet faces
while they were being denounced by their white fellows, and sometimes laughed with appreciation at a flight of invective.

Small boys took politics as passionately as their elders and early
learned the language. Tillmanites were the scum of the earth, con-
signed to Hell and cast into outer darkness. Justice, glory, honor, all

the words that men use to drug and enslave their fellows, rolled off our tongues with the self-righteous assurance of invincible ignorance. Tillman's offense, in the light of the time, consisted in bringing injustice up to date. (Renewed truth is always in bad taste.) The enemy was no longer the Yankee, who was gone now, but the aristocrat, the planter and his social equals. Small farmers, who year round wore black felt hats grimed with sweat and dirt while they scraped a mean living from their worn-out land, were being driven into tenantry or worse by falling cotton prices. Economists would now say that the real enemy was overproduction, but who can hate an abstraction so abstract? South Carolinians liked their hatred to be personal, and the "Wool Hat Boys" whooped with delight when Tillman ripped the hide off the "Columbia Ring" and the Charlestonian gentleman, whose dignified literary replies were unheard in the general din.

To a state inured to oratory, Tillman's was another language. Instead of transporting his hearers to a mythical past and dulling their souls with praise of what they never were, he used the words of cotton patch and cornfield, and waked men to their present. "I'm fits on facts," he said. "The war is over and we are whipped." Overwhelmed veterans struck back with a question as to his own war record, although they knew that his missing eye gave the answer. Wade Hampton's periods were forgotten, but Tillman's words stung and stuck. In Columbia, "the head center of devilment," members of the Ring, "rapscallions and scalawags who scramble for a place at the public crib," took country legislators to the Columbia Club and gave them a taste of high life. "No wonder," he said, "the corn-bread-and-bacon fellows like it." When he had been governor for two years, he ran for the United States Senate. "I went into the fight for the biggest plum, and I shook it down, and now I'm after another." No gentleman ever spoke that way, whatever his private thoughts might be. "The poor man is a farmer, the rich man a planter" put into simple words the economic foundation of social distinctions, and brought forth a reply that, with a change of a name, might be used today: "Tillman has built up class against class; there is but one name for it, Communism—Russia over and over."

My father, who was the only one of the family who had any sympathy for Tillman—Uncle Ellie strung along with the other side, while learning the language of Tillman—often told of the campaign of 1890, the year this charge of Communism was made; how the crowds, drunk with oratory and corn liquor, howled speakers down and broke up meetings, and how the gentleman, in the moment of defeat, uncovered his savage nature. At the meeting in Columbia Tillman pointed to his opponent, who had just finished speaking, and said, "When I touched him a moment ago on the stand, he stood back as though I was an adder and said, 'Don't touch me.'" My father sometimes said, after some social humiliation, "I have often wished I had been a gentleman," but when he told the story of Tillman and the gentleman he was the proud poor boy from Colleton County.

One flaw reserved Tillman to mediocrity—his hatred, which was fear, of the Negro; a hatred that, dripping from the tongues of his followers and successors, has poisoned the soul of South Carolina. And yet he, as they have not, put his prejudice in its only terms: "for the simple reason that God Almighty made him colored and did not make him white." Otherwise he saw as clearly as a politician can. . . . When he took over the running of the state, public education on the higher level—I do not use the words facetiously—was concerned with the making of scholars and gentlemen. (Ladies were presumably home-made.) Tillman established Clemson and Winthrop, colleges for farm boys and girls, not without opposition, particularly as to Clemson. Thomas Clemson had inherited the estate of John C. Calhoun from his wife, who was Calhoun's daughter; when he died childless he left it to the state for an agricultural college. The Charleston *News and Courier* objected to its acceptance, on the ground that it would mean robbing of her ancestral rights the only surviving granddaughter of the old statesman. . . . Tillman wiped out the saloon and set up in its

stead a state dispensary, incurring alike the anger of the wicked and
the pious. The W.C.T.U. raged in a manner that belied its middle
initials, and the liquor interests tried to cut off all sources of supply.
When it looked as if they would succeed, he went himself to Ohio and
found a distiller who would sell, and forced his reform on the state.
(The bottles, with a palmetto blown in the glass, are now collectors'
items.) . . . He cowed his opponents with his single blazing eye and
scornful jibing tongue. Editors and orators whipped at him with screaming anger; he loved it, and let no chance go by, as he said, "to grind
the grit in 'em." In the days of his crusading nothing could buy him off,
neither honors nor money, offered or withheld. By a paradox he was
trying, through dictatorship, to make democracy a reality where before
it had been only a name. He failed, and lived to see that, under leaders
who were followers, an ignorant, mean, and prejudiced mob can be a
dreadful thing. Here was the spiritual progenitor of Huey Long.

The climax of his ruthlessness came when I was too young to know
about it, but memories are long in South Carolina, as among all who
live in the past. When he became governor in 1890 he ordered the
legislature to refuse re-election to the senior senator. The best people
and the next best were horrified at the sacrilege, but he was immovable.
And yet there was a question as to who won, for when Wade Hampton
was facing his last defeat and his friends were pleading with him to
go to the State House, if only to walk through the halls and recall the
legislature to older loyalties, he declined . . . When Tillman was ap-
proaching the end of his life, after years in the Senate, he wrote a
pleading letter to the voters, begging that they remember his services
to them and let an old man, who was too ill to make a campaign, die
in harness.

VII

My father was being less and less of what he wanted to be, a teacher,
and more and more of everything else; he grew restive when he found

what the job of a college president really was, manipulation of man and thing rather than dissemination of ideas. Some of it he liked, for it gave room to satisfy his love of action and ingenuity. Rushing to catch a train and swinging onto the back platform as it pulled out; issuing and reissuing orders; raising money and spending money, making the last penny do the work of a dollar; preaching unfettered by a medieval congregation, speechmaking, leading his world toward the twentieth century and salvation in his time; planning sewage systems, water works, courses of study, people's lives—all these he loved; buying in quantity, coal by the carload, bed linen by the gross, grits and rice, dozens of bags at a time, whole carcasses of hogs and beef—a left-over passion, I think, from his meager childhood in a home where there was not always enough to eat. Once he bought hundreds of cases of canned fruit, a novelty in the nineties, and since that time Sunday night supper has recalled to me green plums swimming in sweet water. He showed one element of greatness: he never acknowledged his own mistakes, however overpowering the evidence. Predilection for the new led him into installing a recommended privy that had to be burnt out once a week, when, among other inconveniences, it made the whole neighborhood smell like a slaughter house. We went about holding our noses; he never even sniffed, and calmly went on to plan a cistern that also did not work.

He was admired as a man of action, but it would have been more accurate to call him a man of motion, unless action be understood to include getting others into action while doing nothing with one's own hands or body, for in this he was awkward. He had grown up on a farm, and yet could not wield an axe without danger to himself and the bystanders, and a hammer in his hand went straight for his thumb. It was not so much that he lived in a world of ideas as that everything was potentially hostile. All nature was either a hindrance or a nuisance. With animals he wanted nothing to do. A dog was a capricious foot-stool, the more likely to get in the way; a cat something to be removed from a chair. A horse was an instrument, to be used and abused. No livery man would hire a horse to him more than once; the poor beast came back exhausted.

There was no inanimate nature. A door knob that came off in his hand, a faucet that would not turn on, a desk drawer that stuck, all these were treated as if they acted out of evil intention. Nature had no business playing tricks on a serious man. When automobiles came in he was convinced of the conspiracy against him. A flat tire was a personal affront. When the car broke down his first act was to get out and shake it, and then, if it still would not go, give it a kick. The funny thing was that it sometimes worked. I remember the satisfaction with which he made the lights come on by this simple procedure, and his climbing back into the driver's seat with all the assurance of a superior moral being.

People were not so simple in their response. His dropping "Female" from the title of the college, making it bare "Columbia College," left a growing doubt as to whether he had proper respect for the sanctity of Southern womanhood, a doubt that had sprouted when he removed the wooden fence. He put up another in its place, this time intellectual, in the form of entrance examinations; other college presidents recognized it as a criticism of themselves, and parents, who knew what they wanted, were annoyed to learn that it now took more than a tin trunk and a roll of blankets to get their daughters into college and off their hands; nor could he meet their demand that the college should be a temporary burying ground, from which graduates ought to be handed back as they had been handed in, innocent of thought or idea. The students thought of him as stern, never knowing how often he acted as a foil between them and sadism, an occupational neurosis among teachers.

There was not much time left him to be a husband and father, and we saw him so seldom that we came in time to form a close circle from which he was shut out. Sometimes he put our four rooms to the uses of a home, loosing there the pent-up irritations of the day, but rousing in his children not sympathy so much as fear. Occasionally he tried to play with us, but it usually ended in tears, for he did not know how to play, with us nor in any way at all. A caress was a blow, and when he tried to tease, we slunk away in shame at his clumsiness—Uncle Ellie had set a high standard. Even when we were ill and he stood worried above the bed, we felt that somehow it was our fault. Sometimes he would come into the room when we were having gay and happy laughter with my mother over some foolishness; silence clamped down on us as we waited for the inevitable question. How could foolishness be explained to one who had no folly?

Loneliness came to him in another way, making him an alien where he wanted most to be at home. The foundations of his faith were beginning to crack—not his faith itself; of that he was never unsure— and he had to find new premises for old truth. (Like all true believers, he never confused premise with conclusion: conclusion was beginning.) Rumors were heard from the outside world of new ways of looking at God and man. William James, while holding firmly to puritanism with one hand, was tentatively sketching with the other a disturbing picture of the children of God. In far-off Vienna a really dangerous inquirer was preparing to frighten the whole·Western world with one word, but as yet Adam and Eve and the literal apple explained and explained away the vagaries of the human spirit, and Southerners had not even heard of the man with the ironic name. But Darwin, who gave man and even God a new history, had brought into speech an ominous word, and a man had to take his stand. Many found an easy way out, by following the bent of their ignorance; some could not. From German universities came the report of a new attitude toward the Bible, a scientific method known as the "higher criticism," which was being applied to the sacred word by scholars who thought themselves dispassionate. No one took the trouble to inquire, "Higher than what?" or to ask whether the methods of biological research were indiscriminately applicable to everything under the sun. At the time all scholars were crowding into the big tent, where it was assumed that one thing was as good as another, provided it worked. The Bible, these German scholars said, was itself a record of evolution, and there was no refuting them on their own ground; or they called it "literature." (Professor Frye, a colleague of mine at the University of Nebraska, used to say that as soon as people heard that the Bible was literature they quit reading it.) Most "defenders of the faith to the fathers once delivered" did not take the trouble to find out what it was all about; they resorted to abuse. Bitterness such as only the faithful can distill began to divide the church, which was my father's real home, and fundamentalism was set aflame. Argument was answered with epithet, and no honest man was safe. Only those who have lived close to enraged piety can know the lengths to which it can go. Bishop Warren Candler, "da' man wid de waffle-iron jaws," as Uncle Melt called him, whose brother was in my time to float a university on Coca-Cola, was using honest words like "free-thinker," "agnostic," "skeptic," as missiles with which to protect his apostolic see, which included all ignorance, from the new, or any, learning. The center of the higher criticism in this country was at the University of Chicago, where John D. Rockefeller had early begun to make his peace with an evolving God by setting up a fountain of heresy. Within a few years it would be said of my father, "Oh, he's gone to Chicago," as to say "gone to Hell."

I didn't know the higher criticism from Adam's off ox, and had never heard the word "psychology" until one day my father sent for me to come to his office, where I found him surrounded by a circle of tittering school teachers. I asked him if he wanted me, and he said, "Yes, I want you to bring me a carving knife." I was startled, as I was evidently expected to be, but before I could answer he swept his audience with a confirmatory smile and said to me, that was all right, I could go now. I went, and straight to my mother. When I told her what had happened and asked what it meant—I knew I did not dare ask my father—she laughed unsweetly and said, "Oh, that's that child-study business, what he calls his class in psychology." Then, when I looked more puzzled, she said, without smiling—and I knew I would learn nothing more— "Studying children with a lot of childless women; tell him if he wants to learn about children he might begin with his own."

Children will accept anything, if it lasts long enough, and I had so taken for granted her critical attitude toward him that I was unprepared for the change in her when he became ill, this time really ill. At first she gave him perfunctory attention and sympathy, for he had used this trick before to find a way to her heart; but after a few days the doctor said it was serious, that he must be moved into a room by himself, where he could have a night nurse. Then my mother forgot all about my brothers and me and everyone else. I wandered in and out of her room and up and down the hall, trying to catch her attention, and feeling like an orphan when she gave me a curt word. Why, if he was such an ogre, should she care?

On the day he was moved I stood disconsolate outside their bedroom, when, supported between a nurse and my mother, he tottered across the hall. In that moment he became in fact a complete stranger to me, for his head and beard had been shaved and his head covered with a yellow transparent coating that looked like dried molasses. If the disease reached a certain point on the crown of his head, I was told, he would die. From the time I heard this I was in the grip, not of affection nor even sympathy, but of abstract curiosity, as I awaited reports of the race between him and death, and when at last the doctor said he would get well I felt cheated out of an exciting game.

Death meant nothing to me then, not so much as an intimation of mortality; but soon it would, and childhood would be gone. Shortly after my father's illness my Grandmother Smith died and I made my first sad journey to Lynchburg, but the sadness was not mine, not yet. Funerals were not then the hasty affairs they since have become, got through quickly, as though death were a shameful thing; they were celebrations, punctuations of the continuity of life, where kith and kin gathered in subdued joy to praise the deceased, not as an individual but as one of humanity, and to rejoice in being alive, and eat great quantities of food, for nothing makes one so hungry as grief. Men sat up all night with the corpse, and after a decent interval of solemnity gossiped and smoked and ate, and, in less pious circles, drank. I can still smell the cigar smoke that came up the stairway and hear the laughter. I also remember my mother's face. She did not weep, she did not speak, and in her eyes there was a questioning look, as if to ask, "What shall I do now?" The next morning when we returned from the burying ground the look was there still, as she watched Uncle Ellie caressing the split-bottom chair in which his mother had sat at the end of the porch, and vowing with tears flowing down his cheeks that the kerchief that she had left lightly knotted there should never be moved.

Not long afterward she herself was dead. That is the only way I can say it, for I remember nothing, not even her illness. My brother Mike (McLeod) who at that time was about eight years old, has told me in detail, remembering everything; but all has gone from my memory, all except one thing, its beginning. I see my mother staggering across the hall with a mattress on her shoulder. Some relative, Uncle Charlie, I think, had come for an unexpected visit, and she was dutifully preparing a bed for him, lifting the weight that was to cause her death, for she was soon to bear another child—but of this I learned long afterwards.

The next thing I remember is the giving away of her clothes, to relatives, friends, and servants, who chose in priority of relationship, inspecting and pawing over the dresses and things that had been hers. Among the dresses was one I remember well, black lace over orange satin, the one on which she had been sewing the day I sat underneath the machine and started the treadle, and became a listener.

Many years after her death I asked Aunt Kate why she had died so young. She said, "Well, John, I have never known for sure, but I think she just got tired living. Your father was too much for her. And yet I never understood that either; she was a strong woman. I don't know."

The disposition of her children was not so quickly made. There were three of us, my brother Liston McLeod, named after the families of our maternal and paternal grandparents, and another brother five years old, Coke Smith. My father was completely lost, more helpless than we, and for a while we lived together in strained intimacy. He tried fumblingly to do for us what he could hardly do for himself, choosing our clothes in the morning and trying to button us up with nervous fingers, while we stood dreading the moment when he should come to our collars, for he always pinched our necks. After a few days of this mutual torture he gave up and turned us over to Jack.

Jack, who had practical ideas about the conduct of life, giving and directing attention only to the absolute necessities, accepted his new irresponsibility with pleasure. He took us for rides in the carriage or on the street car, a novel treat, and put us to bed at a reasonable hour; a clean face once a day was all that should be expected; necks, and other parts, could wait until Saturday night, when we bathed all over by rite. At first the holes in our stockings gave trouble—boys wore them long, and black—until Jack's genius and skin told him what to do. Whenever a hole now appeared, he no longer sewed it up, making a knotted lump, but got out the bottle of black shoe polish and, after the stocking was on, daubed the hole to a matching color. The next morning, unless we pulled our stockings on in the right order, this had to be done again, and by Saturday night our legs were polka-dotted, but freely, like an abstract drawing. This happy life did not last long, for even my father noticed our condition, and called in a succession of cousins to play mother to us, for which some had natural aptitude. Jack was offended at the implied criticism and removed himself from our lives by marrying a mulatto girl, who dazzled him into matrimony and spurious paternity. Shame thereafter kept him out of our sight.

Then our exodus began. My brothers were distributed among relatives and I was sent to live in Uncle Willie's boardinghouse. It was a dismal place, gloomy as only a home for the homeless can be in a land of private hospitality. Since that time I have known other boardinghouses, but the Southern was a step below all, for as yet hospitality was not recognized in the South as a commodity, to be bought and sold, but was still a gift, at least in form. To me, however, this one was interesting, for here were the first unrooted people I had ever seen. All of them now move in and out of my memory as shadows, all except one, the landlady's husband. At first I did not understand why he sat quiet in his rocker and often did not seem to hear when he was spoken to; then I was enlightened by the whisper, "He drinks," final condemnation in the puritan South.

My next dwelling place was in a grove of magnolias on a hilltop near the edge of town. The magnolia has in it something of the character of my native state. Its slow-growing leaves—the same green, season in, season out—deceive the passing stranger with their look of coolness on a summer's day, and at night their dry rattle will sound to him like rain; its blossoms are in color and texture like the cheek of a young girl newly dead, and they stain quickly at a touch and fade soon to a rotten rusty brown. (They are the favorite metaphor of lewd orators at girls' schools.)

Hiding in this grove was the Methodist Orphanage, where I was to be for a few months what would now be called a paying guest, and become acquainted with another kind of outcast. The orphanage had certain advantages over other forms of philanthropy, universities, museums, libraries, in that it was relatively inexpensive, not subject to invidious comparison—the only test being whether most of the inmates remained alive—and gratitude was assured, at least in expression. The kind of life the children led, the treatment they received, were put under the general head of charity, which was assumed to be good, for the orphans, who were not encouraged to forget their debt. The

Methodist Orphanage had the special advantage of being an outlet for piety also. Nothing is more cruel than self-conscious charity, more degrading to the spirit of giver and receiver alike, and charity in the name of God is worst of all.

The first few days I lived in the home of the head of the orphanage. Here all were oppressed with piety; nothing was proposed without the tag, "The Lord being willing." In one respect the Lord had obviously been willing indeed: there were five children about a year apart in age, and another on the way. The man's wife was frighteningly huge, her breasts threatening to burst from their holdings, which were, at breakfast, folds of a wrapper fastened precariously by safety pins. Every morning began with prayers, as was to be expected, but with lack of forethought in the choice of scripture. Prayers without reading were the rule in my family, but in the homes of relatives I had suffered this added interval between face washing and food; on these occasions, however, the passage had been selected with an eye to appropriateness, or innocence. But my hostess always opened the Bible at random and read whatever turned up. One morning, when by all the signs she might have been absent, she was plowing her way through a chapter in the Old Testament when she ran smack into this: "Give them, O Lord, what wilt thou give them? Give them a miscarrying womb and dry breasts."

Life among the orphans was pleasant. I had a room in the infirmary —I was said to be ailing—and here I slept in a bed high off the floor, almost as high as the four-poster at my grandmother's, but otherwise different, for all the furniture was white, and cold to the touch, transmitting its chill to everything. I was envied by the orphans because I had a father, and I was rich. The difference between twenty-five cents and nothing can be great, if one is on the nothing end, especially if the receiver of a weekly allowance is lordly and not addicted to secrecy in his spending. Ten of the twenty-five cents of my allowance went to one of the boys who came in every morning and made my fire. I still think that to lie in a warm bed while a fellow relatively human being shiveringly lays one's fire is the ultimate in class distinction. Perhaps that is why the British object to central heating. But more than money, which they might hope some day to have, they envied me my father, and whenever he came to see me they stood as near as they dared and looked on at father and son.

At the end of a few months my father came one day and told me that he was going to the University of Chicago, and that my brothers and I were to live in Colleton County with his mother and sisters.

I was not unprepared for the news, nor for the life I was to lead the next three years. A year or so before I had had my first fight with a total stranger, an Irish boy about my size and twice as tough. It was not the beating I got—my cousins had hardened me to that—but the provocation to invasion, which was simply that he did not know who I was, he only knew I had no business in that part of town. I told him my name and said I was on my way to visit the son of Governor Ellerbe. This tenuous connection with the aristocracy I offered in the expectation that he would be impressed. He was. He was also my introduction to unreasoning hostility.

CHAPTER III

Grandmother Rice's Plantation

M^Y FATHER'S FAMILY LIVED IN THE LOW COUNTRY, A HOT MUGGY malarial land that sapped the strength and drained ambition from all except the toughest. The sandy soil, shading in color from grey on hillock and hammock to deep black at the swamp edge, merged into canebrakes and slow-moving rivers, whose black waters were tinged with ocher from the tannin of cypress stumps. The sand was the home of the hookworm, and from the backwaters came death-bearing mosquitoes; but no one knew of hookworm yet, and the mosquitoes were merely a nuisance—and not to all at that, for wealth accumulated to vendors of tonics for chills and fever. (Except in textiles, the only fortunes made in the South have come from putting things into the human mouth: patent medicines, Coca-Cola, tobacco.) Farmers planted the same crops on the same land year after year and spent most of their earnings on fertilizer, invoking experience—"Cain' tell me nothing 'bout farmin'; ain't I done wore out more'n one farm?"—and tradition, in their scorn of this new-fangled thing called science. The "faith to the fathers once delivered" was inclusive. Occasionally one of them pulled himself together and cleared a piece of new ground—this was all right—inviting in his neighbors to a logrolling; but, when they had cut down his trees and hitched them to the edge of the clearing and eaten his food and gone home, he was left with a forest of resinous everlasting pine stumps that meant years of broken plow points and prying and pulling and hauling, for dynamite was not yet a farmer's tool. But in winter these roots and knots—"light 'ood" knots, we called them—were a comfort; they make a fierce and brilliant fire and have a wonderful clean smell.

Everyone was poor and everyone accepted poverty as an act of God, like too much or too little rain, and children. Home-grown corn and pork and store-bought sow-belly, flat slabs of tallow white, were standard diet. The corn was ground in the slow-moving water mill, so slow that taking corn to mill was a prized task, for it meant half a day's fishing. One had to wait one's turn; there were always others ahead of one, or alleged to have been. The siftings of the ground corn were meal, the rest grits, which we had for breakfast every day. From the meal were made oval pones, dunkers' delight, baked in oven or spider, or dropped into pot licker and then called dumplings. These sank to the bottom of the stomach and stayed there. Pot licker was the water and grease in which cabbage or its cousin, collards, the only winter vegetable, had been boiled for hours, with a piece of pork siding or, rare treat, a ham hock. Biscuit and undunked corn bread were softened with pork drippings; butter was unusual, for the cows were as poor as the people. Only the visiting preacher could count on a chicken in every pot. Men lived from Sunday to Sunday, when they drove over roads bumpy with roots and twisted from years of dodging fallen trees and mud puddles, to arrive at last at the church and hear the promise of a better life to come. Poverty is the seedbed of piety.

My father's kin were sunk in the double poverty that comes of having seen better days. Colleton County, named after one of the original Lords Proprietors, retained some remnants of a gentry, to which the Rices had belonged and still made a tenuous claim of belonging. Even so, it was county as distinguished from state gentry, and very distinguished from Charlestonian, who, while they lived all of fifty miles away, dimmed other lights with their reiterated superiority. In the low country, you were best or you were nothing. This may explain why my Grandmother Smith, who had a teaspoonful of the snob in her, said that she asked only one thing of her children, that none of them should marry anyone from Colleton County. (Three of the five did.)

My father's father, who died before I was born, had been a doctor in Charleston before he moved his growing family to a large unprosperous plantation near Walterboro which had belonged to his wife's people. He tried farming, but the life was too slow and uneventful, and he knew nothing about his new trade; so he turned the place over to hired help and slaves and set out to be a doctor again. He was a huge man, weighing, his family reluctantly admitted, more than three hundred pounds; but their testimony was not required, for his armchair, made to order, remained as witness, large enough to seat in comfort two people of ordinary size. (It made *Gulliver's Travels* quite real to me.) He practiced within a radius of fifty miles and for years lived in his buggy, also specially built for him, carrying quilts along and sleeping under pine trees or in any secret dry place, for when he got home he would find a swarm of patients and kin of patients waiting for him with urgent calls. When he had emptied his buggy of the hams and eggs and jugs of molasses and other things with which he had been paid— there was almost no cash money in all the countryside—and had doctored the ailing present, he climbed into his buggy and was off again. His family spoke of him as if he had been a stranger. He died when my father was sixteen years old and was buried in a great coffin of yellow pine knocked together in the middle of the night by a neighbor handy man, leaving to his wife and children a good name and a worn-out, run-down place. To his son my father he bequeathed all his energy.

The original plantation house had burned down years before I saw the place, and they now lived in a much smaller house that was indistinguishable from the homes of their neighbors. It had five bedrooms, counting the attic in which my two male cousins slept, not too much space for the eleven of us; the sitting room was a wide hallway opening in front on to a piazza that ran along the wing to the end room; the back door led to a runway and the detached kitchen. In summer we ate on the runway, where it was cool if any place was and handy to kitchen and pump. Between the floor boards were cracks half an inch wide, making it easy to sweep, and serving another purpose to the one hired man on the place, a robust lascivious Negro who used to lie on the ground underneath in the middle of the day and peek up at my old aunts.

In the kitchen, where we ate in winter, was a cookstove that required much wood chopping and a big fireplace built of daubed clay, where most of the cooking was done, in spiders and pots. Boil or fry was the rule. Besides the daily biscuits, the only baking done was of light bread, the original of the baker's imitation. The yeast that sat in a crock in the corner of the fireplace went back in ancestry beyond the years of any living member of the family, like the contents of a French soup pot, and was as carefully guarded as the bed of coals. Matches, even in my day, were sparsely used and my elders could remember the time when there were none and dead coals meant a long walk to a neighbor's fireplace.

Near the kitchen, in a corner of the neglected garden—work time was precious and field crops had first call—stood the smokehouse, lean in comparison with my other grandmother's, but in pattern the same, hams and bacon on the rafters, molasses barrels along the side. Not far away was a shed that covered an iron pot about five feet in diameter set down flush in an oven of daubed clay. This was used as the washpot the year round and, in winter, for rendering lard and boiling syrup. Besides these buildings there were the usual barns and outhouses, and a backhouse, or privy, with holes of graduated sizes. In addition to its designated use it was my brother Mike's favorite reading room; when he heard someone coming, he hid the book and confounded his accuser.

Another memorable outhouse stood between kitchen and grape arbor; in one corner sat an iron cauldron now cracked and useless, the last of several that had once been used for getting the year's supply of salt.

In the slack time of winter slaves and cauldrons had been loaded into wagons and sent to the coast, more than fifty miles away, there to boil sea water for a couple of weeks, for salt was scarce and expensive, human labor not. In another corner were some boxes that offered richer food to curiosity: my Uncle Willie had returned from Columbia to his mother's home and was enjoying a long spell of illness; the boxes contained his medical books. Besides the salt cauldron there were other reminders of the time when the plantation had been self-contained— a spinning wheel that my grandmother still used when she wanted a piece of string, a broken loom, prickly carding combs, bullet molds; horse troughs hollowed out of solid tree trunks, hand-wrought nails and wooden pegs that held together the logs of the barn, themselves hewn with an adze—these and other things; worst of all was a rice mortar burnt out of an up-ended log, with an oaken pestle that was suspended from the limb of a tree, to help in lifting the weight—only it didn't, not after half an hour's pounding, when there was the question as to which made one more tired, going up or coming down. Nothing was bought that could be grown or made on the place. Of the three things that had been regularly imported from the outside world, coffee, gunpowder, and plow points, two, coffee and plow points, were still prime necessities and held priority. Coffee was bought in hundred-pound bags and imperfectly roasted in the kitchen oven; but, as my elders liked to say, it was better than toasted corn and oats, the Civil War substitute, much better—I should have tasted that.

We might have had wine. A scuppernong vine of gnarled antiquity grew between the kitchen and the edge of the cotton patch, spreading over an arbor some fifty feet on the side. On the hottest day in mid-summer it was cool here, and one pleasantly reached up and picked the gray-green grapes that grew abundantly in clusters of two and three. The best fertilizer for scuppernongs was the carcass of a dead dog, which added sweetness to the already sweet grapes. These made an excellent wine, sweeter than a heavy sauterne. Not that I was ever allowed to do more than taste it; one had to be invalid and old; "strong drink was raging," and every child was assumed to be a potential drunkard. At a cousin's house, however, one of the McLeod's near Lynchburg, the one whose brother chopped her finger off—on a dare —I had once got its full flavor in a tumbler of syllabub and walked unsteadily from the table; but only once, for my carriage had been marked.

The cotton fields came so close to yard and house as to give the place a kind of pinched look, the cash-bearing stalks being given every inch that could be spared; and yet, from the far corner of the arbor to the woods beyond, a path cut diagonally across the patch, a gash in the spring when the ground was newly plowed, a canyon when the stalks were grown. It was a symbol, not only of man's reluctance to walk through an angled world—college campuses would teach me that—but, since the path took up the space of a long row, of the improvidence of the South.

The woods through which the path went were mostly scrub oak and second-growth pine, nature's slow recovery from the attack of the saw-mill, which was making a desolation of the land. A few of the original trees were left, so huge that it took three small boys, their fingers touching, to reach around their trunks, but these were now being ruthlessly felled and hauled away by the logging teams. When the trees had been chopped down and trimmed the logs were slung between two pairs of great wheels, one to which the four mules were hitched, the other far down at the end.

My brothers and I were friends of the drivers, for a good and obvious reason—the usual basis of the friendship of children: they let us ride astride the logs and skin our bare legs on the scaly bark that came off in patches and flaked like isinglass. The mules were also our friends—not intimate however, for we had better sense than to come too close—and they were beautiful, with thighs as sleek as a Miami bathing beauty's. Mules were the only creatures in the South that looked and were well fed; even a shiftless Negro would work to feed his mule, and the meanest of the poor whites would not let his mule starve, whatever might happen to his family. They got in return the gratitude of a fickle woman. Southern women and mules have a lot in common, including toughness.

The path, which eventually led to the old place, down near the swamp, the other farm that now made up the plantation, crossed abandoned fields that once had grown cotton and corn but were now covered with yellow broom sedge, which had from a distance the look of fruitful grain. On one day in the year these fields furnished the countryman's equivalent of sport. Within the memory of my elders they had been full of partridge and in the woods and thickets wild turkeys had been plentiful, but they had long ago been killed off, for hunger knows no season. The only game left in number were squirrels, which would eat up half a corn crop in the bottoms, and harmless rabbits. But squirrels had to be shot, while the rabbit could be caught with dogs or killed in another way. This was the way of sport. A fire was set against the wind on one side of the field; on the other sides men and boys waited with clubs in hand to strike down the fleeing rabbits. They often killed more than they could eat; but it was fun.

The hunters hoped the fire would not spread to the trees and turn their fun into work. Woods fires—called "forest fires" elsewhere—were a constant terror, and sometimes all the able-bodied in the community had to fight fire for days. Only the careless let a fire get out of hand, but it happened at least once in every year, whether the fire was set to catch rabbits or to burn off fields where crops were grown, in obedience to ancestral science.

Woods fires were a danger also to the long fences that crisscrossed the county, enclosing the community pastures. A journey required the opening and closing of several gates on the highway, for cattle must not wander too far. A few farmers had their own pastures, but as a rule private fences were built to keep animals out, not in. We and the rest let out the cattle and hogs, except when the cows were fresh, which brought another task for the children. When the cows had been milked they were turned loose again, for they could be trusted to come home when their udders were full; but the calves were kept penned up until the afternoon, when we got the dullest easy job in the world, "minding the calves," so tiresome that when the cows went dry in early summer there was some compensation for the lack of butter and milk.

Within the community pastures, cattle and hogs, their ears slit with owners' marks, roamed and mixed and mingled in nature's way. A pugnacious bull that was all sinew begat stringy and unpalatable offspring, and hardly a pig in Colleton County could boast that in his veins flowed the blood of no razorback. (It was like the tarbrush in New Orleans.) Down in the canebrakes was the home base of the razorback; from here he made forays into an easily conquered world, for nothing could stop or hold him, not fence nor river nor moral law. He was the toughest creature, in more ways than one, that ever lived, and fierce. His backbone was a knotted cord that arched under his tightly stretched skin, and the skin was glued directly to his ribs; for snout he had a long slender cone that came to a point in a flat callus the size of a small saucer, with which he plowed—other hogs might root; not he. His legs were long and stringy and took him over the ground, if he chose to run, faster than any but the fleetest hound's, and the hound, if he had sense, pretended it had been a mistake and slunk away, for when the boar turned and spoke, only a fool would approach that terrifying noise. His mate was as fierce as he, and a small fisherman digging worms had to keep his eye peeled for a sow with litter, for she would attack any moving thing. The meat of the razorback was all muscle and tendon; a man had to be hungry indeed to eat it, and few white men ever did—except in Virginia, where this then lowest of pork society is now in the social register, for his hind leg is a Smithfield ham.

The South Carolinian had bred fine horses, but in the general poverty even this tradition was breaking down. A roan stallion of dubious

pedigree served our neighborhood and struck terror into small onlookers with his eagerness to earn five dollars for his owner. His only
rival was a dispirited listless jackass so old that he could no longer even
leer, and he handed on the torch of life as if he didn't believe in it.

But change has come, even to South Carolina. Once again the bar-
barian has swept down from the vigorous North and reformed the ways
of the soft South. One can now drive the nineteen miles from Varnville
to my grandmother's place in less time than it took us to hitch up. The
poor farmer, who once twisted securely along the road in his wagon,
is crowded off to a scared journey on the shoulders of the new highway.
Nature submits to bridle and bit: the roan stallion, the mournful jackass, the wild bull, are gone, for breed has a value in the market place.
But partridge and turkey have come back, on great stretches of waste
land, where they and other game live secure until the day of their death
—not, however, at the blast of the muzzle-loader but by the imported
gun in the hands of the Yankee sportsman. (Game is preserved by
those who do not need to eat it.)

There is resentment among the whites; contempt, both sham and
real. The Negro alone knows how to take the new world serenely. The
mule he loved so well is being plowed under by the tractor, but its
balky place is filled by the broken-down car; he sits by the side of the
road, surrounded by family and well-wishers, waiting patiently for it to
make up its mind to go.

II

In 1860 the South became a matriarchy. The men went away from
home to other battlefields, leaving the women free to manage farm and
plantation directly, without their bungling hindrance; when they returned, those who had escaped heroic death—the rest, the blessed dead,
did not, as Homer would say—they found their surrogates in complete
and competent charge, and liking it. Four years had fixed the habit of
command, which, when I first began to know them, thirty had not

broken, nor could they forget how pleasant life had been when all the men were gone.

Men like to think themselves a necessary part of life, but when the question is raised the answer comes down to a quite small moment; pushed to the fringe of consciousness lies the unflattering knowledge that women enjoy their absence. (What does a married woman love more than she loves a pick-up lunch?) I used to sit and listen to old ladies talking about the terrible war, how they had "worked their fingers to the bone," pinching and saving, slaves to duty, only to see their little all go up in flames set by the invader; but through all their talk ran the sweet memory of happy days, with just enough of sad experience to sharpen their delight. The gravamen of their charge against Sherman was, not that he had robbed them of sons and lovers, but that he had stolen the family silver.

In the business of digging up grandmothers the South is easily first. Hardly a family of the middle and upper classes was without its living or legendary matriarch, keen of intellect and lacking in respect for persons or institutions. Neither church nor school, the most potent whippers-in of Western civilization, were proof against her clarity of mind and will; she saw them and their human heads as what they were, fictions, and used them—for she knew, as unscrupulous rulers know, that fictions were her surest weapons. The world was a man-made foolish thing, from which she chose what she wanted by an unprincipled eclecticism. Daughters and granddaughters, nieces and cousins, looked on and learned from her; when death, her only conqueror, decreed a new election, from the ranks of female kin another chose herself. Her successor might be married or not, it made little difference, for in the South of my childhood an old maid was respected; somewhere toward the North, beneath the sod of Gettysburg or Appomattox, lay a grey-clad lover, real or imagined.

My Aunt Lou was a part-time matriarch. In winter, when there was only man's work to be done out of doors and we lived in cramped intimacy, she was supreme. No action or thought was secure from her gauging and gouging, and only the tough or desperate dared take a stand against her will. She had once been beautiful, it was plain to see; poverty and hard work had not so touched body and face as to obscure what had once been there. Her back was now permanently bow-shaped from bending to her work over the ground, her fingers were as calloused with horn as a Negro's heel, and her face was drawn with wrinkles of determination; but her eyes were still young, and her mouth was like my father's, as sensual as an Egyptian queen's. When she spoke, the words came carefully chosen and carefully formed, for she had a brilliant mind and knew it, and knew that it deserved a decent report. Others might scream, and did, and slop over into Negroid speech, but she never raised her voice, as she often reminded me, nor let it slide into the lazy drawl of kith and kin. Of her language, however, I remember best her left arm. It had been broken when she was young and inexpert setting had left it curved inward at the wrist, giving it the look of a boxer's hook in mid-action; while she was talking it lay quiet in her lap, waiting to be called, when it came swiftly up and finished off the stroke.

From Monday to Saturday she was an old woman, but on Sunday she became young again and clothed herself for church with all the care of girlhood. Her dresses were antiques, but that did not bother her so long as they held together, for she had fixed on a permanent style and disregarded fashion. In this respect her only weakness was her hat, wherein she made some concession to the recently current mode, doing it over at the beginning of each winter in a fashion not more than six months gone. During the preceding summer she never went to church, and my cousins and I had as our duty to report to her what kind of hats were being worn. (My most plaguing heritage from her is milliner's eyes.) She dressed herself according to a strict ritual long drawn out, but how many petticoats she wore remained a matter of conjecture, for I always lost count; peek as carefully as I would, I was thrown off my calculations by the exciting semifinals, when she pinned tissue paper to her penultimate garment and tied about her waist a string from which hung a folded sheet that served as bustle. Then she lifted the grosgrain silk high above her head and let it slide slowly downward. First to appear from the black cloud were her hands, the twisted wrist and then the other; for a moment they hung in mid-air, old and gnarled, but when her face came through, she had slipped off thirty years.

Aunt Mollie never went to church. I noticed that she was always left behind; when the offering in the way of reason proved unconvincing, I, having just begun my stretch of three years' residence at my Grandmother Rice's, had not yet learned to keep my questions to myself and asked, "Why can't somebody else cook dinner?" and got a short sharp rebuff. But in time I found out why.

She was small, almost tiny, and her arms and neck were twisted and shriveled like cornstalks after a dry summer; her face, from forehead to chin, was drawn in an upward curve, for all the teeth were missing from the left side of her mouth; her eyes seemed never quite to focus and her speech was thick and vague. I was fond of her in a dumb sort of way and used to hang around the kitchen and talk to her. She seldom answered with more than a word, but she listened, and that is all a child requires. Sometimes, at a chance word of mine, tears would come squeezing out of her eyes and roll down her dry cheek. When she saw I was looking, she wiped them away with her dirty apron—it was always dirty during the daytime—and sent me away on a long errand.

One day in September—I have not forgotten; every detail is in my memory, the smoldering log-end in the fireplace, the spider covered with coals, the poker leaning against the stove, cobwebs in the corner, her eyes, everything—she kept lifting the lid off the pot and saying "I can't help it. I can't help it." "Help what?" I asked, but she paid no attention to my question, moved away from the fireplace, inattentively busied herself about something, came back again, lifted the lid, and said, "Can't help it. I can't help it." "Help what?" I asked again, raising my voice to a pitch that would have invited a rebuke from Aunt Lou. Then Aunt Mollie saw me and answered, "I can't help it if there're maggots in the ham," and she lifted the lid of the iron pot and showed me the greasy mess with hundreds of maggots floating on the top. "I can't help it," she said again, this time to me, but when I looked up at her and started to say something I saw that she no longer knew that I was there. "I know it's my fault," she said, "but I can't help it. It's all my fault. I shouldn't have stole that money, I know, but I can't help it." Now I was frightened, as much by the way she looked as by what she was saying. "What money?" I asked, but she did not answer, kept on saying, "I shouldn't have stole that money. I know. I'm guilty. I shouldn't have stole it." I pulled at her apron, trying to get her to look at me, but she just stood there, the tears flowing down her face, saying the same thing over and over again. Then I ran.

I ran to Aunt Lou and said, "Something's wrong with Aunt Mollie. Come quick." She did not come quick, but with a hardened bitter face quietly finished what she was doing, got up from her chair, and said, "You stay here," and went to the kitchen.

No one told me what was wrong, no one told me that Aunt Mollie was "touched." For days I went about in terror, keeping clear of the kitchen, and was finally calmed only by the matter-of-fact way in which the others treated her. At first they did not speak to her, and went about their business as if they did not hear; but as the tension rose and even the toughest could stand it no longer they began to argue with her. "You didn't steal any money—well, when did you steal it?" Then Aunt Mollie's voice got shrill—I had never heard it so before—and she shrieked at them, "I tell you I stole it," and burst into tears. Then came long silences, as she puttered about the cooking, letting the tears fall on the stove and disappear in a puff of steam. But silence itself became intolerable; taut nerves snapped and madness entered into the rest. Then they began to jibe, to tease her into relieving speech. "What about that money you stole?" they would ask, and find comfort in the torrent of noise. Aunt Jinny and her four children, even Aunt Lou, joined in the hateful sport; all except my grandmother, who sat silent in her corner.

Aunt Mollie had never been married and she was the eldest child. That was all I ever knew about her history, except one other thing. When my Uncle Willie was born, I was told, the youngest of eleven children, she had wept because it would mean "one more mouth to feed." She herself told me, in an interval of sanity, that he was such a small baby that you "could have put him in a teapot." Thereafter, when I wanted to make her mad, as we said—not really mad; I never enjoyed that sport—I used to remind her of this: "You say Uncle Willie was so small that you could have put him in a teapot? Why didn't you then, and pour hot water on him?" for I knew she worshiped him, as I did not.

Grandmother Rice was a vegetable. In the morning after breakfast she planted herself in a split-bottom chair in the chimney corner and sat rooted there the livelong day, with an occasional excursion into usefulness, when she moved heavily about the kitchen helping Aunt Mollie; but as a rule things were brought to her where she sat, beans to string, potatoes to peel, anything that could be done with inattention. If she had not been perched on the edge of poverty, she would have been a bed-ridden invalid—a favorite trick of Southern women; but the poor cannot afford the luxury of protracted illness. She seldom spoke, and at length even I with all my love of talk grew grateful for the infertile silence; her little samples of speech held no promise of the wisdom I had learned to expect from the very old. Some old people, while they sit waiting for death, give their account of a road once traveled, where it is rough and where it is smooth, and set up for the young some contrast to their hurried present; but my grandmother simply sat, untouched by regret or pleasant recollection, suspended in time, beyond a thing so positive as waiting. And yet she could be stubborn; when her feelings were roused, she made them felt by the weight of her silence. Whenever my father's name was mentioned, or Aunt Bella's, and others were driven into shrill speech, she came down heavy on the side of her daughter Mollie. There was another way, too, in which she gave her silent support: In the late afternoon of a long summer's day she would move from her chair in the kitchen to the front porch, in time to be at and on the side of Aunt Mollie, now dressed in a clean apron, as she waited for the rest to come from the fields.

My other grandmother had taught me to expect, when words were high and so violent as to threaten instant action, a catalytic sentence that would bring all to a sense of kinship once again; but no such sentence ever came from my Grandmother Rice, to strike aside the weapons of anger and restore peace. There was no peace. Every conflict resolved itself into grim silence, silence that picked at the brain with hate, to be renewed later at the same point and carried on to deeper bitterness and contempt. She never laughed, nor even smiled, but turned to the world the thick look that, I believe, had always been there; for, now that I am past the mid-point of a life of seeing many, I am willing to guess that the dull old were dull young.

She was no match for her husband, nor, as it proved, for her elder son. He was, she said, when her husband had died, now head of the family in his father's stead and it was his duty to take over the running of the place. She was not inept at shifting burdens and relied upon the law of primogeniture, which held good in South Carolina, as to responsibility. But he knew otherwise. From the time when his mother had found him, a child of eight, out in the pasture where she had sent him to mind the calves, preaching from the stump of a longleaf pine, he had known what he must do. God caught him young and held him all his days.

He might have begun preaching on the death of his father; he was only sixteen and ignorant, but time would soon make up his lack of age, and ignorance was no bar. There was even some question as to whether a man of God might not know too much, raised by those who did not. Protestantism, as is sometimes forgotten, is protest, and one needs no knowledge to protest, only strong feeling, and my father had plenty of that. There was no great body of history and doctrine to be learned, as in the Catholic Church; Methodism had no history except the life of John Wesley, who had himself brought his doctrine to Georgia less than a hundred years before; and there was little of that, not more than a small brain could soon learn to parrot. Nothing was required of a candidate for the ministry beyond an enunciation of faith in traditional words, the ability to quote scripture freely, and a little formal learning.

There were examples of consecrated ignorance. One preacher in the county had come before the committee of ordination and met the test of faith and scripture, but when it came to the examination in logic he had repeatedly answered their questions with, "That ain't in my book." Finally, for they wanted to pass the faithful young man, they asked to see his book. When he fetched it, they found the word "Logic" all right, printed on the back, but inside was bound a Plane Geometry, which he had learned, as he had his Bible, from cover to cover. There were other examples, higher placed.

But my father was to be no ordinary preacher and had an early scorn of professional ignorance. Now he saw the chance that his father had denied him and did not hesitate; with little or no money he began his wild race after education: school in Walterboro, where he tried to learn everything at once, South Carolina College, theological seminary— funny word, in that connection—teaching for a few months each year and hoarding his slight pay, preaching for a small fee or just for practice, selling books in vacation, anything to get on toward knowledge. When he returned home for visits, he found the family divided, in this as in most things: his mother, and Aunt Mollie, and Aunt Bella doubtful but willing for him to go on; my other aunts, Lou and Jinny and

Florence, dead against him, calling him selfish, for they knew that he would wince, and trying all their tricks of domination. He told them to wait, he would make it up to them in the end, if they would only be patient. He did, but they never forgave him for deserting them, nor for proving that he had been right. No one is more hated than the one successful member of a family.

All his life he loved his mother and sisters with a strange enduring passion. When I had come to know them, he and I could never speak of them together; I also had strong feelings about them. By that time their grudging release of him had been transmuted into a generous act; for he, like all the saviors of mankind, was an alchemist of the soul. He never saw them clearly, but always through a mist of love; but by the terms of his election he loved God more than he loved them, more than he loved any one.

The true history of his early life came to me for the most part from words and phrases snatched from passing sentences; for, young as I was, I had learned to distrust his account where it touched the family, while they, in contrast to my mother's people, were reticent, stingy of consciously revealing words. Language was for them on the level of bare communication, except when they were angry; then they used words as cleavers, or, worse still, they were silent. From them I learned what awful things silence can say.

My grandfather must have lacked imagination to a degree unusual. On a plantation surrounded by swamps difficult to cross, sometimes dangerous and always slow, with their causeways of pine slabs—the first cut from the log and therefore curved on one side—that lay in the mud and jolted the eyeteeth out of a traveler, except one on horseback, and even he had to fear that his horse might catch his foot between the loose boards, and break a leg . . . nineteen miles from Varnville, where, after an early morning start, one finally arrived with aching sockets and abraded bottom, unless of course a bridge had been washed away and one had been obliged to turn back and wait for a dry day; after a wait that included all time, the wood-burning locomotive might come at last, and, after another age spent in loading its tender with six-foot lengths of split pine and filling its tanks with water, begin to creep upon Charleston, or toward the west on Bamberg . . . nineteen miles from Varnville, and, far worse, ten miles from any neighbor of the same social pretensions . . . here in the middle of the pine woods, he insulated his five daughters, cut them off from the world they had been taught to believe was theirs by right, and expected them to repress the laws of nature in pride of race. It didn't work, not with all of them.

Aunt Bella had held out until her middle years and then been seduced into matrimony by a neighboring small farmer, who could offer only affection and a good living. From that moment she was the family outcast. Aunt Lou never forgave her nor allowed others to forgive her, not openly at least. "She shall never darken this door again," she said, and the decree included her husband, except for the "again," for he had done his courting from a distance, not daring to come nearer until the night of the elopement. There was something ridiculous and sad in the picture of a middle-aged man stealing a middle-aged woman away from nothing more terrible than family pride. When I first saw them, some ten years later, he knew that he had stolen more woe than joy; his wife had used up all her courage in one act and now felt the weight of her guilt increasing with the years. My father, on his semi-annual visits from Chicago, always went to see her; made a pointed point of it, in fact, and filled his mother's house with sullen anger for days before and after. Sometimes he took me with him, by way of underlining his disapproval of her exile, and blandly stored up later trouble for an ephemeral innocent. The first few minutes of our visit were quiet enough, but when Aunt Bella got out her handkerchief, her husband hastily took me out into the back yard and tried awkwardly to entertain me; but it was no use, for we both stayed in the house in imagination. Aunt Bella whimpered and complained to my father, who sat helpless, as the professional comforter must when his own feelings are involved. When he had left us and returned to the peace of divinity school, Aunt Lou, by the magic of feminine logic, made me the offender and I heard all she would have said to my father if she had dared. My grandmother never questioned her decree, nor visited the errant daughter, though sometimes I saw her, momentarily uprooted from her chair, whispering over the kitchen stove with Aunt Mollie and caught the name "Bella"; but when Aunt Lou was in full spate she sat silent.

In these matters my Aunt Jinny also was firm. She had herself, in the warmth of youth, leapt into marriage with a man who was in some way —I never learned just how—connected with the liquor traffic. She too had been banished, to live in outer darkness with her publican and— presumably—sinner. After some years she had the fortune to bury her husband, sue successfully for grace, and return to her home, bringing with her four mementoes of her truancy. Once forgiven, she had the penitential zeal of the salvaged sinner. She was, however, by nature mild, and her curiosity at least had been satisfied by marriage. My brothers and I liked her, for she alone had any motherhood in her, and she was rarely other than kind to us, except when she was salivated from an overdose of calomel; then her dammed-up hostility to my father broke over us. My brother Coke was too young to see any sense in hate, and Mike, who was a gentle person and disliked strife, went into his usual retreat, leaving me to catch the full flow. I can remember standing by her bed while she berated me for having caused a quarrel between her two sons, one of whom had taken my side against the other's oppression. Her gums were swollen, and fetid breath rushed out at me with her words; finally, when words could say no more, she struck me, and I can still feel the sting of her callous hand across my face. But this was not usual, not usual enough to suit me, for I preferred open warfare.

There was one other daughter living, Aunt Florence, whom I seldom saw, and was content. She had made an approach to respectability in marriage, but had gone down at least two steps: her husband was a Baptist preacher, and came from outside the state. He was, in fact, a Yankee and was alleged to be of good family, but that had no meaning in the South: Yankees, as Americans in England, came into that world socially naked. "Family" meant Southern, preferably South Carolinian, or Virginian.

Genealogy is a death pang, symptom of a coming end. When great-grandfathers become important, generation has gone into reverse. From that time forth the birth of a child is not the beginning of new life, but the delivery of plastic material into bony hands that will bind its feet and flatten its head into a pattern that is old. Life is forced to turn backward, to be fitted into the matrix of old time, and goodness and antiquity are one.

Sometimes a child will not be molded, has in it some insistence that breaks through to its own way. The girl to whom my Uncle Willie was half-heartedly engaged and whom after some years he timidly married, was such a person. Nothing could hold her high spirit, which shattered the aristocracy of pretence, her mother's, and assumed an aristocracy of being. Mother and daughter, the last of the tribe, lived in splendid squalor, in a great house that was falling to pieces. The grass grew tall in a flower garden that had once been the show place of the county, and the long row of slave cabins was now empty; all except one, where an ancient Negro lived, the last of her servants, who feebly grew a little corn and tended a few pigs for his mistress. I used to follow him as he puttered around, and I can still see the japonicas, nature's best imitation of waxed flowers, and smell the gardenias blooming on bushes that towered far above my head.

The daughter, by the act of repudiating aristocracy, had become free to choose what was good in it, but her mother remained completely entangled in the past. I never knew her well, nor did any one else, for manner and presence kept all at a distance; but one could look at her, and sharp-cut nose and chin told the twin stories of lineage and hunger. But she would take charity from no one; for, as the neighbors said, she was proud as Lucifer, and to pride of memory was now grafted pride of poverty. There was speculation among the irreverent as to how even death would have the nerve to approach the grand old lady; but finally he did and took her away. She rests in the graveyard of St. Michael's in Charleston, in the peace that comes to those who lie among the best, and the knowledge that any other paradise is bound to be a comedown.

Meanwhile her daughter became engaged to Uncle Willie, and remained engaged until he should be able to support her "in the style to which she had been accustomed"—her mother's words, spoken without intention of irony. She endured prescribed idleness as long as she could, but when she could stand it no longer she slipped the leash of her mother's pride and became a schoolteacher. The old lady took to her bed, a gentlewoman's final argument. "This will be the death of me," she said; but it wasn't, not for a long time.

Whenever Aunt Pet—I'm sorry; that was her name—came to my grandmother's, I followed her around like a hound pup. On one of her visits, however, I was lying on my face in the attic nursing and cursing a boil that would not let me walk nor stand nor sit. I heard her through the cracks in the floor asking where I was and my elders' evasive answers. When at last they circumlocuted my ailment, she let out a peal of laughter, rushed up the stairs and said, "Let's see your boony." When she had inspected the livid bump and prescribed ox gall, she sat on the edge of the bed and told me a gay story.

To be a country school teacher in those days meant to live a life just a cut above that of the hired hand, the only difference being what one did during the day. The teacher boarded around, that is, lived for successive periods of a month in the home of one of the families that had children in the school, taking pot luck and subject to the hazards peculiar to each house: dirt, bed-bugs and other vermin, leaky roofs, musty bedclothes, and poor folks' food. Aunt Pet told me of her first night in such a place, and added to my vocabulary another expression of the idea of democracy.

After supper, she said, the family sat around the fireplace, the father at one side of the hearth, she, the honored guest, at the other. There was talk and laughter and spitting for a while, and then the head of the house said, "Well, I reckon it's about time for the foot tub. Jim, you go fetch it." Jim went and brought a wooden tub holding about five gallons of warm water from the kitchen stove, and set it down in front of his father, with wash rag and towel and a cake of home-made soap. The old man took off his shoes and put his feet, grimed with the dirt of a day's plowing, into the tub and soaped and scrubbed them well. Then, as he dried them, it was the turn of the sitter on his right to soap and scrub his feet, and so on around the semicircle. When the tub was about half way to her, Aunt Pet began to wonder whether the water would be changed; the question was answered when it got nearer and nearer and blacker and blacker. When it finally reached her, it could have been called water only by a stretch of imagination and courtesy; but, while her neighbor was washing, she pulled off shoes and stockings, shut her eyes, and plumped her feet in.

She was a cultural sport, an unexpected flower growing on the dump heap. As a rule, when an agrarian aristocracy is uprooted from the life-giving soil, it ceases to be fed from any source. The only test of belonging then becomes birth. Hamilton had tried to reserve the government of America to the "rich and well-born," but in the South Carolina of my childhood there were few or no rich, only the well-born—and they took no risk of contamination. (With me, "well-born" meant born on a plantation. I question whether an aristocracy can be founded on A. T. & T.) The aristocracy of England, as long as it lived off the land, was a refined peasantry, constantly fertilized from below and reinvigorated by lust; in South Carolina they no longer had the courage of their lust, to the point of marriage. (After all, there were Negro women.)

So, as in some parts of the state today, marriage was dedicated to the continuance of class that had become caste; pure blood, however, gets thin and watery. Seed-spilling planters must blush in heaven or wherever at the timid choices of their pallid descendants. It was not so in their vigorous life; even a woman could stoop and draw a husband up to her estate.

Every social class in its aspirations imitates the class immediately above, not having the wit to see through and beyond. (Virtue always comes from above, or so men think.) My father's people, being what the British would call at best gentry or at worst middle-class, followed the pattern and assumed the manner and mores of the aristocracy— not the morals; they lacked the freedom for that—and, since the older a society the greater the gulf between classes, their isolation was complete. They lived in a sparsely settled county in the oldest part of the state, at a great spatial distance from their like and as great a social distance from the absent aristocracy and their present neighbors; the result was resentment, double on the part of my elders, pure and simple among those who lived near-by. Sometimes it flared.

Once, when it was decided to clear a piece of new ground, a general invitation to a logrolling was sent out, and for days before came the business of cooking mountains of food for the hungry workers; but when the day came no one showed up except a few impelled by sheepish curiosity to see how the snub would be taken. The rest sent word that "if the Rices wanted their logs rolled, let 'em send for their high-toned friends." This had happened some time before I went to live with my grandmother, and I got the story only bit by bit; but the memory still blistered. While I was there, however, I myself saw the law of class-preservation at work, when the cousin whom we called "Bub"— he remained so, all his life—fell in love with a girl who lived across the branch—"brook" to others.

It began at the first cane-grinding, in early winter, when the days were still warm and the nights just sharp enough to make a fire feel good. After the tautening summer, with its long days of grinding work that sent men stumbling to bed and found its way into their dreams, tempers began to cool in the cool of the evening and neighbors came and were friendly once again. They gathered around the bubbling syrup pot and drank cane juice and laughed and talked, and spat. Even Aunt Lou for the moment relaxed her social vigilance; otherwise my cousin might not have yielded to temptation. The people who lived across the branch came the first night and brought with them a daughter who, the year before, had been a gawky girl all arms and legs; now she was a woman who had burst suddenly into full beauty. My cousin was struck dumb and for the rest of the evening blundered about, spilling syrup and doing all other wrong things. Aunt Lou, relaxed into hibernal amiability, did not see what was happening, and no one wished to tell her, for young love was a pleasant thing to see. The next week the neighborhood gathering moved to another syrup pot, and Aunt Lou, still unaware, stayed at home; she had done her duty. Meanwhile the fire burned bright and by the end of a month was a roaring blaze. Then the girl's parents did a foolish thing: they dressed her up in her Sunday best in the middle of the week and sent her over on some slight errand. Aunt Lou took one look, saw, and struck. As soon as the visitor was gone, Bub was hauled off to the end room by Aunt Lou and his mother, the door was shut—itself an omen—and words were spoken. For once Aunt Lou raised her voice; the presence of others equally curious prevented my getting near enough to hear, but the next few days told the story. My cousin went about with a sullen stubborn look and did not speak. The girl came once again, was frozen, and departed. The next winter at cane-grinding time, she, now married to a commoner, sat silent with swollen belly, hiding resentful eyes. Some years later my cousin married one of his own kind, to go childless but unspotted to his grave.

III

If my cousin had only seen his girl in the hot season, his story might have been different, for with the coming of spring Aunt Lou went into eclipse, and remained throughout the steaming summer. The place was too poor to allow the hiring of more than one Negro, Jake, and all the family except Aunt Mollie and my grandmother were compelled to go into the fields and work, at planting and hoeing corn, chopping cotton—that is, thinning the small plants in their drilled line—and, later on, cotton picking; plowing alone was a man's job; everything else had to be done by men and women alike, all the relentless tasks that nature can impose upon a field hand.

By midsummer life had become amoebic, reduced to the simple business of keeping alive. (Only Negroes, who love the sun, and poor whites, who are really amoebae, know how to endure a Southern summer.) Then, with the bursting of the cotton bolls, existence was pushed to a still lower level. Cotton picking was the cruelest task of the year; it meant hours of bending over until back muscles were burning cords and hands took on a detached mechanical life of their own, weaving in and out and heedlessly wounding themselves on the sharp spines of the bolls. Home-made mittens, cut from lengths of discarded stockings, were incomplete protection, for they left the fingers exposed. I have often seen Aunt Lou and Aunt Jinny drag their bodies up the front steps—Jake had gone to the back, as Negroes must—too weary to have removed their mittens, beyond which their fingers stuck out streaked with blood.

But swollen fingers and aching back were forgotten as their feet touched the bottom step, merged in a greater ignominy from which there was no escape, for the same law that sent Jake to the back forced them to the front. Above them Aunt Mollie, now the lady, dressed in a clean apron smelling of the sun, with hair slicked back and freshly washed face, stood by her mother's side waiting to receive them.

Throughout the picking season this daily ritual of contempt was repeated. It was field nigger and house nigger all over again. Untoiling poets may sing of the dignity of toil; others know better, know there is degradation in obligatory sweat.

The Negro field hand hoped he was as good as the white by whose side he worked, while his fellow laborer, with only the color of his skin to mark their difference, was afraid that he was no better than the Negro. These were the wellsprings of their natures, making the one gay and free, as hope will, the other sullen, angry, and bound. During the summer season my aunts became truculent poor white trash, and their sister's contempt only poured salt on a wound that was already there. But beneath self-distrust there was a fear that ran still deeper, and for this, and another, reason Jake was always set to work apart from them, and Jake was quite content to have it so.

I have seen three other Negroes like Jake: a stevedore on the docks in New Orleans, another field hand on a plantation near Beaufort, and a band leader in New York, all of them as lickerish as a drunken English gentleman, with insatiate eyes that stripped to nakedness every woman, white or black, young or old—D. H. Lawrence turned inside out. In the presence of such lust an ordinary church-going white man felt weak and puny, and sometimes lynched to prove it was not so, while many a white woman was raped in imagination alone. Even poor old Aunt Mollie scuttled away from Jake like a chicken at the shadow of a hawk.

But my aunts were safe from Jake, who snickered at their fright and had his own peculiar reason for wanting to work apart from them. The reason was another woman, a great butterball of a Negress to whom he gave all his wages, eight dollars a month, in return for which she shared his nights, and also shared his days. While he chopped cotton or gathered corn or stripped cane, she sat at the edge of the field, waiting for him to go up the row and back again, back to his day love. She earned her money, if one can speak of earning in such connections, for hers was a twenty-four hour job. The truth was, Southern women were safer from Negro men than from white, whom the presence of Negro men with their implied threat of vigor spurred to prove their potency; nor was the proof discouraged. Through all the trafficking, however, ran the fear of avenging relatives. The gentleman set the pattern in these matters, and he, in case there might be some mistake, just in case his lady might prove frail, loaded his gun and awaited the instrument of her downfall, not infrequently another gentleman. Others aped him and often the whisper spread that there had been a "military wedding," or, if the guilty male was stubborn, as occasionally happened, a killing in the name of honor. (There was some doubt as to whose honor.) Sometimes, however, the man escaped justice by calling as witness a fellow concupiscent to testify that he too had shared the joys; by a twist of folk logic, in this as in lynching, numbers could do no wrong.

Our local nymphomaniac lived on a prosperous farm nearby. Her name was silenced in my grandmother's house, so I had to learn about her from Jake, who told me her story bit by bit, adding details from day to day, but never bringing it quite to completion. He had worked on her father's place, he said, and that was how he knew; but from the sudden fear that sometimes caught his face, I suspected there was more, and one day asked him straight out what it was. He grew pale—Negroes can—and his hands twitched helplessly. "I won't tell." I said, "I'll keep it a secret" (I have, till now). He had resisted her invitations as long as nature would permit, "an' a sight longer than I ever thought I could"—there were few Puritans among the Negroes at that time—held back by the certain knowledge that the end of a rope would mark the end of his life, for in miscegenation the white woman was by definition pure; but even fear had not been strong enough on one occasion, when they were shucking corn together in the barn, "only once, I swear to God." The girl's father became suspicious and sent him away, saying to his daughter, "If you bring a black bastard into my house I'll shoot you," and he meant it. Some time later, when she had been faithful to one lover a little too long, she did bring forth; but, thanks to a white God, the child was white. Her father was so relieved at his escape from murder that he forgave her and even learned to joke about it. "Le's call him 'Mornin' Star,'" he said, "cause he rose too soon."

In midsummer, when the crops had been laid by and were growing, untroubled by plow or hoe, toward their gathering, there came a lull, a few weeks of relaxation from the strain. There also came a swarm of locusts, the revivalists, who swept down over the land and chewed men's souls to bits, leaving behind, when they had made a solitude, shaky resolutions and lean larders. The impious went fishing, hook, line, and sinker. The countryman knew nothing of rod and reel, flies and weighted casting lines, only a heavy cord and a cane pole cut from the brake and hung by its tip from the eaves of the barn until it should turn from olive green to pale yellow. Some set traps against the law—freshets had carried away last year's—but a fish trap was an act of faith, and when one was drawn up and a fish was really there it was a question which was more surprised, fisherman or fish. My cousin Bub preferred shooting, or perhaps more accurately, missing fish with his muzzle-loader. For this sport long preparation was required, for he molded his own bullets. He had for this a single bullet mold, like the one Uncle Ellie had used to pull Uncle Melt's aching tooth, and it was a slow business, heating and pouring the lead and getting one good bullet out of three pours. When he had enough made and had filled his powder horn, we set out across the cotton patch toward the swamp, passing on our way the place where the old house had stood and left as mementoes a few cedars and holly bushes and crepe myrtle squared off in the middle of a cornfield. At the fishing hole he sat in the crotch of an overhanging limb and dozed, and I sat on the bank fishing and dreaming of the day when I should be president or locomotive engineer or something. For variety we sometimes "muddied the waters," stirring up the bottom of the hole and catching the breathless fish with our bare hands; but this was work, unworthy of a true fisherman, who fishes not for fish but peace.

We spent other hours at men's work, tinkering with broken wagons and sharpening plow points, splitting shingles from the straight-grained white oak or rails from logs of yellow pine, with which to mend the fence that snaked itself around the cornfield. The best rails were cedar, but all the large trees had been cut down by my ancestors and, when I went to live with my grandmother, most of these heirlooms had also disappeared. Some years before, a smart Yankee had come and bought from my family and other innocents the cedar rails, offering in exchange a small price in cash or woven wire for a fence. Most farmers chose the shining wire, only to find that it soon rusted and was poor substitute for everlasting cedar. The Yankee hauled his plunder away and made it into pencils, with which to figure how he might beat the Southerner some more.

After the midsummer rest the cotton bolls began to pop open and, unless they were soon picked, spilled their cash upon the ground. This was the saddest time of the year, for, besides back-breaking toil, September was presently around us, the worst time of the year. Food began to run low; pork by now was rancid, cabbage was burned by the heat of the sun and collards had not yet felt the sweetening touch of frost, turnips were tasteless and beans rattled in the pod. This was the time of dysentery: heat-weary bodies became so ill that they could barely drag themselves out of bed to do the necessary tasks for keeping alive, and still work had to be done. There was little fruit on the neglected trees and we had no milk, for the cows had long ago gone dry, and butter was a distant memory. In the spring, short season of plenty, Aunt Mollie had tied pats of butter in corn husks and immersed them in brine, but these she hoarded, for presently my father would be coming for a visit, when cakes and other things requiring butter must be baked for him and he must have butter for his hot biscuits. "I don't understand, John Andrew," he would say, "what you mean complaining about the food; I never tasted better," and discouraged explanation. He did not understand: there were always chickens, guarded from hawks and relatives by Aunt Mollie, for brother and preacher, and at least one ham that she had hidden from hungry mouths.

One summer, the one when Aunt Mollie had showed me maggots floating in the pot licker, my father wrote that he had been to see the stock yards and that he was sending us some hams. I felt warm inside and, as I waited for the coming of the hams and devoured them many times, I enjoyed the discomfiture of his detractors, who never lost a chance to call him stingy. When at last they came, they were souvenirs made of baked clay, the size of walnuts.

From sunrise on, the days were streaking, blinding heat that pierced stinging behind the eyeballs. Chickens came from under the house, unrefreshed by their dust bath, holding their bills wide open and gasping for breath, hogs squshed themselves deeper into the iridescent mud, and a plowman on a distant hill flickered in the haze. He had better be wearing a hat, else the heat would strike him down in the furrow. Seen close up, the lower part of his face was burned to an Indian brown, and when he removed his palmetto to wipe his forehead, he looked like an Englishman recently returned from the East.

After the sun had set and Jake and his temporary mate had retired to privacy, the summer night came down, still and quiet. Out of a rich imagination we called it the "cool of the evening," but it was not cool, only a different kind of heat, sodden air that smothered tired bodies in a blanket of trickling sweat and, when one gulped a breath, stuck in the lungs like balls of warm wet wool. No one spoke, for speech cost

effort, and presently we closed doors and windows to keep out the
night air that gave one chills and fever, and dragged ourselves to beds
that were hot to the touch and hotter still from the canopies of mosquito
netting, for screens were not yet known and only Negroes could sleep
without protection from the poisoning beasts.

To bodies less weary the beds would in another way have been a
discouragement to rest, for from Sunday to Sunday they went often
unmade, it being the rule that each should spread his own or leave it
as it was. We boys never bothered; weeks might go by before the mattress had sagged far down between the rows of slats, its ribbed surface
looking for all the world like a miniature cotton patch, a grid that even
a boy could no longer endure. One's elders were brought more quickly
to reform by much discomfort and some pride, though there was little
enough of pride for everyday use. Aunt Mollie and my grandmother
might have taken all housekeeping as their province, but no one
habitually did anything just for another's comfort. One benefited from
indivisible tasks, like cooking, sweeping, washing clothes; whatever
could be separated was assigned as a private burden and kept firmly
there. With "That's your job," one's fellows washed their hands.
Necessity and kindness do not always live together.

As I look back on it now, it would have been more sensible and
more simple to live under the rule of grace; but grace is pervasive love,
and there was no love. I also realize that I no longer feel the bite of
corrosive poverty, the eternal restlessness of fear, and do not touch
exposed nerve-ends in bodies weakened by poor food and the perpetual
cargo of quinine—against the coming of malaria—and the periodic
dose of calomel that made one feel oneself all intestine, until, when
the pain could be borne no longer, benign laudanum, the other sover-
eign remedy, dulled one to stupor; and above all and in all and through
all, the everlasting heat. No wonder the little seeds of love were parched
to dust.

IV

In cold climates men look forward to the coming of spring; in South Carolina it was the fall of the year that held out promise. When the nights became really cold and we knew that we could once more get a good night's sleep, quilts were got down from the attic, still smelling of summer heat, and mosquito nets were put away, for one gratefully roused from life-giving slumber to slap the few hardy survivors; after supper the pitch-pine fire sent a glow over the room, softening the walls and ceiling to a deeper brown and, as it flashed and sputtered, sending great shadows leaping, the way it must have done when the cave men first discovered giants. In the hot ashes we buried sweet potatoes and toward bedtime drew them out, to fill our stomachs again and bring fantastic dreams. This was the time of rich living after the lean and desolate summer that left men gaunt and skinny. We began to fatten on food that a month before had churned a queasy stomach. This furnished heat that the fireplace never gave, nor was expected to give, for no effort was made to keep the whole room warm, only a little space in front of the fire, where one might toast front or back but never both together. On the coldest day doors were left open—no South Carolinian ever shut a door except by request—and the winter traveler might see from the road the roaring flames behind the silhouettes of the hovering dwellers. It was not that being cold was a virtue, as in England, but that no one had ever been warm all over in the winter.

The official opening of the fall season came with the stripping of cane. We began to hunt up heavy gloves, or rags to tie around our hands, for the blades of the ribbon cane were really blades and could slit a palm wide open. Presently, where there had been a jungle of green, welcome cover to a hen with chicks at sight or sound of hawk, purple stalks stood in naked rows, to be chopped down at the roots and hauled away to the mill that was just beyond the washpot. The twin cylinders of the mill set upright in hewn timbers were rusty from a year's disuse but soon they would gleam, rubbed by the fiber of the stalks and washed off by the squirting juice that fell into the waiting barrels below. From the top of the mill a beam of hardwood about fifteen feet long reached downward, holding in its nose an iron ring to which a singletree was fastened. A horse—there were no motors then —usually the oldest and most useless, or a mule on its last legs, was harnessed with a collar of leather or plaited corn shucks and hitched to the singletree by iron trace chains, for the load was heavy.

Building a fire under the pot; drinking the sweet cane juice from the time when it first ran clear and all the rest of the day, with the fore-knowledge that a porous small boy would have to get up more than once in the middle of the shivering night, for it was quick and sure in transit; the first taste of the first run of the syrup; comradeship in work that was play—all this was pleasant, but there seems to be no pure joy, and not even these delights could blind one to the fate of the horse. As he walked round and round the circuit, the outer chain pressed against his side, first rubbing away the hair and then the hide until, by the end of the day, he wore a long bloody streak that was often cut to the ribs. Nothing could be done about it; rags were tied about the chains, but they became soon a second red streak. When night came and the wounded horse was led away, even hardened grinders found it a relief and settled down to an untroubled evening.

To the softening city dweller we seemed callous, but we were not; we still lived in the world of nature, who includes pain in all pleasure and teaches men to say "Nothing can be done about it." Pain and its crises, disease and death, were acts of God, to be avoided for a little while, God willing, and then endured. The horse suffered pain, but so did man; both were pounded in the same mortar. Some of us who watched the horse's side grow bloody have since become enlightened, turned from cathedral to hospital, joined the revolution and learned to say "Something can be done about it—about anything"; but a boy toting light 'ood knots could not know that some day even heartache could be cured.

During the daytime the syrup was methodically boiled and ladled out into barrels and sent to the smokehouse, but with the coming of night boiling became a ritual, for expert eyes watched to see whether the juice, as it turned from yellow green to brown in the glow of the fire, was properly skimmed and taken off in time. It must be not too thin, just right to sight and taste, for syrup was an indispensable article of diet. We poured it on hot biscuits and corn bread, and into coffee, when it was known as "long sweetening"; mixed it with water and called it a drink, or with sulphur, and took it for spring cleaning. White sugar was sparsely used, for it must be bought, and only the visiting preacher might, and did, shovel it like sand.

The scum of the syrup was fed to the hogs, by us; lax neighbors let it ferment and then distilled it. The product was a clear liquor that looked like corn but was more triggerlike in action, half a small gourdful being enough to strike a man drunk. It was dip, drink, drunk, as quick as that.

As the nights grew colder we waited eagerly for the morning when the ground should be covered with frost, for that meant fresh meat, and meat meant pork (beef was caviar). But the cold weather must hold; otherwise a hot spell might spoil the hams and bacon. By this time we were famished for tasty food, and the first hog killing was an occasion of general rejoicing, and illness. From one year to the next we could not resist the temptation to gorge ourselves, take another helping, just one more bit of skin to chew, until with distended stomachs we went into a terrible night and a following day of inward quaking.

As the New Englander professes to tell the difference between one pot of beans and another, and the Louisiana Cajun really knows bayou shrimp, and a Philadelphian, whatever approval he may give to religion in general, makes no such mistake when it comes to ice cream, so we were expert judges of pork, from head to tail—from hog's-head cheese to pig tails roasted to a crunching brown, and all the good things in between, spareribs and backbone and cracklings, which were the pieces of "tried out" fat that floated to the surface when lard was rendered in the washpot, and other parts preferred by foreigners, chops, fresh ham, and sausages in casings and out. To the attendant Negroes who followed hog killings around the neighborhood was assigned the offensive task of preparing the casings, "ridding the chitterlings"; the pulpy matter had to be scraped from the intestines with a dull knife, leaving a thin membrane into which the sausage was stuffed. As part of their pay the Negroes took home—"toted" was the technical word—the intestines that were left over, whose viscid coils had the look of elongated oysters. These they boiled or fried. Some whites also ate chitterlings, but in general this was a stigma of low origin.

Once or twice during the winter we slaughtered a lean cow or bull and, by a long-standing arrangement with three families who lived nearby, sent to each a quarter, hind or fore without discrimination, for beef was beef and one part as good as another. The wringing of a chicken's neck and letting him flop himself to death on the sandy soil— the neck always kept some of the grit and was passed up at table by the knowing—skinning and gutting a squirrel or rabbit, sticking a squealing pig . . . these were common sights of everyday life and, coming under the general head of work, were avoided; but the death of a bull was exciting, and transforming. He was always a familiar, some-times gentle pet of the children, who perched atop his perilous back and rode him around the lot; but from the moment when the decision was made that he should be killed soft thoughts were put away. One of my brothers, Mike, who was himself a gentle creature—but he did suck eggs, a nestful at a time—would never look on; he went away and hid himself and was suspected of tears, but the rest of us were in at the kill, bloodthirsty. Sometimes the plate of the bull's forehead was so thick that blows from a sledge hammer left him only stunned and puzzled; then Bub got his muzzle-loader. We watched with hands covering ears, and when we saw him shudder and sway, and, buckling at the knees, roll over on his side, we let out the Rebel yell.

Winter held other good things besides eating, some of them mixed however. My brothers and I wore shoes and stockings, and, while feet splayed by a barefoot summer protested at enclosure and had to be let out from time to time for a breath of air, still there was compensation: the foot tub was no longer a cause of angry battle; we assumed ourselves to be clean from one Saturday night to the next and the accuser had to make a case. But the shoes of that day were, like education, certain torture, made to fit an idea that had no counterpart in reality, fictional feet as fictional students. My cousins allowed Negro boys to break theirs in and limp around for a week afterward in return for one Sunday of glory. To a Negro a shoe was a shoe, if he could squeeze his foot into it; when he owned a pair, he exercised the privilege of his class and slit them where they hurt. A visitor at my Grandmother Smith's was asked by Uncle Melt whether he could spare a pair. "What size do you wear?" "Any size," the old man answered "any size —but tens is coolest." But at my Grandmother Rice's there was no Negro anywhere near my size, and I had to break in my own shoes and do my own limping.

In winter it was also pleasant to go to bed and pull up the quilt, knowing that daylight, the countryman's alarm clock, would not come so soon, and in the daytime there was some sense of leisure, now that work was not so urgent as to make one feel guilty about doing nothing; and the cool of the evening was really cool, and tempers were no longer quickly inflammable. But best of all was the reading out loud after supper. There were books of all kinds and in plenty, my father's one wild extravagance, piled on tables in the hall and overflowing into the bedrooms. Aunt Lou, now in the ascendent, approached equanimity; but not too close, for she paid me in kind for my insolence of the summer by refusing to let me listen, never discovering that, when they had gathered in the end room, I crept along the piazza and lay on the floor with my ear to the door, grateful now for the habit of leaving it open. Sometimes I got so cold that I had to give up and go to bed; but there was one author, Hardy, who could hold me to numbness. Dickens stood next on the thermometer, and after him Thackeray; but even a sharp nip in the air could drive me away from Scott, who was as sensitive to frost as informing works.

Besides these delights, there was another, secret and my own: I got a medical education, with special reference to anatomy. One warm winter day, my thirst for approved reading quenched for the moment, I sneaked into the outhouse where Uncle Willie's medical books were stored, pried the lid off a box, and entered a new world where knowledge came direct, without the mediation of birds and flowers. That was a memorable winter.

v

When I went to live with my Grandmother Rice I was, by the reckoning of the calendar, thirteen years old, but vastly older in my own conceit and tick-tight with vicarious experience; not so old, however, as Bub, who could prove by arithmetic that he was eighteen, nor in years the equal of his brother, though I would not admit their superiority in any other ways. When I reached into the future and drew myself up another two years, I should put on long pants, the South Carolinian equivalent of the ephebic rite, and then there could be no argument. Meanwhile I lived in a between-world, no longer a small boy and not yet nearly a man. My hands and feet grew farther and farther away from my body and set up on their own, reminding me of their distant connection by getting in the way and declining generally to do what they were told. I would have been glad to get rid of them and go handless and footless through life, and did not realize that they were as unhappy as I, hiding themselves under chairs and tables. Years later I was reminded of this tripartite existence when I was helping to coach a play. "Bill," I said, speaking into the gulf between his ambition and his talent, "a clergyman never puts his hands in his pockets." He drew them out and looked at them, and asked, "Where does he put them then?" I was carried back to Colleton County and felt my divided self trying to come up the aisle in Cross Swamp Church while the whole world looked on, wondering whether my clutching hands and stumbling malicious feet would ever let me make it. It was a relief on Monday to return to childhood with my brothers, especially if, the day before, phlegm had risen in my throat during church services and I had stopped the universe with a cough. Sometimes I got the loan of a horse, and Mike and I set out, leaving Coke crying at the lot gate, for, as we were glad to remind him, he was too young to risk long expeditions. We rode off clinging to reins and mane and each other, presently to draw up at a stump and climb down; pride, when no one was looking, was not equal to the discomfort of doing splits on the back of the pot-bellied horse. We led him through the woods over the mat of pine needles, going fishing or swimming, or gathering nuts, or simply going. It was on one of these trips that the beauty of profanity burst upon me. We had filled the crokus sacks with hickory nuts, tied the two together, and then heaved them onto the back of the horse, but, every time, the string broke and we had to gather the nuts again. After the third or fourth try I was about ready to join Mike in tears, when suddenly out of my mouth streamed strange exhilarating words. Most of them I had heard before, but some were inventions of my uplifted soul. I listened in wonder and awe; I had never felt such ecstasy before, nor would again, until I fell in love.

Profanity is poetry in the real sense of the word, the making of language; drawn up out of the symbolic world of dreams, it is the moral equivalent of hate, a protest against the impurity of puritanism. The South Carolinian gentleman and the lowest of the low whites, members of the two free classes, could say what they felt in words of their own choosing; all the rest had moved into the nineteenth century and become subjects of the queen, wordbound. When once language is circumscribed the circle goes all the way round, timidity becomes general, and it is as impossible to be tender, in one's own words, as it is to be tough. The Greeks knew no such boundaries, nor did the Eliza-. bethans; they could make love and make hate. The question was, not whether a word was fit to be spoken, but whether it was fitting. This is what the scattered nuts told me on that autumn afternoon; and they told me another thing, if I had had the wit to hear—that I should never be a teacher.

That first year my brothers and I were sent to the country school, three miles away over a sandy road. Mike and I walked ahead while Coke, who had an amazing repertory of doing nothing, dawdled behind, showing in this more foresight than we, for the dullness of school was to be no fair exchange for the known dullness of home. The teacher was a country boy, himself just out of school, as touchy as a rattlesnake in spring, and scared. He had no imagination, his ignorance was profound, he needed the money to go to college . . . these were his qualifications. He was, in fact, the average teacher of his day. It would not have occurred to anyone that he could be made into a teacher, for Education, the sow's-ear science, was only in its beginnings. Normal schools, where they teach how to teach, were still foetal, and that other medieval institution, the graduate school of Education, where they teach how to teach how to teach, was yet to be sired by ambition out of ignorance. Meanwhile our teacher did the best he could; he made a quick cast in the pool of memory and fished up a teacher of his own as model. He divided the scholars, ranging in age from seven to seventeen, roughly into classes, assigned tasks, fiercely told us to keep quiet, and went outside. Presently he returned with an armful of peach-tree switches, from three to six feet long, stacked them in a corner, and set up as teacher. By midmorning the whipping began, in the palm for the smallest, across the back for the rest, boys and girls alike. Two of the scholars, however, he never touched—for, I hope, diverse reasons— myself and the biggest bully in the county.

I learned nothing from my teacher except that I could learn algebra, which neither of us had ever seen before, faster than he; but I learned a lot from my friend the bully. He and his sister, who gave promise of an irregular future, were children of a farmer who held in contempt all book learning and passed on to his son his natural gift for ignorance. I remember the old man well, for he was the first person to use a word of which I had never heard nor could guess the meaning. Mike and I were passing his place one day in a wagon, on our way to the general store, when he came out and asked me to get, "an' put down on time," a "Johnson's flustrator." I said I would, wondering what a flustrator might be, and Mike and I speculated, turning it this way and that, but could get no clue to its meaning. When I asked the storekeeper for a "Johnson's flustrator," he turned without hesitation to the shelf behind him and drew down a "Johnson's First Reader." His son, in all his schooling, bought no book beyond the flustrator; but we never discussed books, he and I.

He was tall for his age, more than six feet, unjointed, gawky, obscene, and smelly. His shirt, dyed a deep brown with hickory juice, went back something in time to its last washing; his corduroy trousers held in seam and crotch all the odors of all his sweat, with more than a trace of tobacco spittle, for he chewed and spat all the time. We sat by a window, which must always be kept open, even on the coldest day, for even he did not dare spit upon the floor. My lessons were easy and quickly done; the rest of the time we talked and he told me all he knew, for the most part directly and explicitly, with an occasional teasing hint of darker secrets—this when his sister came into the story. I pressed him, but he became sullen and angry, and frightened. Then he answered me obliquely.

There was a woman, he said, who lived a couple of miles away with several children but no man; not regularly, only for a few hours at a time, he snickered, and then with any man. He had been a visitor when he could squeeze two bits out of his old man; and Lordy, Lordy, what a time he'd had. Hadn't nobody ever told me about her? Everybody knew, and some high-toned gents who went to church every Sunday knew as much as he; it was no secret, not from anybody, not even from her own children. Up to this point I was a ready listener and believer, but at that I bogged down. He, seeing unbelief in my face, beckoned to a little girl, an undersized eight-year-old. She came and stood by his side at the end of the desk, and kept her eyes on the floor, confirming by her silence all the filthy words he poured into her ears. When he reached the limits of even his language, he sent her away with a message for her mother and turned to me in triumph. "See," he said, "whut'd I tell you?" Then he laughed. "The kid didn't say nothing, better not. She don't even know who her own pa is," and he climbed to the heights of legitimacy.

After a year of this kind of tutoring my father, suspecting that I was not learning enough, sent me to Bamberg to what was called a Methodist "fitting school," which fitted its scholars for pure bliss hereafter and deep depravity here. My friend of the county school was multiplied in numbers and experience; the only difference was that these boys were Christians. They ranged in years from seven to seventeen, in nature from boyhood, when they first came, to rotten old age. The stars were those who made the greatest show of piety and sang in the choir; beyond this the headmaster and his help made no inquiry, being particularly incurious on Saturday nights, when, red-faced or defiant as the younger boys watched them go, these models set out across the hill to milltown, for their weekly easing, obedient to folk hygiene.

This was the first time I ever saw mill hands—not close up, for boys of fourteen are as fiercely virginal as girls; but from a distance it was easy to see why Tillman despised them and received their allegiance with contempt, not knowing that they were to supplant his "Wool Hat Boys" and send his distorted picture, Cole Blease, to sit in chairs that he had not disgraced. Enticed from backwoods and hilltop by the promise of weather-tight houses, with a communal pump in back yard and near the pump a privy, a job for every member of the family young and old, and on Saturday night cash in hand, in return for all of which they had only to work ten or twelve hours a day and vote as they were told, no wonder they went wild in their new freedom; and yet, underneath, deep down within them, they were ashamed that they, descendants of men who were really free, should work for any man. They were the first unrooted Southerners, for there was no stock of ancient wrong to which they could be grafted; slavery was for Negroes.

When I returned from the fitting school I was a grown-up young man, I told myself. My hands and feet had tentatively decided against secession, my voice no longer jumped suddenly out of register, and I wore long pants without confusion. My cousins could not now think of a good excuse to exclude me from their pursuits—that was, the girls. Besides, I hinted at experience and built up the picture with borrowed paint. There had been a girl in Bamberg, I said. There had been a girl in Bamberg in fact, but if I had told them the truth they would have thrown me across the gulf that now separated me from my brothers, for it was a noble, inglorious affair. On Saturday nights, while the big boys were in milltown, I sat in her respectable parlor listening to surprised feet scuttling across the floor above, the pouring of water into a bowl, and the sloshing of one having a good wash, while I waited moonily for the moment when she would come quickly down the stairs and burst into the room—sun-burst, for her face was red and shining from its recent soaping. When the end of the year came, and good-by, I asked if I might kiss her; but she said no, she thought it wouldn't be right, and I agreed. These things I did not tell my cousins.

During the week I was willing to play with my brothers, but with Sunday came all the cruelty of the child that was left in me and the arrogance of the coming man, and without so much as a look at their unhappy faces I climbed into the buggy, where I sat creased and starched between my cousins, ready for new and strange adventures, more thrilling then than in their pale reality.

The creasing and starching had been done by me. My aunts and female cousins did the rough wash, work shirts and the like, but when it came to ironing white shirts and collars and pressing pants—they must have a razor edge—they refused; all foolishness, they said. Shirts and pants were easy; trouble came with the collars, which, by the fashion of the day, were three inches or more in height, and their ironing took skill. For a fine finish the best kind of iron was a kind of oven filled with charcoal, but its use took skill, for it was very hot and at any moment a spark might fly out of the chimney and make a smudge. I was the best ironer in the family, which gave me great pride and was to give me as much uneasiness.

As we drove off into the bright future, I felt to see if my hat was in shape; all week I had kept it tied up with a string in order to make its brim curve sharply upward on the sides—in the current mode—and give its wearer a startled look. It was good for several hours, I said to myself, though I knew that by evening it would have resumed its honest shape; by that time, however, history would have been made.

Our first goal was Cross Swamp Church, which got its name from having been so placed that every worshiper should impartially be obliged to cross at least one swamp. But we sometimes went to three different churches in one day, for at each would be a new batch of girls—in the main, at least; some girls also were itinerant, as were all the preachers, who traveled from one church to another, for no congregation could support a full-time professional, and they often preached the same sermon at each stop. One I remember well; in the morning he gave out as his text, often repeated as he wandered along, "Thou art neither cold nor hot, but lukewarm, and I will spew thee out of my mouth," and when he came to "spew," he did. In the afternoon, at his next church, he preached and spewed from the same text. By this time I could not only repeat the sermon but also time the spews, so we decided to go to a church where we were sure he would not be; but when we arrived, there he was, spewing away.

These expeditions were, however, not all untinctured pleasure. I had to go just so far in success with my several pursuits, else one of my cousins whispered to the girl, "He's only fourteen," and her eyes would glaze.

Once a year there was a glut of churchgoing, when "protracted meeting" was held, in fact protracted; all day long and into the night for a solid week relays of preachers deafened the ears of the deity, and worshipers drifted in to feed their souls and out to feed their bodies. Housewives baked and cooked and fried, and piled the tables under the trees high with lordly food—ham and fried chicken, cakes and pies, hidden among mountains of light bread and beaten biscuit.

The preaching at protracted meetings was ordinary; extraordinary preaching, springing from the doom of man's sinful nature and immediate danger of Hell-fire, was offered to the wide world at camp meetings, which were revivals held, not at churches, but at grounds set aside for these general gatherings. Cottages, occupied by the determined pious, surrounded a huge shed that covered rows of backless benches on which a boy sat and made pictures in the sawdust under foot and felt a growing ache in back and thighs until he could stand it no longer and offered an incontestable excuse to get out. Sometimes, in an interval of quiet, I thumbed through the hymn book, wondering how they got their names, "Duke Street," "Annie," "Elizabethtown," "State Street," "Sessions," strangely irrelevant and enchanting; but when the going got personally hot and I felt Hell closing in on me I sought the cool woods, where the talk, and action, was of a different kind.

Somewhere in the bushes there was a furtive dispenser of corn liquor, which unregenerate sinners drank, and staggered under the blow. Here was sin indeed, for anyone to see. I remember a farmer boy who lay on the ground in a drunken stupor while his father lashed him with an ox whip five feet long. The old man whirled the whip around his head and snarled with every stroke, "I'll teach you not to be a sinner."

The bushes also offered cover for more secret delights. A couple strolled casually away when, as they thought, no one was looking; but someone always was; women bit their lips in anger and groups of men standing under the trees guffawed and, their eyes glittering with desire, used short highly-flavored words. The frenetic outpourings of the preachers had unintended results.

Singing School was the nearest thing to secular entertainment that we knew, and it was held in the church. Once a year a peripatetic teacher, the only official representative of the muses in South Carolina, came to Cross Swamp Church for a week of instruction. The meetings took place at night and opened with prayer, but we had done our praying beforehand, for a full moon. Singing was loud and free, the teacher beating time on the pulpit and stopping the noise only when some loony palpably missed a shape-note. First we ran through the scales, Do, Re, Mi, and so on up to Do again, which was an isosceles triangle; Re was a semicircle, Mi a lozenge; the rest I have forgotten. Next the teacher chose a song, and we went through that in the same way, Do-ing and Re-ing and Mi-ing. Then, when we had got that with fair pitch and plenty of volume, we sang the words. Among singing teachers there were two schools—round-noters, the moderns, and shape-noters—who swore death and damnation to each other. Our teacher, a good native of the state, stuck to shape-notes, as his father had before him, and gave us all the arguments. We agreed, as who would not on a soft night with a soft girl at one's side? He thought himself called to save singing and we let him; he never suspected that he was a bemused chanticleer, calling up the moon.

He is gone or going into oblivion and may some day be followed by God's other lightning rod, the preacher. Aesop tells the story of a gnat that lit on a bull's horn, and after a while, having cleaned his wings and sunned himself, asked whether it would be all right if he should go now. South Carolinians of middle age and beyond are quick to anger at disapprobation of the church. I wonder what it is they remember, their worship of God, or themselves when they were young.

VI

Conversation among South Carolinians was entirely personal. Even the common openings of the countryman, crops and the weather, were God's instruments, and God was a person, vengeful and capricious, straight out of the Old Testament, where he had recently finished off enemy and innocent alike with impartial savagery. He marked, the hymn said, the sparrow's fall; also man's, with pleasure. He was awful and we feared him; death, and everything else disturbing, was the will of God (the expression was never used on happy occasions). In politics, however, there was some straining at the leash, some fiction of free will; the deity was assumed to be inattentive, and besides, God himself couldn't be expected to understand South Carolina politics. With factional, that is, personal politics, one must be intoxicated in infancy, and God had never been young. When these preliminary topics had been quickly run through, South Carolinians swung into the main current, which skirted birth, marriage and its correlate, death, and of these marriage was most inclusive, as furnishing promise of birth and being in its nature itself a kind of death.

My mother was hardly dead—"cold in her grave," they said—when my father's friends and acquaintances began to choose her successor, thinking nothing of my presence as they weighed one candidate against another. When I went to live with my Grandmother Rice I hoped there would be no more of this kind of speculation, but there was, only more pointed, pointed at me. "Just you wait until you've got a stepmother," they said, and told the usual folk tales of the accepted cruelty of stepmothers. "You just wait; then you'll see." But for once I knew my father and was untroubled. He still loved my mother, in his wild and passionate way, and his love was mingled with hidden guilt, now that she was gone. We seldom mentioned her; when we did, his face became helpless with grief, and then, and once only again in the years of my knowing him, tears came to his eyes, personal tears—preacher's tears were different; they were part of his acting. After something more than a year, however, I felt a change in him, while he was on a visit to Colleton County. A small thing told me: he had always been careful of his clothes, but now they were creased and baggy and spotted, and when Aunt Lou said to him, "John, you need somebody to look after you," and he answered "Yes, I know," there was something in his tone that told me he was looking for love again.

He was always looking for love. As fierce as his desire for heat and food was his desire for love, but here his very desire defeated him, for, just as he wanted to swallow all the food and drink all the heat in the world, so he devoured those whom he loved. One could not go part way; one must be completely consumed, binding over to his demanding love all one's will. One had to submit or rebel. Some rebelled.

If he had lived in another age he might have become a legend, spreading his seed far over the earth; he would have been a happy lover, and his loves would have been happy too, for a tiny part of his passion was equal to any ordinary man's. If he had been the father of a hundred children, each would have had enough of him and not too much. But we were only three, and my mother made the fourth, for to him she was both wife and child.

Unsolaced at home, in desperation and anger he poured his welling love over his congregation, most of whom also fought it off, for its demands were implacable. Some, however, accepted his love and came to life in it, for it was life-giving, when diluted. Wherever he went, about a third of the congregation worshiped him as a saint; the rest feared and hated him. Only hardy sinners could stand out against him; they knew their lives were at stake.

He was also afraid of love, afraid to lose himself in love. With him there were always two loves, his and another's; never, even in union, unity. He kept something of himself in reserve, outside and independent, free from the bonds of love. This was where his fear lived, in this part of him that was outside love. It is often so when one has not known love in childhood. His fear of love had odd ways of expression. Whenever he came back from a trip he brought presents, but—and here fear kept him outside, kept him from final commitment—the presents must always be useful things, such as perhaps we would have had anyway, never merely delightful silly things. He never brought my mother flowers; they would wither and die; better a shawl or some other apparel, or some fixture that could serve around the house when the glow of the gift had departed. To us his sons he usually brought cravats and socks, and here parsimony also entered in; he could never pass a bargain by, and buying things wholesale added, or supplied, virtue. I shall not forget a dozen socks of sickly purple, nor cravats ready tied and fastened with rubber bands. (I offered mine to Jake, but he declined them, with grace.) With books it was different; only the best would do, for us and for my mother, who, however, not infrequently suffered from the disadvantage of receiving as gifts books that he himself wanted to read. But there was another flaw: the books had inscriptions, written boldly on the flyleaf in his nervous hand. My mother flinched when she had to open hers in his presence, for she dreaded "To my dear wife" or "To my darling." We boys did not mind; we were too glad to get them to cavil at the words of affection; but as I grew older I also began to flush and squirm. For years I kept hidden away a Bible on whose cover was stamped in gold, "To John Andrew Rice from Father." He seemed to feel that what was written or printed was said and not said. In the early years of his preaching we sometimes came in for loving reference in his sermons, and sat with ears burning, knowing that the eyes of the congregation were upon us as he proclaimed in the public security of the pulpit the love that he could not express in his home.

All this, inarticulate and unspoken inside me, I knew and remembered, but even so I knew that his love had been stronger than his fear, and I was sure that he would love my mother forever, that death itself could not break the bond. What I did not know was that one love does not need to drive out another; knew nothing, in fact, of the love of man and woman. My father was unhappy and restless, but he had always seemed so, and I was quite unprepared for the meaning that came through his voice when he said to Aunt Lou, "Yes, I know." I was frightened.

Not long afterwards a letter came saying that he intended marrying again, and praising, with restraint, my future stepmother. She was, he said, a schoolteacher from Tennessee, he had met her at the University of Chicago, they would be married soon; that was all. In a few days a picture came, a photograph of a middle-aged woman with a face that, while it was not exactly stern, was certainly firm. (I was later told that it had been taken for a teachers' agency.) Aunt Lou took the trembling picture from my hands, turned it this way and that, and then said, with a satisfied smile: "She's a tartar; now you'll catch it." In all the time I knew my aunt, that was the only time that honest thought was conquered by honest wish; but honest wish was strong.

A few years ago a visiting Englishman said to me, "I say, what does a skunk smell like?" I answered, "I can't tell you what a skunk smells like; you'll know when you smell one." There are some things like that. If his question had been about gardenias, my answer would have been the same. Some experiences are, as the Latins said, of their own kind, unique, disparate, all themselves and nothing else. I had read and been told the usual stories about the cruel stepmother—she was always cruel—but she had been another's, not mine, not conceivably mine. That night I made my first acquaintance with sleeplessness, and when at last I dropped off, claws and fangs followed me into my dreams. Fear and anger and shame, all of these, and yet none of these, clutched and held me.

My aunts and cousins were jubilant, in my presence, all except Aunt

Mollie, who reached out to me in a dumb way. "Now you'll catch it," they said, "just you wait; she won't take any of your back talk," and ingenious variations. "Better not raise your voice to your new stepmother," Aunt Lou sang, and Aunt Jinny chimed in with "Better not quarrel with Mike and Coke when your stepmother comes." It was "better not" this "better not" that, all day long. Bub said, "I wouldn't be in your shoes for a pretty." One Saturday, when I was ironing a collar, Aunt Lou found another theme: "Better not let your stepmother find out you can iron. She'll make you do the family washing," and the others took it up, endlessly. Whenever they saw me with an iron in my hand, the tune was repeated, "Better not let her. . . ." "No danger," I said to myself; "that's one thing she'll never know from me," and when the day approached on which I should see her for the first time I did up enough shirts and collars to last through the visit, and longer.

But I didn't see her for a long time, not until she had been married to my father for nearly a year. He put off his coming to the next autumn, when he intended to return to preaching. In the meantime I lived in misery and terror.

Finally the day came. Bub hitched up in the morning and asked if I would like to go to Varnville with him to fetch the visitors, but I declined; until nightfall, at least, I would be free. As I awaited the end of the world a thousand wild plans chased one another around inside my quaking mind: I would run away, I would drown myself, shoot myself, do something, anything; I would even go so far as to ask my grandmother to let me stay with her. But I knew I would do nothing, that I would submit. Also, I was curious. Perhaps she might not after all be like other stepmothers, perhaps I might even like her, perhaps her picture hadn't done her justice . . . perhaps and perhaps, but I didn't believe it.

They arrived after dark and I could not see her face when I came slowly to the carriage and greeted her and my father with speechlessness. Aunt Lou and Aunt Jinny, now the loving sisters, took them to their rooms. Presently, when they came to the kitchen where I was drinking in Aunt Mollie's silent sympathy, they looked puzzled and were silent. When supper was ready they went to get the guests and I went into hiding under the porch, from where I could hear greetings and shuffling feet, and her voice, which was quiet and calm. But how did I know she wasn't just being polite, putting on her company manners? I stayed away as long as I dared, for any moment my aunts might mark my absence; then I crawled up the steps and slipped into my chair at the end of the table, from where I could see my father, diagonally across from me, smiling at his new wife in the lamplight. I put tasteless things into my mouth and chewed and choked. At last, when no one was watching me, I leaned cautiously forward and looked down the table at her. It was the most beautiful face I had ever seen.

The next morning from my room, which was next to theirs, I heard my father laughing, gay and happy and free, as I had never heard him laugh before. I laughed too, to myself, at my luck, and at my aunts. That was why they were puzzled—her face. After breakfast I spoke to her, something casual and meaningless, but senseless noises of good will, the amalgams of life, took on sense when she listened; and she only listened, for she was a wise woman, putting in a word or question, but saying nothing to stop the flood of love that was going out from me to her. When the tide was at full, and all was calm and peaceful, I went to my room and brought out some of the shirts and collars I had ironed against her coming. "Did you do this yourself?" she asked. I nodded. "You're a wonderful boy," she said.

CHAPTER IV

Montgomery

M Y FIRST INTIMATE ACQUAINTANCE, AND ENEMY, IN MONTGOMERY was a cow. My father, lover of simple country life, in imagination, and for others, calling himself and yet never having been a farm boy, thought it would be good for my character to have a cow to milk and to have to milk a cow. The seed of this fruitful idea was a stable that sat on the corner of the parsonage lot. Southern houses, when they moved to town, brought with them their country nature; so the parsonage, where we lived a convenient stone's throw from the church, had, besides a detached kitchen and runway, this stable. If, instead of "good" for my character, he had read "evocative," he would have been right, for with the advent of the cow all my meanness came out and stayed out. I was fifteen years of age at the time, standing at a fork in the roads, where, my mind might have told me, others had stood before; but this knowledge would have meant nothing to me then, just as now, to know that I do not stand alone at my present age, means nothing. (One ceases to be lonely only in recollection; perhaps that is why people read history.) I stood hesitant: if I should take the one road, I might in time acquire a character, not my own but one that would do, one that would entitle me some day to be called a good man; if I took the other—the cow led me down the other.

Sunday was the special day for the development of character, mine and the cow's. I didn't mind the morning milking; it was followed by

Sunday school and church, when I was willing to be offensive; but afternoon milking time was just an hour before the meeting of the Epworth League, after which came sweet and secret meetings of the young. Mine could not be sweet, however, not with the smell of cow teats on my hands. There is no smell like it, the clinging subtle pervasive smell of cow teats, unconquerably itself, proof against soap or any other deodorant. I washed and scrubbed my hands until the smell was gone, along with most of the skin; but it was not gone, it had only retired. A couple of hours later, when I lifted my girl's hand to my lips, there was the smell, come out of hiding and growing stronger every moment, until at last it struck her nostrils too; then her fingers grew clammy, clammy as the cow's teats.

This was not the only trial; there was another. I had to decide every afternoon whether to change my clothes completely, or take a chance with what I had on; to risk my good clothes against the ingenuity of the cow. On Sundays, as a rule, I was not so rash: I angrily changed to overalls and met her as an equal. One Sunday afternoon, however, after an unsmirched week, recalling the amiability of her liquid eye at the morning milking, I went into the stable, bucket in hand, all dressed up in my best. As I stepped through the door the cow turned and took one look at me, a detached amused contemptuous look. We stood for a moment, she and I, communicating mutual hate, and then, as I moved closer, she lifted her tail in a leisurely arc, as if to swish a fly from her far side, and brought it whirling back like a whip lash across my face. My foot flew out as automatically as a cuckoo out of a clock, and flew and flew until I was exhausted and she subdued. But when at last I started to milk her, there was no milk; she was, as farmers said, holding it back. That was all right with me, quite all right; it was, in fact, inspiring. The next Sunday night I simply kicked her and went to church. This happened several successive Sundays, with no great harm to the milk supply, and I might be milking her yet had I not been invited to a party on Monday night. After that, kicking became the rule until offended nature brought permanent release. "Why aren't you milking, John Andrew?" my father asked. "The cow's gone dry," I said. "That's funny," he said, "they told me she was fresh." I let silence tell my lie.

I had already become adept in deception, but I was never a happy liar. Some boys seem to slip easily into the adult world and accept without shock the knowledge that what their elders say to the young and what they do among themselves are wide apart; I did not. Christianity, to which about this time I thought I became converted, seemed simple and inclusive, and where I saw the law of love followed, it met the American test: it worked. The trouble was, and is, that its statement is too simple; no one told me, or approved of the fact, that saying and doing are themselves wide apart, and when there was failure I condemned as severely as the God of Israel; but the censure was for others, not myself, which meant that most of my lies were cushioned on unconsciousness, the final infirmity.

Conversion was as inevitable to a bursting boy in the South as psychoanalysis is to a pimply-souled New Yorker—and with the same result: underneath every exhortation to repentance one heard the loud unspoken assurance that a Christian could do no wrong, a king's immunity to which any democrat was now entitled. This was one of the nets that drew me into the church. Another net was the sense of sin; one never got away from its immanence. "Brother, are you saved?" or "Is your heart right with God?" was likely to pop out at one from the most casual conversation and under otherwise decent circumstances. Doubt was permissible as to other doctrine or dogma, but there was one tenet common to all the evangelical sects, the belief in "original sin"; of that there could be no possible doubt. As to the merits of sprinkling and ducking there was some question between Methodists and Baptists, and Presbyterians found themselves in a logical difficulty with their doctrine of predestination—"There are infants in Hell not a span long,"

I heard one of their preachers say—but they got themselves out by saying that one should be good anyway, presumably just for the fun of it. Underneath all the talk, however, ran the menace of destruction. We lived in peril of life hereafter and were not allowed to forget it. Others, members of ritualistic sects, Episcopalian or Catholic, might go to Hell in bliss; but not we; we had to be saved and keep saved.

The city church, holding to the country ways of its origin, conducted an annual revival—decorous, but still a revival. The visiting evangelist in the year of my conversion was a restrained Englishman who led me readily up his alley, which was "the Bible as literature"; but when he got me there his delicate gesturing hands and modulated voice were obliterated in the general fog of old-time Methodist feeling. I see myself now, standing saved in the corner of the parlor, wondering why tears were flowing, a little angry, much bewildered, and knowing myself inwardly as pure fake. Nothing had happened.

I soon recovered, however, and went about being a Christian; my self-esteem grew lustrous, gleaming in the doubtless sunshine. A natural talent for censure bloomed into genius in the spurious comradeship of the elect. Spotting a sinner at sight became as easy as hog calling, and more fun. I was enjoying being one of the boys.

This also did not last. Doubt crept in and took away my joy. How was I to know that Christ and Christianity have little in common? I woke to the bitter knowledge that no one was saved, certainly not I, and not even my father. (As I see it now, the fault of Christianity is in promising salvation.) It was my first taste of a complete negative. All Christians were fakes, I said to myself, and out of the security of this insecurity I saw my father as the chief, as one living in two disparate worlds and happy in neither.

There was evidence. I see him looking on helpless while my youngest brother lies dying. There is no light in his eyes, no belief now in immortality. Here is the end of a life not yet begun, and the end of his hopes. This boy was to become what none of his other three sons now promised, was to match his own dreams and blot out his failure. As the small skeleton breathed less and less, he died with his son; and there would be no resurrection. All the words that he had confidently said to suffering mothers and fathers, the love that he had poured out on others to make them want to live and believe, came to the full stop of silence. His face became twisted with pain and slow reluctant tears fell unnoticed down his cheeks, and mingling with the pain was fierce resentment of death, anger so deep as to be ready to turn against his God and curse him for his blundering ways. The next Sunday the child, now in his grave, reappeared transfigured into the promise of eternal life. God in his infinite wisdom, the God of Love, the blessed Saviour, had received him in his all-embracing arms. Again tears, not now reluctant, came down his cheeks and into his beard. The true faith had been restored, the pattern of Christianity once again set upon his mind. I sank down in the pew and stared at him through angry stinging eyes. My memory traveled back to a day six months before, when there had been angry speech between my father and mother about the doctor who had been called to see her ailing child. She had objected to him, said he knew nothing, that even if he was a good Christian and a regular churchgoer, he wasn't fit to tinker with a sick cat, much less a sick child. (There is a close correlation between piety and incompetence.) But my father had stood firm; the doctor had tinkered and the child had died. Why then these tears?

Truth is an easy thing to come by when one is young, but once life is fitted into sharp-edged words, imagination begins to lose its wings and sympathy admits constraint. We learn to live in a world of words, no longer able to see things as a child first sees them, to live uncontaminated by thought, letting images, ideas, feelings, flow in and find their own resting place. Some of us live wordbound the rest of our days, unless love comes to make us free again; but even love can wither in the bonds of language. Only poets and fools would have it otherwise. Our practical elders give us words, and words can be swords.

As I looked up into my father's foreshortened face and saw his eyes above the full fan-shaped beard, the word came to me: "Hypocrite," I said; "O ye hypocrites and liars," quoting the textbook.

From where I sat in the pew reserved for the pastor's family, second on the right, I could miss no detail of man or thing. Protestantism is green and raw, formless—there is no form to protesting—without the patina of old time, and its outward show mirrors its inner nature. Here was no dim religious light, only glare, that gave to every thing its own shameless reality. The stained-glass window that framed my father's head bit at my eyes with its reds and blues, and the murky green that flowed along its sides was like a first attempt at colored icing. The organ pipes were furry with dust, the chancel rail, just under my eyes, grimed with sweat. The professional boredom of the paid choir, the nervous starchiness of the voluntary singers, the beads that formed on my father's forehead as he warmed to the theme, were picked out in the glare from varnished golden oak. Years later I was to see the same kind of thing in the evangelical chapels of England, confirming a doubt as to democracy in matters spiritual. Furniture and furnishings, the awkward choir, pulpit and preacher rather than altar as the center of worship, and all asserting their right to be seen, became for me symbols. Out of the Reformation came individualism, and here it was, and here was chaos.

The Methodist Church was itself chaos, a curious mixture of democracy, oligarchy, and despotism. At the top sat the bishops, for the duration of life and good behavior. (What the latter meant was not clear.) They were elected at the general conference of the entire church, held every four years, by delegates from the state conferences; but they were chosen beforehand, by an undetermined oligarchy of politicians, ecclesiastical politicians. Sometimes a good man slipped through, but that was divine accident. The bishops presided over the annual state conferences and made appointments for the following year, with absolute authority to send a man where they pleased; but, most of them being politicians, their inclinations were tempered by their habits.

Friday was the fateful day on which appointments were announced —as to how they were made, few were certain. Whatever of brotherly love had prevailed until Friday now disappeared in the general panic: every man became for that moment the enemy of every other, as they drew apart and sat in dark silence waiting for the words of doom that would send them up among the rich and well-born or down among the poor. Sometimes they broke down and cried, and once or twice I heard of one forced to his feet by anger, to protest and be covered with hot shame. When the annual conference was over we could breathe again, for now we knew whether we should or should not have to move. The word became an omen, finding its way into many family consultations and being near the center of most quarrels. As soon as we had settled in one place my father began to worry about when he would have to move to another, and what that other would be; forever afraid—this lasted all his life—that some vengeful bishop, of whom there were plenty among the princes of the church, would, as he said, "send him to the sticks." For a long time I did not know what the "sticks" were, or their variant, "the tall timber," but I knew I did not want to go there. Nor did he know what influence would determine the bishop's action.

Portents were not infrequent, for the parsonage, besides being a clearinghouse for church activity and curiosity, was also a kind of lodginghouse for traveling and wandering preachers, who put up with us as a matter of course. There were few hotels in the South at that time and these were merely adult boardinghouses, musty and dirty and Negroid, as they still are for the most part. Besides, they cost money, while lodging with us was free. We had a special room set aside for transient divines—we hoped they would be transient—and family and servants understood that when the doorbell rang and one stood waiting, he was to be invited in and shown to his room without question. Usually he stayed only a day or so, but sometimes he was a clerical bum, and stayed and stayed as long as the brotherhood of man endured. When that gave out, getting rid of him was a nice business. The easiest way was to pay his fare to the next town, a device since borrowed from us by charity agencies; but a seasoned sponge had sometimes to be given a bit extra, a sort of tip. The hardest task of all, however, was to obey my father's injunction that no guest, during his stay or after, should be discussed disparagingly. My grandfather, a minor Charlestonian by birth, had bequeathed this rule to his son, who did his best to enforce it and never seemed to realize that his own pointed silence was sometimes like a headline.

Occasionally, however, this rule of uniform respect for a guest was too much even for him. One Sunday night, when my elders were at church and my brother Mike and I had been left to mind the door, the bell rang and there stood a tall bundle of a man who stepped quickly in out of the cold and as quickly demanded to be shown to his room. Evidently this was not the first parsonage he had visited. When he had seen thus far to his comfort, he called for food. We told him that the cook had gone, we were sorry, there would be nothing to eat until breakfast. He expressed dissatisfaction. We crept away, wondering what we had drawn this time. The next morning told us. When the breakfast bell rang he came downstairs dressed, in other details, like a preacher, black on white; but around his head he wore a vari-colored fascinator, a kind of knitted muffler like the one Uncle Coke had once given his mother at Christmas, worn, so far as we had known up to that moment, by ladies alone. But that was not all: atop the fascinator sat a black derby hat, far too small by now to fit the padded head. This was a test of our rearing, and my father's eyes nailed us to silence. Even Uncle Ellie, who happened to be visiting us, had to content himself with twitching the muscles of his face to show that his contempt for preachers had reached a new depth. My father gravely asked the newcomer to ask the blessing, which he did at some length. Then he explained: he had to wear these things, he said, because there was something wrong with his head. None of us looked at Uncle Ellie. My mother—I never thought of her as a stepmother—filled the space by giving an extra sharp tinkle to the bell that called the cook. Presently we heard her come lumbering, for she was large and slow-moving, along the runway from the kitchen. When she opened the door and caught sight of the apparition, she stopped still, as still as if her feet had suddenly stuck to the floor, and began to swell with laughter. But she had first to get rid of the plate of pancakes and out of the door, and, ungluing herself, she started toward my mother, who sat at the far end of the table, when she caught Mike's eye, which closed with a comprising wink. With a burst of speed she slammed the plate down on the nearest corner of the table, rushed from the room, and, pounding toward the kitchen, let out peals of shrill Negro laughter. Uncle Ellie made a small irrelevant joke and we all roared with grateful laughter, and for once my father liked his pagan brother-in-law. Presently, when the cakes were all eaten, my mother rang again. There was a long wait, but in time cook came, opened the door slowly, slammed the plate down and ran again. In the full two weeks that the visitor stayed she never got quite used to him, and when at last he was bribed to leave she said to my father, with deference, "If dat gemen wuzn' a preacher, I sho would call him crazy."

These impecunious derelicts were a terror to my father, who saw in their obsequious and defiant ways his own old age.

The clergyman was a servant of the Lord, but he had to look elsewhere to find a paymaster. In England the foundation of the Established Church rested solidly upon the land, from which it drew its support in tithes and other special taxes, a device that left the incumbent —beautiful word—somewhat free of dependence upon local powers; but Protestantism in America was for the most part evangelical and, like its parent bodies in England, had laid its mudsills in democracy. Contributions more or less voluntary were requested of those who were to be served and saved. If a churchgoer disapproved of the particular brand of salvation offered by his preacher, he could refuse support and, if he could get enough of his fellow worshipers to agree, would show the errant shepherd who was boss. Under this dispensation, Jeremiah or other thundering prophets would have led a tough life, if indeed they could have managed to keep alive at all. No wonder many a preacher reserved his tongue-lashings for the absent, atheists and infidels who never went to church, and the dead. And yet, in the South Carolina that I had known, the preacher still had some authority left, was still looked upon as a man of God to some extent, for South Carolina was eighteenth century, and the eighteenth century was conscious of its narrow escape from Catholicism and had respect for its saviors. (The violent rejection of Al Smith was no surprise to those who knew the South.) Dependence upon average opinion had not yet degraded the church to its present level, where the preacher is usually a mere mirror of opinion—and low opinion at that, for, in matters spiritual, average is always low. But by the turn of the century a new kind of shepherd was coming in, one who followed his sheep, who could spot a banker at sight and knew where to get, and use, his butter; whoever refused to crook the knee and had the strength to castigate contemporary sinners rather than the ancient Hebrews was beginning to live a perilous life. Montgomery had more than one sheepish shepherd. My father's resentment, as I see it now, sprang from the knowledge that in a competitive world there is no certain test or proof of a preacher's worth. The merchant's goods wear or wear out, the doctor's patient lives or dies, the lawyer's client pays or is paid, and even the teacher can offer in evidence a parroting pupil, or, if all else fails, he can write a book. But the preacher, the real psychiatrist, the healer of souls, what coin has he that will pass in the market place?

There were ways of getting on. The word "publicity" had not yet been turned to its present use, but there were preachers even in the sleepy South who, like their fellow actors, knew its virtue if not its name. They were beginning to learn that the surest way to rise in the church was, not to be known—Heaven forbid—but to be known for something, to be labeled, which is the essence of publicity. One young preacher had a minute knowledge of genealogy, an asset in a land of ancestor worship, and climbed rapidly to the glory of God. Polished manners, a soothing voice, a spate of language, the unction of inferiority and other sycophancies—all these were useful. Admirers of the late Ivy Lee, the first of the great public butlers of the rich, should have shifted their admiration back a generation, for his father taught him all he knew.

These methods were no temptation to my father, who was honest as well as honorable. He did want to be a success—these were the success days—but not at that price, and it enraged him to see mountebanks going to the top in ways no decent man would use. Always eager and usually willing to see the truth, he now became an unhappy martyr to his own clarity. But if he would not get ahead by such means, he could at least have the satisfaction of exposing their employers, to his family. To have uttered his thoughts publicly would have ended his career in the church, so he sat at table and dissected ecclesiastical scoundrels so dextrously that we ourselves became expert. I listened with delight, not knowing that some day I should be plagued with my then acquired skill in detecting another's weaknesses, nor that, when it comes to people, clarity unwed to charity can be an evil thing.

This violence, in my father and in us, his three sons, this electric hate that crackled at every mealtime and was an inner current of our lives, frightened my mother, who was not used to such ways. Her own father was an ordinary Methodist preacher, shiftless, cheerfully lacking in learning, willing to let the day come and go and bring what it would, grateful to the bishops for whatever small change they doled out to him, grateful for the little gifts of coffee and sugar and the like that came from his poor congregations, receiving and expending good hard cash as carelessly as if it was a smile—he was, in fact, like the gentle Christ; not the hard one; he would never have driven the bankers out of the temple, never driven anyone anywhere, and least of all himself. He was a poor introduction to life with my father, to whom he was incredible, monstrous—and to life with us, whose nerves had been grated raw by three years of abrasive anger. My mother had to discover her own toughness and set it against ours, and make it work; and, in time, it did work, for its center was love, which is the toughest thing in the world.

Ignorance is a wonderful thing, much more wonderful than knowledge, and of all ignorance the most wonderful is ignorance in time. If it were not for ignorance of the future, the human race would have perished long ago. To be about to know, what knowing can match this in sweetness? If we knew the future as simply as we know what we ate for breakfast, half the human race would commit suicide. All the important things in life rest on the solid foundation of ignorance. If, then, my mother had known what she was letting herself in for, she would, I think, never have been married to my father. But I may be wrong. There are compensations in marriage that only those who know can know, and only two can know. In his last years, when I was far away from him and deep in my own experience of marriage, he surrendered to love, I am told, and became a gentle old man. On the wall of my brother's office in Dallas there hangs a picture of him taken a few months before he died in 1930. A shrunken neck stands out of his gaping collar, the flat surfaces of his face are drawn tight between cheekbone and jaw; everything is gone that I remember, even the close-clipped mustache, everything—except the eyes and mouth. But they too are gone, the ones I knew, that spoke scorn and anger and violence. These lips and eyes speak another language. They speak of defeat, and victory.

In the years that I knew him, however, there was no hint of what could be, not to me. The flames that had been kindled in me when I, a child of eight, heard my first mother speak of her unhappiness now flared anew, and I became my second mother's champion. I did not know that she needed none.

It took the courage of invincible ignorance for her to hold steady the scales of mercy—not justice; justice is cheap, to be had at any cross-road. But somehow she held them steady. She had been until middle life a schoolteacher, and teaching is parenthood without responsibility; now there was responsibility, not only for us, three wild boys, but for her own beginning family, in a home where everything came from a life she had not known, every piece of furniture—there were not many, but the fewer the worse—every book, every picture.

Besides my turbulent father and his three sons, each an unique exasperation, there were the Negro servants, with whom she had never had any dealings before. They took one look at her and took her in, went about blandly wasteful, slovenly, careless and content. "Law, ma'am, dat ain' dus' under de bed, dat jes house wool." "Was dat soup in de pot? Lawsey, I thought it was slops." "I ain' never done dat way" —Mother had been reading a cook book—"but if you tells me to do it dat way, I sho' will do it dat way," and the cake came out flat, the roast raw burnt, the Yorkshire pudding sole leather. One nursemaid, whose skin had the color and surface texture of charcoal—not all Negroes are shiny—was looking for a man to lead her into sin and when she found him was, in her purring contentment, more puzzled than ever as to what her mistress was talking about. Another preferred to sleep in the basement, and did, until it was discovered why and with what results. This time my mother was frightened and hurried her off to a doctor. I overheard the word syphilis. Then there were various degrees of thievery. We, who had thought of the good life, if we thought at all, as applying only to whites, found all this very funny; but I think it was her fumbling belief that began a way of feeling in me, brought Negroes into humanity, brought me to see that between me and Negroes there could exist human as well as personal relations.

One of the advantages in being married to a businessman is, I suspect, that he will be definitely out of the house all day. A preacher's wife enjoys no such comfort. Her husband is always there, or about to be there, or absent when he should be there. One of the most difficult things my mother had to do was keeping the study door closed, when my father had returned for the acquiring of further knowledge. Visitors were insistent, and to be firmly refused; for—and this was a trouble—it was almost impossible for him to stay at his task of learning.

It was a painful thing to see him trying to learn from books. He attacked Hebrew with the same impatience that he put into fixing the car. But he stuck to it until he learned and became as much of a scholar as he could be, without the flavor of scholarship, which comes only with a sense of leisure. As he sat at his desk with books piled in front of him he was never relaxed, never quiet. His muscles were tensed as if he was about to spring, and any legitimate call to action was a great relief. With writing, which he began in his later years, it was the same way. The language was kicked and hammered, never coaxed, to do its job. As a result there were few overtones. It was all straight journalistic prose. His letters were the same, full of stock meaningless phrases, and ending "Affly, Father." If he had written the word out it would have taken too long and besides might have meant too much. When he had an excuse to leave his study, when the spring of action was released, he leapt into motion, racing upstairs and down, hurrying every one and every thing into motion, walking at a terrific pace along the street.

And yet, he really wanted to know. I have known few people that were hungry for knowledge; my father was one of these, and he persisted in getting knowledge, hard as it was for him. He had come to Montgomery after three years of pursuit in the University of Chicago, where he had sat in mystified awe and listened to the learned scholars —whom he innocently supposed to be also wise—and set about to be one too. I never quite knew why he wanted to get knowledge, for when he got it he got little satisfaction. He was not content to wear it as a cloak, the way many scholars do; he was looking for a deeper meaning than books or professors could give him, but his very intentness kept him from finding it. He was looking for an answer to a question, but the way in which he put the question kept him from the answer: it had to come in the form of Christian morality. He was uneasy in company, for he had no small talk and could never learn to make the meaningless noises that express good will or attentive indifference. The common coinage of unmeant compliments, stereotyped grace, the little word that turned one away from unpleasant truth, the amalgams and emollients of social intercourse, reduced him to angry silence. Their practitioners were hypocrites and liars—the lips never said this, but the grey eyes under the heavy brows did. In his own family, in Colleton County, speech had been used for two things, as a means of communicating facts and as weapons. Days went by without a word above the level of cotton and cane. Then, suddenly, at some slight misdemeanor, his sisters would hack at the offender with the axe of words. There was nothing in between, no tentative approach to thought or idea, no light play with words, no fun—for they never laughed except at one another.

This was one reason why my father had always been uncomfortable at Grandmother Smith's. He never knew whether the talk was serious, and he had no means to measure nonserious talk. To him all the storms were real, all the abuse intended to hurt, every lash of the whip carried a sting. He could never understand how Uncle Ellie and his sister, my mother, could be almost literally at each other's throats, and the next moment be laughing gaily together. He could never do that way. In his own home, on the slightest offense, he would go into private retirement and sometimes sulk for days.

He never wore new clothes without self-consciousness, nor old clothes without a sense of inferiority; that is, he was not an aristocrat, was not born into the aristocracy, and had no natural aptitude for its graces. But he wanted to be. I often heard him say, "I should like to have been a gentleman." But he could not be a gentleman because he had no gracious tolerance of the past, which was always called upon by him to defend itself with a statement of purpose. He was never at home in any world, and the gentleman has at least one world, however specious, in which he is at home—as has, presumably, the saint. He had something of them both in him, but not enough of either to bring him security. In later years, when he became pastor of rich congregations, he was always awkward in their social affairs, and awkwardness in the uncertain civilization of the Middle West was unforgivable. They were no more aristocrat than he was, they were trying to learn how, to form an aristocracy (I got quite a surprise in St. Louis when I found that one might be in the social register and the Methodist Church at the same time); meanwhile, when they were uncertain as to a point, they looked it up. He was at length persuaded to buy a dress suit; but he was not instructed, and did not bother to find out, the rules as to time of wearing—never before six o'clock—and made his first public appearance in it at an afternoon tea. Many souls were lost to the Kingdom on that day.

From these clashes with the world of fine people he came away angry and hurt. Fashionable weddings in particular upset him for days, but he took a mad delight in marrying off plain simple people and would go to any lengths to help them out. Elopements gave him special pleasure. The doorbell would ring late at night and there would stand two frightened people stammering their wish. He would hustle them into matrimony, and then quietly reassure them with gentle words and send them away with a feeling of deep tenderness for him and for each other—but not before he had had his little joke. After the ceremony was performed the groom gawked around trying to ask "how much would it be"; my father never helped him, and when the question finally came out, he said, "As much as you think she's worth." It always happened the same way: the gleeful haste, the joke, and the calm blessing.

Once in Montgomery a middle-aged man came to the door and hesitantly explained that he wanted to get married but that his lady refused to get out of the buggy. My father went with him and out of the darkness we heard him talking in his most persuasive tone, and then presently the toneless words of the wedding ceremony, which he knew by heart. He had climbed up into the buggy, sat on the dash-board, and made them man and wife.

Another time a boy, but old enough to be married as attested by the license which he brought, came early in the morning and told his story. The parents of his girl were on their way out west and were taking her with them, for they disapproved of the match. The boy had followed them on the train, knowing they would have to "lay over" for three hours before they could start on the long journey that would take his girl away from him. My father sprang into action and within an hour brought the frightened couple in his own carriage to the parsonage and performed the ceremony. He had bribed the washroom attendant to sneak the girl out through the window. When he had married them and said his gentle words, he went with them to confront the angry parents. He believed in love.

He was also afraid of love. Love was madness and must be con-strained, or confined. Here his puritanism stood out strong against the laxness of the Southern gentleman, who in this respect was a genuine cavalier, concerned, if at all, only with the integrity of his own class. If, then, one had not the "gift of continency," the only way out was marriage. His face would flush at the very mention of "free love"—as if there were any other kind.

He came straight out of the stern Old South. There was a stern Old South, as grim and stern in its puritanism as New England; and long-lived and tough. At the turn of the century every third Southerner was an uncompromising and fanatical puritan, as ruthless as Cotton

Mather. This was no sudden emergence; it had been there all along. There had been another Old South, the technicolor South. Thomas Nelson Page had been one of its authors, Stark Young was another, and John Crowe Ransom and his "Southern Agrarians"—the only plowing they ever did was in the classroom—wrote a book to prove that the way back was the only way out. The pink cloud of memory held, no doubt, a drop or two of fact, and that is enough to water a myth. But now, whatever it had been, this Old South of the cavalier was withering. Perverse fortune reserved its full privileges to the Negro; he alone was free to enjoy its vices and its virtues, gambling, leisure, loafing, the right to say what he thought to his equals, drinking and the correlates of drink. The seedbed of Southern puritanism was evangelical Christianity, for the most part Baptist and Methodist; its flowering, prohibition, laws against miscegenation—the cavalier had not been so squeamish and in the only state where puritanism was weak, Louisiana, no miscegenation bill could be got past the legislature —and blue laws that would have pleased the Plymouth brethren.

The puritan in the South was, however, different in some ways from his Northern like. He lacked a single vent to his violence, such as business offered to the Yankee (the Quaker was a calm and just man, outside of office hours), and as a result explosions were whimsical. He was also socially inferior, as the Nonconformist was in England. The roster of the Episcopal Church was the social register.

But there were no absolutes in the South. A boy, soon to become a man by the reckoning of the calendar, was not allowed to be pure puritan; he must also preserve within himself the cavalier tradition, he must somehow manage to be what no one could be, a Christian gentleman. But that was not all; there was another turn to the screw; in school he was told that he should become another contradiction, a gentleman and a scholar. How was a boy to know that Christian gentleman and gentleman-scholar were impossible equations?

II

To the outsider there is one South, and that solid. If the word were used as one might say "solid England" or "solid China," what it lacked in accuracy would be made up in grace, and there would still be truth in it. But as it is used, it casts a shadow of deprecation in which lurks "hopelessly" or "stupidly" or some such opinion. The South is indeed solid, for there, as nowhere else in America, is homogeneity, a certain inner unity. A mountain white, strayed to the flat lands and squatting, quid in jaw, before the country store, will soon find himself at ease with the low-country man. There may be some difficulty with the dialect, especially if his fellow Southerner be from Georgetown or Charleston or that neck of the woods, where the speech of the Gullah Negroes has left shade and tone in the language of the master race; but, speech aside—and speech may be of no great importance where other means of communication are in plenty—they will be one. They will understand one another, for their likes and dislikes are the same, particularly their dislikes; they will boil at about the same temperature. The South is solid, in its own peculiar solidness; and that, I suspect, is one reason the critic also quickly comes to a boil, whether he be pure down-Easter Yankee, or hybrid, like Mencken, born and bred in limbo.

And yet, since without diversity there can be no unity—that would be monotony, and the South is not monotonous—there are, to the seeing eye and the cocked ear, differences; rather, the differences are at first felt, and may later on be catalogued and docketed. So it was with me when I moved to Montgomery. I felt the differences—I was fifteen at the time—and responded with discomfort, a kind of alienation such as I would find in school, in Tennessee and much later in New Orleans. When, still later, I became detached in fact and to some degree in feeling, one of these differences became quite clear.

This was in England, at Oxford. When I met my first Canadian he seemed awkwardly familiar. I had seen him somewhere before, and, as one will be teased by a scent or tune until it is placed in memory, so the Canadian plagued me. Then at last I saw him and knew him. The Canadian was the Alabamian. Now, hot on the trail, the South African became the North Carolinian, Mississippian, Tennessean, and the New Zealander and Australian together the Georgian. The last was pat and clinching. We used to say in South Carolina, when a neighbor under suspicion of crime suddenly disappeared, "Well, I guess he's gone to Georgia." These fellow Southerners were colonials, excepting those from my native state and Virginia.

They were the mother states of the South, Virginia and South Carolina; the rest were colonies, and subject to the disabilities, and advantages, of that condition. (I do not include Florida, which can hardly be called a state, nor Louisiana, which is half-caste.) The North Carolinian will serve as an example. The saying is old, but here worth repeating, that "North Carolina is a valley of humility between two mountains of conceit." Scorned alike by the Virginian and South Carolinian, deprived of the title "gentleman"—I think I never heard the words "North Carolina gentleman"—he might have sunk into schizophrenic ignominy; he chose rather to bestir himself and is today the South's most thoughtful man, and thinking comes hard to a Southerner; but he remains a colonial.

Colonies lack the mellow inconsequence of the mother country. Where each is fixed in status at birth and change comes long and slow, a man can stand out as an individual within his class and be seen across class lines; but where change is rapid and lines are forming, differences of class are more sharply marked, and reverenced or despised. An old name was worth more to its wearer in Montgomery than in Richmond or Charleston. There were contemptible Randolphs and Hamptons in their native states, but in Montgomery their names alone comprised all virtue and covered all sin. One needs to look long at things of a kind before differences begin to appear, and Alabamians had not seen enough of aristocracy to see through it. A prosperous middle class was rising in the South, though we did not know it by that or any name; the old aristocracy had been depleted by valor and cheap cotton, and a new and other was ready to take its place. Men and women whose grandparents had been welcome at the back door of the big house were now crowding to the front; they would soon put forth claims to something more than wealth, would wish to be called ladies and gentlemen. Meanwhile the vendor of sheets and pillowcases, plug tobacco, and soft drinks aped his betters and humbly crooked the knee in the presence of the real thing. Some day his children would be a name; he had the price clinking in his pocket. Where class is lean, the skeleton shows through; shrewd in all things, the merchant knew that aristocracy begins with money. Also, having been none too nice in the building of his foundation, he was ready to overlook shady practices, especially if the practicer's name was good.

This came out sordid and clear when a member of an old Virginia family returned to Montgomery after many years of asylum in Costa Rica, beyond the arm of extradition treaties. He had held an office in the city government, treasurer as I recall, or some other that admitted his hand to the public till. One day he had put it in deep and at once departed, to a land where he could live in a style to which he was weary of being unaccustomed. Aristocracy and wealth belonged together, he knew; now he had them both. But he grew old, and the city's pile grew small, and there was talk of an extradition treaty with Costa Rica which would empty that country of its shady immigrants. The officers of the law in Montgomery, mindful that he was a gentleman and had done his pilfering long ago, answered the inquiries of interested friends and relatives, saying that, if he returned, they would look the other way.

He returned, and, to read the papers and listen to the talk, an unknowing stranger would have thought that a hero had come home. A committee met him at the depot and with honors. There were, however, a few dissentient voices, my father's among them, and loud, uttered from the pulpit the following Sunday morning.

On Monday morning nervous friends warned my father that he had gone too far. The gentleman from Virginia was making threats—such as would have landed a Negro in jail or worse—and my father had better tote a pistol. This he refused to do. Would he then at least stay off the streets? No, he would not do that either. If Montgomery was the sort of town in which a man could be murdered for speaking his mind, well, let the embezzler shoot. The suppliants shook their heads and went away worried and uncomprehending. He was a tough customer, for fair.

Meanwhile the hero was beginning to be something of a nuisance to others, with conduct unbecoming even a gentleman. He did not shoot my father. He went out after other game, more profitable, he hoped. A nephew received a note demanding money. When he refused, a message followed: if the money was not delivered by a certain time the next morning, when the uncle called for it, his kinsman might expect to be shot at sight. Promptly at the appointed hour the old man stepped into his nephew's office and received, not the money but a load of buckshot. The gentleman was taken on his last journey, without honors.

Sometimes the conclusion was not so painless to the living. Near the parsonage lived two old ladies in black, lived and mourned the death of a son and nephew. His life had been flagrant, almost taxing the patience of his own class; everyone, even the mother and aunt with whom he lived, knew that the cabin that stood empty in the back yard had been the dwelling of his Negro mistress. But now that he was dead his little sin was forgotten and he became a saint, and, as became a saint, deserved a monument. The mourners were unexpectedly members of my father's church—this occasionally happened in the best families, perhaps because some renegade ancestor had gone religious—and they asked their pastor for advice. He suggested that they build a needed addition to the church and this they were glad to do, but when my

father announced the gift there was a mixed response. Most of the congregation were as pleased as he, but dominant members stipulated that
the memorial should not carry the name of the dead gentleman's family.
Sin must remain anonymous.

At the time it was a puzzle to me—most things were a puzzle to me
at the time—that those who looked askance at the old Virginian, although they were glad enough when he was dead, condemned in life
and death alike the wild young man. He had been honest, if not honorable; the honored thief plainly dishonest.

My dismay increased when I took a job in a store and began to see
the business world close up, where a good name might not be good for
a bill of goods. Many old families lived precariously in the sickly city,
no place for an aristocracy, where, in the competition of business, their
expansive habits undid them. The horse trader, in the moment of trading, recognizes as superior only the more crafty trader, and, as most
business in the South was still on the level of horse trading, the gentleman became an easy victim to his own graces and sank down and down
until, when he asked for credit, he met a glazed eye. And yet, when
the names of the indigent gentry appeared in the society columns, they
were read with unmeditating envy.

One name appeared suddenly in another column. The body of a
young gentleman had been found on the roof of a bank building. He
had tried to cut the electric burglar alarm with a pair of pliers. The
only condemnation I heard was, "The damn fool, didn't he know he
couldn't do that with his bare hands?" When the loss of silverware and
jewelry among the families of his friends was traced to his pilfering
hand, it was their carelessness rather than his theft that was disapproved. They should have taken better care of their things.

There was a woman of the town who, while not openly on the town,
lived in a haze of suspicion. She had a daughter, beautiful, as my own
eyes were witness, and without reproach. But when a boy of good fam-

ily married her, it was as if he had offered personal affront to prospering citizens.

Here was confusion, and confusion that would last long, longer than the astigmatism of youth. It had been hard enough in South Carolina, admonished to be at the same time puritan and cavalier, Christian and gentleman, honest as well as honorable; but what was I to make of this: dishonesty that was honorable, honesty unhonored, honesty and honor alike despised?

These small comedies were not in themselves extraordinary, they might have been enacted elsewhere; what made them significant was their reception by the people of Montgomery. Most of them knew little, nor cared, were amused or contemptuous, because they were tired or unambitious or happy; but there were some who did care, and of these a few who cared in a peculiar way, showing bland complacency toward one kind of actor and sharp resentment toward the other. They were the few who were hopefully on their way up, puritans changing into their notion of cavaliers, imitation gentlemen; but—and this explained their complacency—they were taking their natures along. Sharp practice, which lives next door to theft, was their practice, and therefore to be condoned. The Southern puritan in the street was honest, but these few were no longer in the street; they were climbing the hill and leaving inconvenient virtues behind, and of these the most inconvenient was honesty.

At that time in the South it was almost impossible for a just man to get rich; but, if one was to become a gentleman, wealth was an absolute necessity. Every aristocracy in the Western world had been based on wealth. After a few generations the gentleman might forget, might even become contemptuous of money—the coeval gentleman often was—but still wealth was the ground beneath his feet. The climber had therefore dropped burdensome honesty at the foot of the hill. That made sense. But why this concern with honor? Why was he more perturbed than the authentic gentleman at its violation?

The answer to that was long in coming. When the Southerner moves out of the South he takes with him in detail the memory of what it was, and, if he can learn to hold the picture steady, after a while it may come into focus. A laborer pulling his forelock in an English village, a week end in the home of a London brewer, an evening of fun in the University Club of Lincoln, Nebraska, the dean of a New Jersey college calling herself a lady with insistence . . . these and a thousand others, and constant return in thought, and after a while there was less blur here and there.

When he began to imitate the gentleman, puritan virtues were dropped, or transmuted into useful climbing implements. Sternness became ruthlessness, truth-telling turned into truth-making, candor into bluff, thrift into parsimony, justice became legality, and there was no mercy, for mercy was never a puritan virtue. He was taking his nature along, but his nature no longer restrained by the virtues of his native class. Nevertheless there were virtues that restrained him, misunderstood virtues. That was when honor came in, not honor as the gentleman understood it, but honor as his imitator understood honor. But why this resentment toward the gentleman without honor? He would soon be gone, the gentleman, and the climber would take his place. Why not let him dishonor himself and come to his end the quicker? Because—here was glorious laughter—because the gentleman must keep the garment of gentility unsmirched until the climber should stumble over the last boulder and take it from his shoulders. If there was any dirtying to be done, and there was plenty as time would tell, he would do it himself. Meanwhile it must be kept, as his orator liked to say, "pure as the driven snow." Ivanhoe, Lancelot, Galahad, these were the heroes, not of the gentry, who never read anything, but of the newcome gentlemen.

The end of the story was told me by Atlanta, Durham, Charlotte, and Charleston in its way. I saw the gentleman, in 1933, the new gentleman of the New South, when, as Uncle Melt would have said, he had "done clumb." Hating—that is, fearing—enlightenment, he had cynically founded two universities and doused them with wealth; despising the poor, he had used charity. He had set up a foundation in the Carolinas that professed to protect the orphans of the poor, but in reality protected his own orphans, by tying both legislatures to his will.

He was proud, in his way. He had done his best to imitate the pride of the gentleman, and his best was arrogance. Buck Duke, staggering drunk along the streets of Durham, was rebuked: "Aren't you ashamed, Mr. Duke, to be seen this way? You belong to the Methodist Church." "I belong to the Methodist Church?" the old man roared, "Hell, the Methodist Church belongs to me!"

III

In the eighteenth century an awaited illness among young girls was the "green sickness"—the words convey the meaning. The cure was marriage. When the bride turned from the altar and hooked herself to her new husband through the crook of his arm, parents and relatives accepted the symbol with gratitude and dismissed her from their thoughts; for them she ceased to be a person at the moment she became a wife. So it was in the South; a fiction, of course, but fictions are fertilizers of culture.

For a boy, however, there was no such fiction, no easy step into oblivion. He had to become a man, whatever that might mean, and the eventual crook of an arm would only add to his troubles. It was as if he stood, not at the fork of the roads—that figure is too simple—but on the depot platform of any Southern city, surrounded by bawling hack drivers inviting him to perfect destinations; or, to bring him up to date, at a clover-leaf intersection with hundreds of signs and no time to read them, honked at by impatient travelers who think they know where they want to go. It is now that he would like a little peace and quiet, but there is none. Awkward, stumbling, aching, with voice and limbs that fly incontinently out of register, every morning he wakes to the shock of change, and at night, when he reluctantly drags himself to bed, he knows that even his dreams will italicize his fears. This is the time when wise elders will surround a boy with unsolicitous love and leave him to find his own way into manhood. This is the time when nobody lets him alone. He cuts a swath through the room, stumbling over chairs and rugs and thoughts, and his father glares. This awful thing was an infant, then he was a boy, now he is a monster. Even his mother may love him too much.

While he was an infant he absorbed knowledge, taking it in through his tissues, without thought or care. Then, in boyhood, he became a collector, of birds' eggs, stamps, tobacco tags, baseball averages, dates —anything that can be arranged in series. But if he is to become a man —some do—he grows tired of counting and collecting, and a terrifying thing happens: he ceases to be a scientist; he begins to ask, "What does it mean?" and with the coming of this question there comes the first step into manhood. To know is not enough.

It hit me about the time we moved to Montgomery. Until then I had been a whole, a self-contained universe; but now when voice and shape and thoughts began to change, this other change came, this disrelish for mere knowledge, this hesitant desire for meaning. At times I scrambled back into childhood, searching for my lost wholeness, wondering whether I should ever be whole again; then there were other, frightening, moments of certainty that I would never be whole again, not in that wholeness.

My father could not understand. No blame to him; he had leapt from childhood into middle age and had forgotten or never known the torture of second birth, of birth into meaning. He thought he knew meaning because he thought he had found final meaning; he had become a Christian and elected to be a preacher at the time when other boys were mere collectors; thought, in fact, that there was only one meaning and, somehow or other, everything must be packed into that. Music had no meaning to him, for music eludes dogma, as painting, and literature, and every created thing. Meaning for him meant purpose, and there was only one purpose. For me, religion had already proved an ineffectual midwife.

The ordeal of parenthood is to admit new premises for old conclusions. In the multiple premises of the nineteenth century there was one constant, God; in the twentieth, none. As to conclusions there was no argument—they were deep in all of us, these old conclusions—we were only seeking new constants; but, by the irony of conflict, there was the center of alienation.

This lapse of communication, long preparing, now became clear to me. I had just made the disturbing discovery, new to me as to every generation but old as Adam, that experiment and experience were not the same thing, that there is in action a quality beyond the reach of the imagination. I hung around my father's study, a very small Lady Macbeth, in manly hope and boyish fear that he would ask me why I was troubled. At last he turned in his swivel chair and said, "What's the matter with you this morning, John Andrew? Why are you so restless? Why aren't you at school?" I told him what had happened. It was like striking him in the face. He sat looking at me through twisted muscles and heard me silently to the end. Then, to my horror, I saw him getting down on his knees and as they touched the floor, heard the familiar words, "Our Heavenly Father . . ."

A man may remember his childhood with pleasure, but where is one who does not wince at the memory of his adolescence?

I came sodden to the breakfast table and nibbled where I once had gorged, apologetic because my tossing had rattled the parsonage bedsprings and again waked my father, apologetic when my reports came from school, apologetic for being alive. The doctors were called in. My father remembered, as I more vividly, the year I had spent in bed not long ago, kept firmly there on doctor's orders, and he became afraid. I was in a panic; a year in bed was just what I did not want. They came, looked me over hurriedly—we were preacher's family and there would be no fee—and said, "Take him out of school." What was I to do out of school? "Get him a job," they said, and went.

The next Monday morning at seven o'clock I went to work in a furniture store. My father got me the job, as he would get me others, by a mild form of blackmail. The proprietor, a good man of simple piety, was offered the Methodist equivalent of an indulgence. Nothing of the kind was spoken in words, but the impression somehow vaguely floated to him that, if he would take me on, he would profit in some way unspecified, here or hereafter. He knew, for I was not reputed energetic, that, if at all, it would be hereafter; but he was a patient Christian and loved his pastor, so he offered me five dollars a week, twelve hours daily except Saturday, when it might stretch to sixteen. The wages and hours were reasonable by the standard of the day. Daylight for work, dark for sleep, that was what the farm had taught him, when he, like most other merchants, had been a farm boy and lived under its tyranny.

The first thing I saw, when I got the dust out of my eyes—I dislocated the dust of the previous day with a turkey feather duster—was that an honest man had a hard time. The proprietor tried, and at last failed, to put into practice what he learned and believed on Sunday. The customers were against him; they wanted to higgle and haggle and beat him down, and could not comprehend his honest nature. There must be a catch somewhere, they thought, and after extensive battling they went to other stores where they could find salesmen no more decent than themselves.

He loved furniture, and when they had gone he would stand and look at the piece they had rejected, rub his hand over the surface, pull out a drawer, tilt the headboard to let the light catch the grain, and shake his head in hurt wonder. Presently others came, and, lest they too despise the things he loved, he cut the price to where there was no profit. In a few years he was back on the road, from which he came, a drummer, as we called a traveling salesman in that day.

I became a collector, sent out to get the weekly payments on furniture bought on the installment plan, and saw Montgomery bottom side up. I was not the only one. The poorer parts of town swarmed with collectors, of payments on sewing machines, furniture, funeral clubs—twenty-five cents a week, and the promise of a casket, a hearse, and two carriages at death—building lots, newspapers. The last, the newspapers, were the widest detour around value; subscriptions were solicited with an offer of a set of dishes after so many months, and the daily papers, rolled as they came from the tossing hand of the delivery boy, were piled in the corner for kindling. Collectors were thickest in the Negro quarter, and in the segregated district. The sleepy madam counted dimes and quarters into a trembling hand held to its hired duty while glittering eyes peered over her shoulder into the dark hallway.

In Columbia, from the shelter of childhood, I had seen something of my fellow Southerners' inhumanity to the Negro; in Montgomery I saw and felt it directly. Here as there, he was half country, half city, living in the same kind of niggertown of unpaved streets that were rain gullies in winter and dust chutes in summer, beside which flowers, as tough as their inattentive owners, grew and bloomed, defying all the rules of gardening. The houses gave off through unchinked cracks a peculiar pungent acid smell that reminded me of Uncle Melt's cabin; mongrel dogs—"fice" they called them—barked savagely at the white intruder, following the rule of "like master, like dog," but, while not being constrained as their masters were to a show of servility, seldom savage to the point of biting, again like their masters. Sometimes the dogs were away on private business and I had to pass the silent stare of a cat. If I found courage to knock and enquire for Mary or Sue or whatever the name of the one I was sent to find, no one knew where they were nor ever knew them, until some one recognized me, laughed, and said, "Ain't you Dr. Rice's son? Sho, Sue's right nex' do' in de back room." But sometimes the search was longer, and I met more than one "ficety" Negro leaning against the front gate and warning me with sullen eyes that I had better be gone.

The Negro, of course, was everybody's game. Unless he kept accounts, any contract he made went into eternity. A cook we had complained, "Don' seem like I ever will get my sewing machine paid for." My father found that she had already paid them three times the price agreed upon; when he asked for an accounting, the agent let him know how he felt about nigger-lovers. White men spent their daylight hours squeezing nickels and dimes and quarters out of Negroes, and went home at night to their families, superior. Sometimes payment was had in other currency. An old Negro said to me, when I was slow to accept his offer of deferred payment, "New account bring fresh meat, boss."

As I had known him in South Carolina the Negro was a person, and my and others' relations with him were personal; but here in Montgomery he was sunk below the level of humanity; he was a thing. The savage that is just beneath the skin of every Southerner was ready to spring at him; but, restrained by law, he was compelled to take it out on the Negro within the rules of his own age. The rules were, however, flexible; such a thing as police protection being hardly known, the law was held to have done its full duty if it kept the white man from murdering a Negro.

I was a successful collector, because I brought to my job my childhood liking for Negroes, and also because I was not trying to cheat them. Others, boys of my age and older men, hated them; in reality hated themselves when they worked their mean little game of chipping off a nickel here and a dime there. When we gathered at midday to eat our lunches—we were a fraternity—they often laughed and boasted of their skill. That dam' nigger's family would find out when he was dead that they'd have to pay another five dollars before the hearse would come; tomorrow a dray would haul another's furniture away; what if they had paid up, they had no receipt; the collector mimicked, "When I go'n to git my dishes, boss?" They laughed, but it was uneasy laughter, and they were quick to quarrel, haul out their brass knuckles and bloody one another.

They were, as a Chicago gangster said of his necessity, coming up the hard way; one man in town had found an easier. He sat in his small office on the main street and let them bring their money to him. On the walls hung blueprints of a projected Negro community, and its future dwellers came and gladly paid their money down on the lots they had bought. "Where'd you say mine wuz, boss?" they would ask, and he would swing his great bulk round and point, "There it is, Joe, right next to the post office," or, "Up in that corner, Ed, near the canning factory. Yep, you and your family won't have to go far to work." The devout had theirs in the block where the church was to stand, and on another wall they saw sketches of the coming glory, a real white-folks church, stained-glass windows and all, and all for them— niggers. When he had pocketed their payments—"I'll remember to put it down to your account, Sam"—and they were gone, he would lean back in his swivel chair, take aim at the spittoon in the corner, spit, and laugh; and his admirers laughed with him.

Years later I saw him and his kind again. I was having dinner with a friend in a roadhouse near Charleston and, not long returned, I looked and listened, as a man will when he comes home. Most of the voices and faces were pleasant, like remembered flowers, but there was one group of men that stirred an unpleasant memory. They laughed and slapped each other on the back, and yet, in all their laughter, there was no mirth. I asked my host who they were. "Oh," he said, "those people? They're collectors for Negro funeral societies. They have an organization now, you know, and this is their annual dinner."

IV

Boswell gave his approval to the class system, to what he called the "grand scheme of subordination." But even in the eighteenth century in England a man might rise from his class and acquire the privilege of looking down on his fellows. In the South, however, there was no rising. The servant was forever fixed in status by another device, this time of Nature herself, by the grand scheme of pigmentation. We are told by some scientists that we are forever determined as individuals by the biochemical pattern of the genetic cell. This is a theory, which we are at liberty to accept or not. But another biochemical phenomenon we see operating in life in the South, implacable and relentless, and we must admit its existence whether we like it or not. Some day history may record with amazement that a man's whole life was once determined by the color of his skin, that the presence of a modicum of dark pigment cut off the individual, however fit he might be in other respects, from much that men called good in life; and the absence of dark pigment in a man, however unfit he might be, gave him a chance that biochemistry denied his fellow. That is what is known as white supremacy. I have often asked my fellow Southerners in what white supremacy consisted, and, when they have answered, it has come down to pigmentation.

The Civil War destroyed the class system in the South, but it left untouched the barrier of pigmentation, the caste system. To a small boy growing up there at the end of the last century, there was trouble enough to differentiate between the gentleman real and the gentleman ideal, between the lady he knew and the lady of fiction; but, striking deeper than these, bringing a profounder disturbance within him, was the shadow of uncertainty and doubt thrown across his life by the barrier of caste. He was dismayed by the phrase, "sanctity of womanhood," when he learned that it meant white womanhood, while women of another color were sacred to none, not even to himself; the unmistakable stamp of family resemblance on the faces of his mulatto play-mates made him wonder; the mother of these mulattoes, who never worked as other Negroes did and lived undisturbed by economic care, was a puzzle; the savage anger of the gentleman when caste lines were crossed without his approval or connivance; all these left the small boy in a cloud of doubt. The encroaching knowledge that the Negro children with whom he played must some day forever live their lives behind the barrier of caste worked in him a strange deep sadness.

This barrier that lay across the whole South, setting up divisions wherever white and black were gathered together, was again characteristically Southern in being, from the Negro's side, more inclusive than exclusive. Over it the white man leapt at will to deal as insolently as he pleased with Negro men and to claim the right of master with his women, and to ease in some measure the frustrations that came to him through the code of conduct that he himself had imposed upon his own womankind. Sometimes he was caught by something stronger than desire and found himself a willing and unwilling victim of real affection; found in his bungling way personal equality across the barrier of human inequality. There is a chapter to be written in the history of the South on the influence of the Negro woman on the nature of the white man. When he invaded their world, he went seeking not their grace of life, but unleashing the savage that was in him, and, like the invader and the immigrant everywhere, found it easier to adapt himself to the vices than to the virtues of the found land. The guilty unease that is often seen in the face and mien of the Southern white man is the stigma that his excursions have put upon him. One needs but to recall the sad look of shame in the eyes of his white mate.

But every human institution is both good and bad, and the caste barrier was bad and good. Behind it, and protected by it, forever free from the fierce competition of the white world, the Negro developed a gracious life all his own. There is an advantage in knowing that you can never be President. There is an advantage, as the artist has always known, in the limitations of a medium. The white man is an individualist subject to all the terrors of that lonely state. The Negro was free from this care, for he was always one of the race. It has been a constant surprise to the stranger in the South that the Negro blandly accepts what, to the white man, would be a personal affront. Here the barrier of caste is the Negro's protection. Call him a "nigger" however insolently, and the insult is never personal. It is quietly diffused over the whole race and absorbed. Behind the barrier of race the Negro has developed a personal dignity seldom equaled by that of his white brother, the individualist. A visit to a Negro school is a revelation; here are calm and quiet faces such as are seldom seen in a white school, calm and undisturbed by the cancer of guilt. (Here is a problem for the economic determinist.)

Some of the finest practitioners of the art of living learned their art beyond the barrier, but grace is pervasive, and much of the grace of life in the South has come from the gentle nature of the Negro. We laughed and called him lazy, but laziness needs only occupation to become leisure. His very laziness was an embodiment of the double nature of every human attitude. He had learned, and we learned from him, that what is human vice may be personal virtue, and laziness is both. (The man who is busy with business finds the artist a condemned puzzle.) They used to say among themselves that the reason a Negro never committed suicide was that when he got to "studyin'" he went to sleep. He knew how to live in the present, a lost art among whites. He was our best teacher in this, as in all the realm of human and personal relations.

Sometimes he reminded the gentleman of the difference, quietly and graciously. The father of Judge Henry Hammond of Augusta had a Negro body servant whom he trusted until at length he trusted him too much. Money, small sums always, began to disappear from the compartment of the desk into which the master emptied his pockets at night; after a time he began slowly and reluctantly to suspect Jim, and with even more reluctance at last he set a trap for Jim. One night he left in the compartment nothing but a five-dollar bill. The next morning, when he opened it, he found four dollars and seventy-five cents.

The Negro was also brutal, still half a slave, filled with trickery and subterfuge and servility. These a boy learned from the Negro, learned them at the very moment when he thought himself superior.

As the Southern gentleman sanctified his lady and made her the repository of all the virtues, so he desecrated his servant and made him the repository of vice. What he did not want, or dare to do himself, he allowed the Negro. The lady was by definition moral, the Negro immoral. The gentleman lived in a limbo between the two, committed finally to the assumed value of neither. I say "assumed" advisedly, for both pictures were fiction, and the gentleman was unwilling to trust either one. He did not completely believe in the immorality of his servant, and he was right not to. But from this repository of evil, from this assumed concept of the corrupt darky, there was a seepage into his own life. What he generally tolerated in others of a different color he sometimes came to overlook in himself. The sensual Southern gentleman had a competent tutor.

But the Negro affected not the men alone. Much that is admirable and much that is deplorable in Southern women is, in its origin, tinged. We know, now that we have begun to think seriously about human society, that no element in it is isolated or isolable. Everything colors, changes, modifies everything else. The Negro mammy has been overpraised, and the lady's maid, who exchanged corruption with her mistress, each encouraging the other to slithering irresponsibility and laziness without virtue, is part of the dark history of the South.

v

When, after an absence of some twenty years, I returned to the South, I found change, but between and within all classes, themselves shifting and changing, there was still a sense of community. They all speak the same language and are moved by the same feelings. The same fears and hopes hold all. One common fear is very old, so old that the Greeks had a name for it, xenophobia, fear of the stranger. Outsiders are dismayed at the roaring alien-baiting Southern politicians. It is the voice of old fear, for the alien in the South is almost a stranger. Bob Reynolds, the junior Senator from North Carolina—and very junior—regularly hoarsens his vocal chords with abuse of the alien. He is quite safe; there are practically none in his State. Anti-Catholic feeling is also fear of the stranger. Except in the seaports there are few Catholics, but the Southerner carries in him his seventeenth-century grandfather's fear of Popery. Individual Catholics and aliens are as such seldom mistrusted or mistreated. But there is also a better side to the sense of community: once a good idea catches on, it travels fast. The Southerner's attitude toward the Negro is incredibly more humane than it was in the South I knew as a child.

The gentleman is almost extinct, appearing once in a while on stage or screen, an unconvincing figure, or embalmed in the pages of literature for which fiction is too soft a name, so red the rose. The lady too has almost disappeared and is now rarely seen in the South. Her enemies, the mill and the city, have changed the basic pattern of the Southern family. The plantation has gone and taken her with it. Her granddaughter, the lady as we now know her, has, by the persistence of memory, only her grace and charm, with little to grace and few to charm.

The Negro remains, but he also is not as he was. When I knew him in my boyhood he aspired, if he aspired at all, to be like white folks, and by "white folks" he meant the gentleman and his lady, whom, and alone, he recognized as superior. Now that the gentleman and lady are gone, the Negro seeks his model elsewhere, in the now dominant middle class—the aristocracy was, by the reckoning of numbers, always small—and is assuming their manners and even their morals. He is no longer free in the borrowed freedom of his master, and has begun to forget. A young Negro student under Professor Charles Johnson at Fiske University elected to make a study of "The Southern Gentleman." He had to get a very old Negro to find one for him.

They are gone, these three aristocrats—or going, for the old Negro will follow his master and mistress into oblivion—and few will wish to stay their passing. But every democracy needs them or their like, detached observers who may be also vocal or silent critics. Such observers can exist, however, only when there is something in their nature or status that protects them from the leveling judgment of the average mind.

The gentleman and lady occupied their position through favorable injustice. They were the privileged class; but there is another privileged class in the South, or caste, created by unfavorable injustice. The Negro, through no wish of his own, and no fault, has been set outside the center of Southern life and has been unintentionally elevated to the status of critic. So far, in the main, his criticism has been inarticulate. Now, however, it begins to be otherwise, and from the pen and tongue of Negroes there is coming a detached and dispassionate picture of the South that makes the Southerner squirm. One needs only to hear a Southern Negro gentleman and scholar describe a railway journey through the South or an attempt to find decent lodgings—all this in a quiet, amused, uncontemptuous voice—to realize that from this privileged caste may someday come the South's best critic. He is already the best critic of his own race, for here again race prejudice has done race a useful turn. A good many Negroes from the South are recently getting as good an education as any white man can, thanks to the hospitality of Northern institutions of learning, but—and here there is a tinge of irony—when he wants to teach he is obliged to go back to his native land. The South may yet present to America the picture of an oppressed race getting the best education in the nation. Sometimes in history the oppressor has met with subtle defeat at the hands of the oppressed, a thing that the white Southerner, and others, might well remember.

CHAPTER V

Webb School

AS A MAN WHO HAS BEEN CHEATED IN BUSINESS OR LOVE OR ANY OF
the things that happen will toss on his bed through the sleepless
night, going over each step in the transaction and saying to himself, "If
I had done this," "If I had not done that," and rises with the sun, full
of anger and violence and despair; so the South after the Civil War.
At every crossroad, in every country store, wherever men gathered, the
Confederate veteran was present to tell how the South had been—not
defeated, never that—bilked, cheated, tricked out of victory, overwhelmed. In the North, I am told, which is what we called all of America outside the South, listeners grew impatient at the talkative old man
(another's victory is a bore) and walked off into the future, but for
the South there was no future. Stunned by their overwhelming, men
and women wandered about in a dream world, a world of incomparably
brave men and women every one a Helen, and listened eagerly to the
words of the old men who had returned from the bright past. Boys
listened too. "If we'd just 'a had one more company, we'd 'a licked
'em," the old man said, and the boy became that company.

Anger, violence, despair, all were in us and in all of us, and longing
for another chance we knew would never come. (If Wilson had remembered his childhood, he might have brought peace to Germany;
but Wilson was also a Southern Presbyterian, coldly violent.) We knew
the chance would never come, but we got ready for it. We kept our
violence in condition, by fist fights (many of my age-fellows carried

brass knuckles), cutting scrapes (every one carried a knife), brawls at political rallies. (Ben Tillman often could not make himself heard above the din.)

Our violence was schooled, literally, in another way. The South was, and still is, dotted with military schools, academies and colleges. Violence was also curbed, channeled, by them. When Clemson College was established in South Carolina for the training of farmer boys, some one asked Ben Tillman why he had made it military. "How'n hell do you think we could keep these wild boys down?" he asked in answer.

Tillman, the first of the Southern dictators, knew what he was talking about, as he always did when it came to knowing his people. The Southerner, for all his easy ways, is quick to anger. "Techy" (touchy), "ficety" (like a fice, a mongrel pup, nervous and misunderstood), "meaner 'n a blue-gum nigger" (the bite of a "blue-gum nigger" was poisonous)—these were some of the regional words to describe the extremes, but we were all, in our several ways, wild.

The first task of a school was therefore to tame a boy, to match violence with violence; by means of the rod and peach-tree switch to make of him a gentleman (chivalry is codified violence) and, hopefully, a scholar. "School" meant private school, if a boy was to be prepared for college or for life—the preparations were the same. The public school, even as late as the turn of the century, was in its infancy, and there remained, for it died at the end of the eighth grade or thereabouts; also, education at public expense offended the genteel tradition.

Among the relics of the Civil War there was a young man who returned hatless to his home in North Carolina. He had ridden part of the way in an open flatcar and his army cap—"tattered" was the word he used to describe it—had blown off. He remained hatless, for there was not enough money in the whole family connection to buy another. This was Sawney Webb, soon to be a teacher, whom one day I should know when his beard, which he wore even then, had long turned grey.

There were many who came home, inured to ordered violence, angry at their defeat, only to find that the farm, which had remained green and fruitful in their memory, gave them a stingy welcome. Men who had been bred to the law took to the plow, and others in their several ways had to bury their ambitions and go about earning a living, and by living they meant bread and meat. Only two professions offered a sure living—and that lean, too—preaching and teaching. If a man could not quite go the church, he set up as a teacher, and even to this day, if you scratch a Southern teacher, a preacher will wince.

All that the founder of a new school needed was a little learning and a lot of physical strength. Sawney Webb, one of the founders of Webb School, had both. He had attended the Bingham school in North Carolina where he had been an admirer as well as pupil of Colonel Bingham; had learned from him his Latin, Greek, and math—but more deeply his autocratic ways. He was a graduate of the University of North Carolina and had gone through four years of war, enlisted as a boy and discharged as a tough young man. He had, as he liked to remind his pupils, taken a cold bath every morning, even if he had to walk miles to find a stream; he had also been wounded in an arm, and sometimes, when his left hand had been scratched by a briar, he allowed it to bleed unnoticed as the boys sat in awe at the brave show.

He had needed all his vigor in the early days, for it was a convention in the South that, when a new school opened, the big boys should beat the teacher up on the first day. These boys had been too young to fight when the war ended and cheated them of their natural rights, so they took it out on the new teacher. If he proved a match for them with his fists, the rest was easy, for they knew nothing.

The other founder was John Webb, who had been too young to be taken to war and, while his brother fought and learned the ways of fighting, remained a student at the University of North Carolina.

The two brothers had taken Emerson at his word, often quoted by Sawney with no intention of irony: "Make a better mouse trap and the world will beat a path to your door." Their door was in Bell Buckle, a village in Middle Tennessee. In the beginning they had no money and no backing; nothing, except ideas. By the time I came along the path was well beaten, for their ideas had met the American test and worked. One that sounds odd in a world attuned to tests and measurements and psychographs was, that no boy should be refused admission. "Every boy deserves another chance," they said. One result was that the greatest scoundrels and scholars in the South could boast attendance, long or short, at Webb School. The assumption was, as I should discover, that one had been a scoundrel; but in the narrow world of education the scholars were known. Twenty years ago it was true, and is here recorded without prejudice—may still be true—that more Rhodes Scholars came from Webb School than from any other in the world.

My mother had been casual in her mentioning of the school, for she knew that the only way to catch a crazy colt was to creep up on his blind side; then, as I began to listen, she told me more. She had known the Webbs, both Sawney and John, when she herself was a teacher in Tennessee, and been befriended by them both. When she talked of Sawney she was like someone who has just come from seeing an exciting play, but when she spoke John Webb's name, her voice changed and her eyes changed, and her words became vague and incoherent, which was a strange thing in her, who could always say what she meant. My father was not so easy to convince. He distrusted Sawney, although he had never seen him, and his distrust was deep—and, as I should know in later years, well founded.

Women say they cannot remember the pangs of childbirth. Crafty Nature blots them out, lest there be no more. So also one does not remember one's second birth—not the final birth; that comes much later, at twenty, or thirty, forty, fifty, the birth into manhood—even the second birth, from childhood into youth, becomes in memory a dull pain,

pain of both mother and child, in one, for one is both, in this as in the final birth.

I felt miserable all the way from Montgomery to Bell Buckle. That is all I remember, that and a little sharing of misery with other boys, when I changed trains at Nashville and started on the last long-short lap. The train stopped at the depot, indistinguishable from a thousand others with its grey sanded paint of years before, its signs "White" and "Colored," its spittoons and cinders. I followed the herd up the hill and was greeted by a boy some thirty years old, "Son Will" as he was called behind his back, Sawney's eldest and mouthpiece for routine. I was to live at the home of Dr. Hatch, he told me, some distance beyond the school, in a room with three other boys, sleeping two in a bed. (Double beds were the rule in the South.)

Dr. and Mrs. Hatch have long since gone to their reward and have, I hope, got their deserts. He was a mean old man who spat on the floor wherever he might be sitting, and bullied whom he could. His wife was the sort of woman who has lived with that sort of man forty years, patient, kindly, slowly moved to anger, but bitter when she was. She earned their living by taking ten boys as boarders, the most the school would allow in one house; cooked, cleaned house, kept the garden, and did everything else that had to be done, while her husband sat and chewed. He was the first shiftless white man I had ever seen close up. I had known shiftless Negroes, but their shiftlessness had content, was firmly grounded in purpose, a bold assertion of their right to be themselves. I am sure that Dr. Hatch—he had been an M.D. we were told by his wife, but she spoke as if she herself didn't believe it—if he could have known, absolutely and without a shadow of doubt, that he would be allowed to spend eternity as he pleased, sitting and spitting, he would have been dead by the time the messenger of bright doom had got the words out of his mouth.

The boys, my fellow boarders, have as people almost faded. One, as I recall, was the son of a lawyer, another of a doctor; the fathers of the rest were small-town merchants. They represented in little the school at large, except for a few farmer boys from near-by, and about a dozen girls from the village.

On my first morning a roommate, Tom Stokes, who had been there the year before, offered to be my guide. To get to the school we skirted a pond and crossed by means of a crudely built stile the fence that surrounded the grounds—campus would have been too fancy a name. This stile was my first lesson in the customs, traditions, ways of the school, that looked senseless at first and yet were packed with sense. The rule, strictly enforced, Tom explained, was that, wherever a boy climbed a fence, at that point he should build a stile. The building would help him to remember, as I often heard Sawney say afterwards, that a boy in a hurry climbing a fence—and a boy was usually in a hurry, after a ball, or escape—bent the wires, the next boy bent them more, and so until the fence was down. A boy-built stile every twenty feet or so was witness to the honored rule. The grounds were divided into four sections, known as Senior, Junior, Caesar, Beginners, the names of the four classes to which they were allotted.

There were three buildings, a large one in the center of the grounds with two classrooms and one huge room called the Big Room; another building was the Junior Room; and the third was the Senior Room, which was also the library. They were built of Southern longleaf pine mellowed by almost half a century to a deep brown, with cracks under and around doors and windows through which the wind blew serenely cold on a winter day. Pot-bellied iron stoves, heated red-hot, shed warmth for at most five feet.

When a boy was not in class, he could go where he pleased on his own grounds, or stay in his classroom, sit where he pleased and talk. Most of the boys, when they had been in the school for a while and it began to look as if they might stay—the turnover was large—bought themselves chairs and carved their names on the backs. They added to comfort, tilted against wall or tree. If a boy strayed off his grounds or did any of the things that a boy does when he wants to be different, he was put on "exile," the most dreaded punishment in school. He was required to sit in a room other than his own and not allowed to speak to anyone; but—and this was bitter—he could be spoken to, and was.

Trees were sacred, Tom went on to say. They were not to be carved or injured in any other way; one must not even pull a leaf. Sawney knew the boys' and grownups' careless habit of pulling leaves, for no reason at all except to be doing something with the hands while walking or talking. When a boy pulled a leaf he was reported by a fellow student, whoever saw him, or he had the choice of reporting himself, a choice, when taken, regarded with approval. In the case of leaf pulling the penalty was always the same: plant a tree. In tree-planting time a boy toiled all day Saturday picking out a likely sapling, digging it up, hauling it to the grounds, and planting it where he was told. That made sense, as all the rules made sense. . . . If two boys wanted to fight, they should do so, by all means, provided they were of the same size, but it must be without onlookers; they, the onlookers, got a thrashing. To be invited "to the woods" showed that one's adversary meant business. . . . Stay on your own grounds among members of your own class. . . . Don't go off your premises at night (no Southern boy needed to be told the reason). . . . No smoking outside one's room; chew, if you must. . . . If you carved a desk, the desk was yours; the school would prefer a new one, uncarved. Some boys lived on an allowance next to nothing for a year, paying for a desk. Sawney boasted that he knew all the tricks; when a boy pulled a new one, he said to him, with dry respect, "My son, you are too slick," and required the boy to follow him around all day, going home only to sleep: to the post office, to the depot to enquire for a package he knew wasn't there, a stop at every store to chat with a townsman, trips to the barn, to the hayfield, until by suppertime the boy was ready to drop with fatigue. The old man really was tough.

Boys, and the young generally, back into an explanation. They are poets still, their minds unbound by logic, and poets are impatient of exposition. My guide was a poet, and into my bewildered ear poured jumbled information in a foreign vocabularly, "over," "exile," "dink," "trap," "slide," "books," "holiday." The last sounded familiar, and I supposed he meant Christmas and such; but no; about once a month, when the day was fair and work in the school had been good, Sawney stepped onto the platform and said, "You may have the day," and boys exploded from doors and windows. When Tom stopped to show me how to make a shinny stick—shinny was primitive hockey—by bending down a hickory sapling and building a fire to set the crook, he saw incomprehension in my face and laughed. Once or twice in the history of the school, he said, there had been a teacher who was not a graduate: he had given up in despair; the whole thing was too intricate.

The routine, however, was easily understood: chapel first thing in the morning, lasting from ten minutes to an hour or even more, if Sawney happened to be talkative that day; after chapel the first class (Greek for me, with John Webb, "Old Jack," for I was to be a junior); an interval of about an hour and then the second class, Latin for everybody. At noon we went to our boardinghouses for lunch—dinner we called it, and it was—and at two o'clock the last class met, math. At around three o'clock we were dismissed and the rest of the day and night was ours. But when Tom went on to tell me of other things, I got lost again. And yet, when I had lived myself into the school, everything became as simple as child's play, and it was just that, as anyone can testify who has ever tried to learn a game from children.

The teacher in the school, it seemed, was not strictly speaking a teacher at all: he was a kind of referee, for the classes of the first three years were conducted under the "head and foot," or "trapping," system, something like a spelling bee, and all the teacher had to do was to settle disputes between boys as to who had answered a question right, and thrash the ones who missed the most often. But to explain how it worked baffled Tom, as it baffles me. I have tried it on friends, and lost them all. That was Webb School, as simple as child's play, and intricate beyond explication.

In later years, when I bore the dubious title of educator, and at last was tagged with the still more dubious "Progressive," I visited schools and listened to breathless accounts of the latest thing. I could match them point by point from the Webb School I knew as a student, and go them one better—two better, for the school had both order and intellectual backbone. As to the rest, its government was for boys as no school I have since seen. Sawney Webb had once had an active mind, and an intuitive knowledge of boys and their ways. He grew to be a tyrant, filled with his own glory, but once in a while there was a flash of the young man he had been. A boy ran away and the teachers were frantic. "Go down to where the railroad track crosses the creek," he said; "you'll probably find him there," and there the boy was. Sawney laughed and said, "A lonely boy can't stand quiet. He's got to see something moving."

This was the story that began to unfold as we climbed one of the stiles and walked along the path toward the Big Room, where presently the whole school would assemble.

When we got near the main building an older boy came up to me and asked, "Are you John Andrew Rice?" When I nodded, he said, "Mr. Sawney wants to speak to you," and he led me to a beech tree near the entrance to the grounds, a permanent stile of sturdy steps. Here a man in his sixties sat in a split-bottom chair tilted against the tree; sat and spat, for he chewed tobacco all the time, and when he talked irrelevantly punctuated his speech with "p'too" as he got rid of particles that had become separated from the main quid. I was so scared that I hardly heard what he said, and disconcerted because he never looked my way nor turned his head.

"Are you—p'too—John Andrew—p'too—Rice?" "Yes, sir," I said. "Your step—p'too—mother was Miss Darnell." I was about to speak, but he went on without noticing me, p'tooing every third word or so. As one will be charmed by a speech defect and hear nothing, so I was caught by his small explosions and still more engaged when he pulled out a gold toothpick and began to add particles of food to the tobacco. But I got the drift. I had listened to enough sermons to do that while fixing my attention elsewhere. He was praising my mother, whom he was careful to call my stepmother, in words out of an old phrase book. Finally I heard, "You may go," and he sent me away without a look. I was to learn that he never looked at anyone to whom he was speaking except at the end of a castigation, when he suddenly turned and drove it home with his colorless grey eyes.

He had a kind of face I had never seen before. The space from the top of his forehead, where his hair had once stopped—and now a few hairs marked the place, like the last trees at timber line—from this spot to the tip of his nose was a perfect arc, an arc that was repeated in reverse by the curve from nostrils to tip of his short grey beard. His mouth, seen from the side, was a grim gash. In the year 1933 I saw him, long dead, again, when I made my first trip to Connecticut. On every street corner, in every town, stood Sawney Webb—a Connecticut Yankee in Tennessee, though his ancestry was North Carolinian for generations.

While I stood and pulled my jerky nerves together, I saw Sawney get up from his chair, go outside the grounds through the gate next to the Senior Room, and around to the stile beyond. There the teachers were waiting for him to give the signal to go over the stile. From where I stood I could not see them clearly but I could count them, four, and Sawney was the fifth. Every school I had known had been skimpy in the number of its teachers; but even so I wondered how four teachers could manage more than two hundred boys, for Sawney himself taught no longer. Then, somewhere along my thoughts, he put his foot on the bottom step of the stile, and immediately from every side the boys cried, "Over!" and came running from all parts of the grounds and crowded into the Big Room, some of last year's carelessly climbing in through the windows. By the time Sawney and the other teachers had walked along the gravel path that led from the main stile, the Big Room was full of boys, and noisy boys; but when they filed through the door, Sawney in the lead, there was instant silence. They filed onto the platform, and while the others took their seats, Sawney picked up the Bible.

I had found a place on one of the long benches that sat one behind the other from the edge of the platform to the back of the long wooden room. I looked up and waited.

II

John Webb had a wisdom bump in the middle of his forehead, the size of half a walnut. That was the first thing I noticed about him, and the last, when ten years later I told him good-by. We were many then, we who had gathered to give thanks that he had lived; but on this morning, when I first saw him I was alone, completely, stranger in a world of others' friends. Then I looked up and saw John Webb's wisdom bump. Later on I was to see his face, and the eyes behind the glasses, and the grey beard that one day was pointed and another club, for he trimmed it with a pair of pocket scissors as he sat and talked to himself; but in the moment I saw only the wisdom bump set in a full forehead, and I knew that here was something special, here was a man, and a man to know.

He sat cross-legged at the left end of the narrow bench that ran along the back of the platform, his right hand resting on his knee and his face turned toward the window. His brother had just finished reading from the haphazard opening of the Bible and praying in the flat voice of long custom, and was now talking to us, repeating his thoughts of years before in words that then sounded new and exciting but would, within a short time, scratch like a worn-out record. John Webb sat detached with eyes fixed on the window. Presently his lips began to move. Last year's boys passed the word along, "Old Jack's talking to himself again."

An hour later I heard his voice. In a room—the Junior Room—full of noise, of boys greeting and slapping backs and guffawing, suddenly through the uproar a voice pierced, almost a whisper, "Take your seats, please," and there was instant silence. I never learned how he did it, how he thrust through the cacophony of ordinary speech and brought his listeners to awful silence. It always worked the same way, whether in schoolroom or parlor, or on a public platform—but this was seldom, for he distrusted speakers' speech. Even the noise of clatching women was not proof against his quiet voice. He spoke, and they listened.

At first I thought him impassive; but in time I learned to read him. The wrinkles in his face were a clue to his thoughts. There was one at the corner of his right eye that was a book of contempt, and others near his lips that deepened when he was moved by goodness in what he read. And then there was the surest clue, his voice. At first it sounded monotonous, or impassive as his face to the casual listener, but in time one began to hear the cadences and overtones, and in and through it all the counterpoint of thought. It was as simple as Bach, and as intricate. Silence was also speech with him. In my last year in the school, when we seniors spent our indoor time in the library, which was also his classroom, he often sat without speaking for long minutes, choosing in our sight the exactly right colors from the palette of speech. Sometimes, when we could hardly longer bear the suspense, he would smile slightly and say, "You may go to dinner now." We smiled at his slyness, for we somehow knew the thoughts that had been going through his great head, and what he would have said. He had the wisdom seldom to complete a thought for others.

In the intervals between recitations—he taught the seniors everything, math, Greek, Latin, English, history, everything, and things that have no name—he sat in a split-bottom chair in the middle of the room and read or talked aloud to himself. When we saw that his lips were not moving, we went to him with questions which he tried to avoid answering. If it was a technical point, we were shamed into research. One morning he asked us to account for a certain Greek accent, and, when no one could answer, he dismissed the class and told us to come back when we knew. We spent a morning searching, frantic, dogged, desperate, and when our inner clocks told us that it was long past dinnertime, he called dryly, "Books!" (This was the signal for the beginning of recitation.) When we had taken our places in a circle, he asked, "Has any one found the answer?" Our defeated silence told the story. He laughed and said, "It's a misprint."

We learned in other ways to distrust books. One drowsy afternoon I went to him as he sat tilted in his chair and asked him a casual question, more to get him talking than to learn. Up to that moment I had gobbled books the way a dog bolts his rations, and had just finished off another. "Mr. Webb," I said, "what do you think of *The Clansman*?" He kept his eyes fixed on the window, patted his knee with his right hand, laughed three dry cackles, and said, "Some people like that kind of thing." From that time forth no book was my master.

His mind was fertile with ways for bringing boys to knowledge, but he never used the same device more than once, for he was an artist, and the artist never repeats himself. The class in Greek was lagging. He said nothing, but invited the two best scholars to do some extra reading with him. The rest were stung to emulation, but he never said a word. One day he told us all to stand up, and gradually "spelled us down" until only one hardy was left standing. Still not a word of reproof nor of censure came from him. In later years, when I was a teacher in the school, he said to me, when I complained of stupidity among my pupils, "They get something. Why embarrass them with exposure of their ignorance?" He was not afraid of ignorance, as most teachers are. He knew that his pupils would learn something in their future, so he was willing to leave gaps. As he grew older he became dismayed at what was happening in the colleges, where the curriculum began to be based, not on love of learning, but on fear of ignorance. He never fooled himself into thinking that equality of opportunity meant equality of performance. He had the skill to make the learner stretch and do more than he could do, let him rest on that level for a while, and then push him higher. His pupils acquired respect for their own capacity, for he made each of them an artist for the moment, with his own private goal.

Sometimes he set tasks that only the best could perform, without bringing shame to those who could not. Somehow he knew when to call out all one's strength, and he also knew the exact moment. I am a loafer by nature, and it used to worry him at times, but he had the patience to wait. He knew that patience is a goad. One day he told me to translate a passage from Vergil. How he knew that his patience had got on my nerves I never discovered, but at just the right moment he called on me and I answered with a translation that I had worked at and polished until it glittered. There was in the class no envy, only admiration which one could feel in the air. Finally, he spoke and quietly suggested one or two improvements. Then, after another silence, he said, "You know, John Andrew, it is my job to criticize." That is still the highest praise I have ever heard.

In autumn and spring and on warm days in winter we sat outside under the trees in groups of threes and fours and studied together, or read, or talked. Our talk would have sounded strange to Mr. Chips or Mr. Kipling. It was never about games, for we played no other schools, and such games as we had were simple; the sun set on our empire and we were content to have it so; and school spirit, about which one reads much in sentimental records, was unknown to us by name.

Aside from the meaningless noises made by all companies, we talked about what we were learning, and much about what had happened in the debating societies last Saturday night and what would happen next, and who would be elected public debaters at the end of the year. This was long before the present fashion in debate—the lowest known form of intellectual perversion. We took the side we believed in and defended it with complete passion and ignorance; but we were learning to handle ideas and fix our prejudices, and what else is a school for?

In the South nearly all conversation is personal; a Southerner can hardly think any other way; ideas come to him wrapped up in people, and so with us. Besides ourselves, the most interesting packages were Sawney and Old Jack, and we debated about them. Our talk would have shocked the younger boys, who looked on Sawney as a hero and would not know Old Jack until their junior year, when they would begin with Greek. Among the seniors, however, there were few all-out champions of Sawney, only the vegetative minds; we knew him too well and too thoroughly. With Old Jack it was different; here was exploration, with clouds of awe still trailing from earlier years but with lightness too, for there was deep-running laughter in him and we shared its freedom.

Sawney's brutality set our own quivering for action, and frightened us a little. His sayings, by which he was known everywhere—"Don't do things on the sly," and its variant, "Never do a thing that you would be ashamed to have the keen sunlight of publicity shine on"—we recognized as good advice, albeit somewhat difficult to follow, and pleasant variations from parental admonitions. There was a lot too about obedience being the first virtue, and not bringing grey hairs in sorrow to the grave. But he was a man of action, and we liked that; if only he had not bragged so much and flung his wounded arm in our faces and told so often of breaking the ice to take his morning bath. One got the impression that the war had been fought amid snow and ice, and that there was something immoral about warm water.

Sawney was a disciplinarian of outward order, and frightened or shamed the young into a similitude of goodness; John Webb's was an inner discipline, of the mind and spirit, grounded in freedom. Pupils who in after years had become inured to injustice in themselves and others, told with delight of the thrashings they had got from Sawney and were sorry they had not learned from him the whole lesson of caution; others, fewer these, had another sorrow, and delight.

Sawney was an actor; John Webb was a dramatist. The persons of his plays were ideas, for his plays were plays of the mind. If he had written for the stage, his characters would have been his ideas clothed in men, just as Shaw's people are each something else of Shaw, who rediscovered what the Greeks knew without learning. This made him incapable of acting, that is, repeating, and peculiarly unable to act the parts that he himself had created, for he knew that language could die and meaning with it, and a thing said three times is no longer true. That was why, when he had to say the same words over again, for the student must hear familiar words, he set them each time in a new frame, for his own relief. He was quick to see and approve a new garment in his brother's tattered wardrobe. Sometimes Sawney would be droning along, when suddenly the man who had made up these speeches came to life again and wrote a new part for himself. Then John Webb would listen. He would turn his head from looking out of the window, and if what Sawney said was funny, he would pat his knee and laugh; if serious, take the idea and begin working on it, to reject it or remake it for himself.

He never mentioned personal hygiene and he had no sayings; he met every moment as if it was brand new, took us behind words to meaning, and flung them away when they had served their use. We lacked the skill in hearing to repeat the lightning movement of his thought; it was like wit, which needs its setting. In other ways he was elusive, and he never stated his case. We knew him as a man of peace and grace, but we were not yet ready for peace and were unaware of the grace that was in us. We believed that, with rugged effort, we could all be Sawneys, and soon; but Old Jack's nature was out of our youthful reach; he was always drawing us into manhood while we were still half child and clinging tearfully to our state. Sawney's world was not really different from the world we knew, except that all the fun was taken out; Old Jack's was a kind of dream in which were all the good things of the present and many more as yet unseen, only felt. But, we learned from him, it was to be found not by effort, and this was a first-class puzzle. All this we said or skirted around, but in the language of youth: silence, a word or two, embarrassment, laughter, and lots of scorn.

We were in green pastures. The years before had been taken up with rigid drill in the skeleton of knowledge, grammar, the manipulative side of math, and dates and such, memory work. Now we were getting at meaning, which is a leisurely delight; beginning to chew on ideas, for we were eager to emerge into manhood, where ideas were important. Most of us would go to college, and looked with hopeful eyes over the fence to that lush carpet of freedom. Not that we were discontent, but we knew there were still better days to come. We would become philosophers, whether lawyer, doctor, preacher; one hoped to spend his life in the realm of pure meaning—he would be a Doctor of Philosophy; and one wanted some day to sit tilted in a split-bottom chair and be wise that way.

Through the open windows of the library there came a single word, spoken only once, and stopped our talk: "Books," and we picked up our chairs, dragged them in, and ranged ourselves in a circle with imitative tilt. The class might continue for two hours or last no more than five minutes. It depended, whether we were ready to learn; or there might be visitors. John Webb was no strutting actor; teaching was an intimate impersonal thing to him, as learning had become to us. Sometimes we found him with a book in his hand; sometimes he sat for a minute unoccupied, got up, went to the shelves and pulled down a book. We gratefully stored our texts and tablets under our chairs and waited.

The school library was an expression, in choice and arrangement, of the man himself. The books were not adolescent, nor for adolescents, for he knew the young want to grow. He chose mainly what he liked to read himself, and they were put on the shelves in some spiritual order that would make a student of "library science" shudder. The *Origin of Species* might sit between the poems of Keats and Lane's Latin Grammar and be none the worse for the company. He was no Aristotelian; he knew the limits, and poison, of classification.

In his own home his study was across the hall from the sitting room, and here he sat and read aloud. The talk of the family or visitors never distracted him; he was listening to his author. It might be Greek or some other foreign language, but he liked English best, and, for the full range of its expression, prose best of all. Except rarely, his reading was to and for himself, but any might come and listen. The four-year-old son of a neighbor came frequently and sat attentive while his patron read Burke, or Stevenson, or the prose of Matthew Arnold. It made no difference to the small listener. He had come for an hour of music.

The arrangement of his own was the same as in the school library, until his daughter and her new husband, a college professor addicted to order, rearranged his books for him by some system of classification. Thereafter he spent most of his time in the sitting room with whatever book he had been able to rescue from the maze of logic.

Legends grow up about a teacher—if not, he is none. It was said that many universities had tried to persuade John Webb to leave school-teaching and become a professor. This was untrue, or at least exaggerated, for even at that time, the end of the last and the first of this century, the universities were no place for a teacher; the scholar was what they wanted, scholar in their sense, he who pursues truth for his own sake. John Webb was called erudite, and he was, though certainly he did not know the traditional twenty-three languages with which he was credited. The boys said his wisdom bump was a bulge of his brain, like the extra walnut in an overloaded sack, and were ready to believe the whispered story that old Jack had once "gone off his head." Didn't he talk to himself? In this report there may have been some truth: the wise are sometimes called mad in ·a world of fools. The ancients were more discerning. They called them blessed.

A teacher's life is filled with many minor comedies and some small tragedies; it is never a spectacle. It is not what he does that counts, but what he is, and there is no way to describe existence: it can only be felt. John Webb's fame was quiet, carried by experience, and felt in the spirit. One of the tragedies of being a teacher is that one is out-grown by one's pupils. Many outgrew John Webb's brother, but none him, for he, by what he was, entered into and became part of those he taught. When I had finished, and finished with, what is called, facetiously I hope, education on the higher level, I went back to Webb School to teach. There was some doubt and a little fear. Would John Webb prove to have been a mere hero, inferior to the great scholars my manhood had known? The first words, and the first silence, were my reassurance.

Of teachers who "grow old in harness" there are two who will use those words to describe themselves. One likes to believe that he is an aged Man-o'-War, the other hangs the head of Old Dobbin. Both, whether surgeon or nurse, slave driver or comrade, top sergeant or fellow private, have this in common: they try to mold their pupils to some fixed and final form, by persuasion, by violence, by example. They are the ethical men and they know what they want. The question they ask is not "How?" but "What?"—for life to them is not process but formula. They suffer from the worst occupational diseases among teachers, sadism and sentimentality, having been caught on one of the hooks of youth, the unfulfilled desire to grow up and the desire to remain in childhood.

The one, the comrade, is timidly grateful to remain a grey-haired youth, to be one of the boys and to love them. He feels their pains as his own, shares their sadness and their joy, and keeps them as straight as he can in a fuddled world. But he is a teacher for boys, not men, to be forgotten with gratitude and never seen again. One's stomach turns queasy at the sight of an old man shouting on the sidelines or flapping along the towpath, or lifting thoughtless face in chapel. (I am not saying they are not to be found in colleges. I remember one who was said to be the best-loved and least-respected man on the campus.)

The more memorable of these old adolescents are the top sergeants, who are untroubled by doubt or even thought. To admit doubt of themselves would be to doubt the universe, and thought, they unconsciously know, is the enemy of things that were. Thomas Arnold of Rugby is their exemplar. He would no more have questioned his own integrity and rightness than he would have wondered when he went to bed at night whether the dawn would come. He was a builder of empire-builders, and a destroyer of men, for he forced them into the mold of the immutable past. Many teachers, and good ones too, wear knowledge as a proud cloak or hide behind the screen of what they know; but the top sergeants have a deep distrust of learning, unless they can use it as a whiplash. Another, Headmaster Keat of Eton (American private boys' schools are copies of the English), used to say, "It doesn't matter what a boy studies, just so he hates it." The model they set themselves is themselves. If they had been God, they would have pulled themselves together on the sixth day and, by a leap of the imagination, peopled the earth with their like.

A growing boy needs both, comrade and top sergeant, the one to steady him, the other to drive him with savage anger into vicarious manhood. If he becomes a man, he will put them away among other childish things. But he needs another, and once in a while he finds him, a teacher whose face is turned toward the light. Youth is the seed of the secret future. No one knows when, but some day there will be a writer more profound than Shakespeare, painters who will be masters of all who have lived before, a Beethoven who knows how to reach the heights and depths of human feeling, and greater men than Socrates will live. He whose face is turned toward the light knows this, and, while he shares the joy and sadness of the very young, his joy is the prelude to comedy and his sadness stands on the threshold of final knowledge, which is tragedy. His is and must be the peaceful way, for he knows that he cannot compel others to know what they will not know. He also knows that everyone has limits to his knowledge, whatever the will, and so he invites each with him as far as each can go, and has no harshness in him when one fails; there will be weeds in the crop, but only the rash will tell them among the seedlings. A boy who has had such a teacher will fumble for a word; love is too narrow, worship too wide; for, while men worship what they do not completely understand, there was in John Webb the promise that some day we should know.

On Sunday afternoons all the boys were required to go to the Big Room at three o'clock and listen to someone talk, or at least to be there in person. Sawney explained, and it made sense, that a long Sunday afternoon was a time of mischief for boys, because they could not play games—taboo in the South—and they would not be working. Sawney usually did the talking, rather, aimless wandering around among thoughts he had once entertained, now permanent fixtures in the household of his mind. When there was no one else, John Webb was obliged to fill up the hour. He did so, literally: he took a book, something he liked to hear himself read, read for an hour, and closed it on the minute. "You may go," he said, and tucked the book under his arm without a word as to what it was or who had written it. But there was guile. More than one of us asked him the next day what the book was, and, when we got to the part he had read, we heard his voice again, as a musician will read a score and recall its perfect playing.

On Sunday mornings we were required to go to church, and most of us went to the Methodist church because that was where most of us went. Occasionally a boy who knew no better elected his family's leanings and put his preference down as Baptist or something, but a Sunday or so in a strange crowd soon changed his faith. Sawney always went, sat in the front pew, picked his teeth with the gold toothpick, and never looked at the preacher. When something was said that he liked, he twitched the toe at the end of his crossed leg; if heretical, he grew deadly still, toothpick hung in mid-air. John Webb also went, every Sunday. If the preacher was young, he gave him full attention, for there would be talk afterwards between them, unless the young man was already old. He knew as much theology as any man in the South, and anyone could have his knowledge for the asking; but he never used it as an offensive weapon. When the winds of doctrine began blowing loudly from the pulpit, he closed his eyes and withdrew from the general noise. Presently his lips began to move. He was off in his own world.

When I came to know him intimately as a fellow teacher, I discovered that he was not satisfied with his life and I was dismayed; but he sometimes quoted—he was willing to quote others—a saying of George MacDonald, the Scotch preacher, "God is often pleased but never satisfied." In this sense he was pleased, for he had done what he wanted to do and that is as near happiness as a man can come. In his early years he must have been completely serene, and even when I knew him his serenity was deeper than any I have ever seen; but there was one alienation that troubled him, the break between him and his brother. The two had made the school together, disciplinarian and scholar; but when success came Sawney grew arrogant and ceased to learn. John Webb never thought he knew enough. Sawney read the daily paper and became a prophet.

When I went back to the school to teach, the war was just beginning. Sawney stood at the stile waiting for "over" and told us what was what. John Webb stood a little outside the circle and was silent. He seldom spoke, in fact, in the presence of his brother, who was ready to be as brusque with him as with the rest of us. When they had founded the school together they had been so close to each other that there had been no question as to who was head; both were, by tacit agreement, and neither would have thought of suggesting that they write down what the relationship was. But, as the actor became well known while the scholar's fame spread slowly, Sawney let it be known to him that he regarded him as "only a teacher." Then, having done this injustice, he became resentful of its cause. One day when I went to John Webb's house his brother was leaving with three or four books under his arm, looking very sheepish. He had been asked to deliver a course of lectures on the Bible, and, since he knew no more about it than one might learn from opening it at random every morning and reading whatever hit his eye, he had been obliged to come for help. But the next morning he evened the score. As we stood at the stile he said, sharply, "John! There's egg on your chin. Wipe it off."

John Webb, however, never spoke to me of his unhappiness. Only once, when I was troubled about something, he said, "Don't come to me. I no longer have any voice in running the school." When he died, this was confirmed. Sawney claimed that, if there was a partnership, it did not go beyond the life of either; and, as there was no written contract, he secured full ownership of the school to himself and his son, Son Will.

The crafty man who has something to conceal will never let anyone sit behind him while he is speaking; not lest they may not hear but lest they see. The clever actor trains his front; only the greatest dares turn his back to the audience. It is hard to simulate with the back; the muscles of back and shoulders and thighs carelessly let slip the truth. For two years I sat on the narrow wooden bench that ran the length of the platform and watched Sawney talk.

He had not done what he wanted to do. He had wanted to be a man of action, and had found it out too late. When at last his chance came, he fumbled and was confused. By way of compliment he was appointed to fill out the unexpired term of a senator who had died, and when he went to Washington the newspapers proclaimed him, printed his picture and his sayings, but not as a great man, only a great teacher; and he had wanted so much to be a great man.

Sawney accepted without question the dominant beliefs of the South in his time, and of America. The words "success" and "failure" were not long absent from his speech. One of the boys in my house came to me and asked, "Why does Sawney keep on saying that if you are a traveling salesman in middle life, you are a failure? My father's a traveling salesman, but I don't think he's a failure. He's a wonderful man."

Sawney's opening shot on the first morning I heard him speak, and often repeated, was, "We would like to develop both character and scholarship here, but first and foremost we must have character." John Webb said to me, "I don't understand. To me they are the same." . . . Sawney said, "If you hit a nigger, you are no better than a nigger." One of the statements therein contained the Southern boy needed made to him again and again, but the other—Gene Talmadge is still making it. He often spoke with contempt, never compassion, of "niggers"; Br'er Rabbit was their hero, sly and cunning as they, but not a word as to what had made them so. . . . One of his stories, which used to bring shouts of laughter from the boys, ended with the words, "I don't pay no attention to a woman." He boasted, "I never tell my wife anything about my business." . . . He liked to tell the story of how a widow woman had called on him to help her right a wrong. With the aid of detectives he had traced the woman's daughter and her lover to a hotel room. Then he had placed a guard with shotguns and gone to get a preacher. . . . Ned Carmack had been expelled from his school as a boy, but Ned Carmack as a man became a successful politician, and Sawney took the stump for him. . . . Luke Lea, who afterward spent a term in the North Carolina penitentiary for bank wrecking, was introduced to the school as the "matchless and unparalleled young leader of Tennessee democracy." . . . One of his graduates had made a million. His name was always popping up.

John Webb never wanted to be a great anything, and if anyone had used the word of him in his presence, he would have cringed with shame for the speaker. It was only when he lay in his coffin that we could speak without fear of reproof.

For a year and a half I taught with him and he opened to me the stores of knowledge and of wisdom that were in him. He often read to me and we turned ideas this way and that to make them give off their light, and sometimes we talked about people. There was nothing that he had not known about me and my age-fellows, for, by an ironic twist, while the other teachers and his brother kept their eyes fastened on the boys, he had seen more than they; and there were no surprises for him in what his pupils had afterwards become. He had known of every love affair in the class, and yet he had never spoken to us about personal matters, ours or others. He had seen his brother's arrogant ambition issue in desiccated fame, as he knew it would all along. A brilliant boy in my class had the same taint, and had died in full pursuit. In a small number of all he had known he had seen a promise of manhood; a smaller number had kept their promise. But he was not dismayed. There were still books, and ideas, and there was the future.

In this time I found out what he said when he talked to himself: he said whatever he was thinking or remembering, a poem, a paragraph of prose, a funny story, a conversation he would have tomorrow. There was no mystery. Language and thought were to him as scores to a musician.

When he went down for the mail, a ritual denied to city dwellers, he met the villagers with nose-rubbing words about the weather, crops, and other little things; but wherever he was, peace came into the company, and self-respect. They knew that, if he judged them at all, it was not by what they did; and he never questioned any man's right to live.

He took his daily walk along the railroad track—it could be relied upon to be dry footing—and one day when I was going through the village someone called me in a worried voice to the depot platform; something was wrong with Mr. Webb. Down the track I saw him stumbling into the weeds at the side. When I reached him he tried to speak, but his voice was thick.

The doctor said he had had a slight stroke and might live for a long time, but that he must give up teaching. Two months later he was dead. I had known he would not live, that he could not live without his teaching. He had said to me once, "I couldn't have done anything else. I believe I would have paid to be allowed to teach."

Funerals are sad occasions. John Webb's was not. Hundreds gathered, from the village and from far places, and all spoke of the wonder of his life. As his body was lowered into the grave, some of the boys sang the hymn that he liked best, "O love that wilt not let me go."

CHAPTER VI

Interlude Among the Half-Castes

NEW ORLEANS WAS A CITY OF GUTTERS, GUTTERS EVERYWHERE, ON houses, in yards, along both sides of every street, and crossing, each with its perilous little bridge, at the corners. Through gutters hanging under the eaves the constant rain was carried to great wooden cisterns that stood aboveground behind the house, and, overflowing, through other gutters to the street, there to join, in wide and open gutters, drainage from sidewalks and alleys and to mix and mingle with dirt and filth from unswept streets, and be pumped at last over the levee into the mother of gutters.

In the South where I had lived until that time, I had been accustomed to a measure of concealment. Here, in this half-caste Latin city, there was none. The sewage of New Orleans was there for eye to see, and nose to smell, for on hot summer nights the gutters stirred, and effused gagging odors onto the porch and through the windows and upstairs to bed. During the daytime they were placid, covered with oily slime in unbroken surface; but not quite unbroken, not to the hungry eye of a native, who watched the gleaming scum for a sign, and when it came, flicked to the bank a sprawling crawfish or, if his luck was good that day, the length of a squirming eel. For the squeamish and unskillful the gutters served another end: they kept the city from being a swamp. The cisterns stood on stilts, the houses rested on pilings, and even the dead, shunning a watery grave, had their dwellings in the upper air. The city lived with its feet in water.

The air itself was filled with water. When the temperature stood at ninety, one's body became half liquid, and taking a bath a mere exchange of water, a gesture to civilization. I had endured heat before, in the low country of South Carolina, but here was something new. It was as if any moment a hand or leg might dissolve and float away; breathing seemed a little foolish, and was often unpleasant, for scents, and smells, stayed put in the thick air. It could also be cold, as nowhere else; not sharp cold challenging resistant energy, but slow, gnawing, burrowing cold that would not pause until it froze one's marrow. That was in January, February, and March; the rest of the year the names of months had no meaning.

The living body of the city also was menaced by water. When rains upstate filled the river to its brim and sandbags were piled along the levee in the old town, the natives became twitchy, and walked in a trance of fear. It was as if the whole city held its breath, waiting for the news, waiting to hear of a break somewhere above. The break always came, but one could never know for sure. Providence, or whatever it was that opened a sluice and flooded the uplands, bringing disaster to a few that many should escape, might fail this once; watchers on the levee might do their work too well and let the hated city be washed into the Gulf. It was then that the old war was renewed, the war between New Orleans and the rest of the state, payer of tribute to the old hag who lived in the bend of the river. Algiers, the little town that lay below the western levee, screamed hate across the river, but there were other voices, voices that would within a few years become one, the voice of Huey Long, and at last the gluttonous city would be engulfed in hate.

When I came to know the city—the French Quarter, then half Italian, the tenements of Negroes, the docks, and the section out beyond the tracks, all of these below Canal Street, dividing line between the old town and the new; and the new town, strung along the crescent of St. Charles Avenue, beginning with names and houses that were foreign and swinging wide into America—when I knew all this, I knew that there was nothing simple in New Orleans. There was no clear stream of feeling or thought.

The house in which we lived at first, until the new parsonage should be built, was itself a forewarning. It would now be called semidetached, but the word would be misleading, for it was detached from nothing. On one side we heard through the thin partition all that our neighbors said and readily guessed what they were doing; the other side was a match-toss from the street. Hucksters sang their wares or blasted the air with triangles, whistles, cowbells, or simply shouted, and over and through it all a scraggy-toothed barrel organ wheezed an Italian tune. Often the din was so great as to stop all conversation, a feat in itself, and sometimes my father rose and angrily banged down the windows. For a moment there was quiet, as if the noise was shocked at his rudeness; then, recovering, the triangle, cowbell, and all the rest came in again.

There was one hope: Tulane. My brother Mike and I would soon be freshmen there. Perhaps, although general talk stirred misgivings, there would be another John Webb, some professor who would tilt his chair and make a little circle of light.

Tulane was my introduction to numerology in education. In Webb School there had never been a hint that accomplishment could be measured by the clock; how many hours and minutes one spent in preparation or recitation was not in question; the question was, "Do you know?" In Tulane the question was, "Do you sit, and, if so, how long?" The adage was, "The race is to the swift." The adage was wrong. There was no way to sit swiftly.

But, before I should be allowed to begin to count my sittings, I must first be admitted. The chief numerologist, the registrar, handed me a list of questions. How many minutes for how many days for how many weeks for how many years had I sat in the Greek class? I said

I did not know, nor about Latin or English or anything else. "That," he said with patient annoyance, "is not for you to fill out; it is for the school." Tulane required fifteen units for entrance, he explained. Did I think I had fifteen units? Every respectable institution of learning on the higher level—it sounded funny even then—required fifteen units. (The Carnegie Foundation had laid its first mortgage on education.) When I said I didn't know the answer to that one either, didn't know, in fact, what a unit was, he said abruptly, "Send it to your school."

I knew it was useless to send it to the school; Sawney had said a thousand times, "It's not our business to get you into college. Let them examine you and decide for themselves." So I sent it to John Webb. Within a few days it came back all neatly filled out, so many units of this, so many of that, and adding up to exactly fifteen units—loving perjury.

Some time later the registrar said to me, "How do you explain the fact that you were admitted by certificate while Jim Smith, who graduated with you, couldn't get one?" I said, "It does seem odd, doesn't it?" "Odd!" he said; "most irregular."

I entered Tulane University in 1908 and emerged in 1911 with a diploma in my hand; that was all I had to show for three spent years. The diploma said I was a *baccalaris artium*, and when the president handed it to me he welcomed me into the "company of educated men." They were both liars. I had no art, and if I was an educated man, the words meant nothing.

In my second year Tom Stokes came to visit me—Tom, my roommate at Webb School—and I took him to see the town. One of the places we saw was the oldest cemetery, a gruesome curiosity. Here were few tombs, as I recall, such as one saw elsewhere, little marble houses of the dead built above ground, but blocks of brick "ovens," each just large enough to hold a body, communities of the dead. They were leased for a term of years, and, when a lease was up, if it was not renewed, the old dead was evicted to make room for a new tenant who could pay the rent. The headstone was removed from its brick setting, thriftily turned around and engraved with the name of the newcomer; meanwhile the bones of the delinquent were raked out and piled in the corner of the cemetery. Tom was an admirer of Byron and wanted a skull, so we went to the heap of bones and searched until we found one to his taste. It was like any one of my classes in Tulane—Plato, Shakespeare, mathematics—this dry thing had no relation to life. I could force myself to admit, I could not deny the fact, that it had once been carried, proudly or in shame or in mere submission, atop others that lay mingled in the pile, that a human face had once been where now there were ridges and gaping, grinning holes—all this I knew, but I could not believe it. The worms had done their job too well.

I used to think that Tulane was different from other universities, in that its social stratification was the same as the town's; but, having since seen Harvard, I am not now so sure. At any rate, one came trailing clouds of glory or ignominy, or no clouds at all. I, being a Methodist preacher's son, had none; I was like an American in England. This was nothing new to me, a South Carolinian, but farmer boys found it puzzling that a name could amount to so much while its wearer amounted to so little; for Louisiana was next door to Texas, where inquiry as to the name of a grandfather was likely to be the innocent's last. But New Orleans was not Louisiana, and New Orleans had put its stamp on Tulane.

At this point likeness to Harvard, if there was likeness, ceased. I had known the South Carolinian and something of the Virginian gentleman, who lived, or had lived, off the land, and one day I would meet his vegetative like in England; meanwhile I had seen close up the New Southern gentleman in Montgomery, and I would, in time, see one version of him in Boston and another in the Midwest; none were like the New Orleans gentleman. He was a gambler, and his was an aristocracy of gambling. The dominance of this gentleman gambler, with his "here today and gone tomorrow," gave a certain tentative quality to everything that happened in Tulane. One of the satisfactions of a university, as I discovered in Oxford, is that there are some things that are permanent, or at least more nearly permanent than oneself, but in Tulane there were none.

My own private civil war, begun in South Carolina and continued in Alabama, was breaking out again. For a while it had reached a kind of stasis. The puritan had no weakness, the cavalier many. Since by nature and birth I could not be either, I would keep such virtues of the one as did not fatally interfere with the vices—I could not call them virtues—assumed from the other. It had been working fairly well until, with the advent of a third model, the war became three-way. To my dismay, however, the New Orleans gentleman turned out to be an inverted puritan, a hard-shelled ascetic, armored against pity and compassion, love, the play of the imagination, every softness. He was not even a sensualist, as the puritan often was; for, while the sensualist may lose himself, for a time at least, in feeling, my new gentleman was harder than that. He had no passion; he was as cold as his January dawn.

At first, before I became acquainted in the town, I knew him only in his son. I had before seen a few and have since seen others, but nowhere except in New Orleans have I seen so many who proposed prosperity for themselves without compensatory effort. He would get along, somehow; chance would take care of that. He was not like his frequent age-fellows elsewhere, the young man on the make; he was already made, would be at fifty what he was then. He was an old young man, in his nature a denial of change and growth. The rules were all known. It only remained to play the game.

A few years ago a gentleman from New Orleans, having married a

rich Yankee, bought with her money a plantation in the low country
of South Carolina and shortly afterwards gave a housewarming. The
vendor declined his invitation and was rebuked by a friend, a lady
born and bred in New Orleans. "Why did you refuse? He is just as
much a gentleman as you are." "He is not a gentleman," said the
South Carolinian; "gentlemen sell plantations, they don't buy them."
To have was not to have had. The upstart now had the plantation that
was once his, but the having had no one could take away, for its dwelling was in the broad reaches of the heart.

On the streets of Charleston a citizen may discreetly point to a
passer-by and say, "He once owned Medway." In New Orleans it was,
"His family, the Howards, ran the Louisiana lottery." . . . "That fellow cornered cotton and made millions by selling out his partner." . . .
"Sure, he built a big house in Audubon Place, with money he got from
selling Uncle Sam's timber." . . . "I knew that man when he didn't
have a nickel to his name; got his start by winning forty thousand in
the lottery, and look at him now, big guy in the Boston Club." . . .
"Don't you know him? That's Commodore Baldwin. Owns a little
hardware store and worth millions. No, son, he didn't make it selling
hardware; at least, not hammers and nails and that sort of chicken
feed; guns, gunrunning to insurrections in Central America. They tell
me he still does. I don't know. Some say he's mixed up in the lottery
too. It's against the law now, so he takes his yacht out beyond the three-
mile limit and holds the drawing there. Got a big steam yacht. You'll
see it some day, out on Lake Pontchartrain; calls it *Semper Idem*. Latin,
means 'always the same'."

And so it was, always and everywhere the same, easy money, quick
money. The question was not "How'd you get it?" nor "How long have
you had it?"—only, "Have you got it?"

Mardi Gras was also business. New Orleans had discovered, long
before Charleston, that quaintness was a salable commodity. Hotel
proprietors with alien accent invited expenditure and even Rex hoped

to turn a profit; the marriage market flourished, and vice paid a dividend; but none of them nor all together were Mardi Gras.

Mardi Gras was something in the blood of every incorruptible, a time for letting loose, forgetting, leaving the morrow, which would be Lent, to its sufficient evil. He would be penitent then, bow his head and groan "peccavi"; meanwhile he stored up a treasure of precious sin, enough cause of penitence to see him through the lean weeks.

To the puritan, who is never a successful penitent, nor sinner, for that matter—he thinks too much—this was inexplicable, and during Mardi Gras he went into hiding, to sulk, or stick a thirsty tongue out of the cave of reason and lick up a drop or two; or he put on a mask and came timidly out. If he did, if he could, if he was not befuddled by the tinseled antics of the aristocracy or its imitation below, he discovered that Mardi Gras was the outward and visible evidence of inward and spiritual grace; a folk festival in the real sense, which, imported though it was, no longer wore the self-conscious stigmata of importation. It was in very fact a sign of grace, a recognition and acknowledgment of the human wish to belong, to be part of something, to forget for a moment private cares, to be free within general freedom. When the king rode by no one saw his foolish crown or wig or sleazy satin, nor remembered him as yesterday and tomorrow, a broker, plain businessman, fop, bad or good; he was a symbol of kinship, and of man, of the kingship of the celebrant himself. It was no accident that Huey Long chose as his slogan, "Every man a king."

II

To escape the heat of New Orleans, or, rather, to exchange one kind of heat for another, the family took a cottage in the Methodist Camp Grounds near Biloxi, a sort of cheap edition of Asbury Park. Here, while the elders conducted revivals, the youngers accumulated a store of mild sins on which they could draw when they too should be penitent. It was a curious juxtaposition, religious frenzy in the tabernacle, another frenzy out on the dark pier.

I had, however, seen this before in South Carolina, the excitements of religion creating other excitements, and there was nothing new. But in the daytime there was something new, for me. I met Tony, the first, and still in my memory the purest, of his kind. He came from an old French family who spent the summers in an old house near-by, and there made a little island of eighteenth-century France next door to nineteenth-century Methodism. Tony was the only son, and the only man about during the week. On Fridays his exasperated father came from his office in New Orleans, to relax and express his incomprehension that a young lawyer could take off three full months in the summer. When he went back on Sunday, the women took up the theme—they were at least a dozen—but Tony, whose patience was large and tolerant, turned a serene blank face to their questions. Sometimes, however, he found their chatter too much for his good nature. Then he got his rod, gave me a hail, and we went fishing.

We really went talking. He was to me unique, the only completely unmoral person I had ever known. He was not immoral, which implies a certain hostility to the concept of morality. He had no hostility; for him the thing simply did not exist. Occasionally my puritanism broke out into remonstrance; he looked at me as if I spoke a third language, knitting his brow and resting his eyes on mine, graciously trying to understand, but shaking his head in the end and whistling softly to himself. He was silent for a while, then, looking up hopefully, said, "Did I ever tell you . . . ?" and innocently told me something equally shocking. He was my private social register of New Orleans. He knew everyone, and about everyone; opened closet doors and lovingly exhibited skeletons. It was like a class in anatomy, with a change of terminology. Once in a while he went in to town, and returned with his memory refreshed. "Did I ever tell you . . . ?" and out poured another startling stream.

When we had docked the boat and gathered up our tackle, I walked with him toward the house. It was late in the afternoon and the old ladies were sitting. As soon as he came in sight they began to speak to him, or at him, and by the time he reached the edge of the piazza they were spattering him from head to foot with their queer French. He stood a moment, laughed, ducked his head and dodged around the house.

When the calendar said it was September we returned to the city, where presently one of my disabilities was lightened and the other two resumed. My father was transferred to Fort Worth, Texas, and I became something less of a preacher's son, no longer under the church's thousand eyes, freed of prying censorship, free to do as I pleased. There was a moment of elation, and then I was as I had been before, a preacher's son. Ten years later I would be standing at the door of the faculty room in the University of Nebraska, watching a billiard game and intermittently talking with a colleague, Dann, who is now dissecting saints for the amusement of irreverent young angels. He said, "You know, Rice, I'm a preacher's son. You are too, aren't you? . . . I thought so. . . . Well, I am and I'll never get over it. To me the click of a billiard ball is still the voice of the Devil."

As soon as I had said good-by to the family, I went straight to a dancing school. (I had refrained out of respect for my father.) I also bought from a friend the upper part of a dress suit; trousers I already had, not strictly correct, but black at any rate. Thus rendered indistinguishable from any other male, I was ready, with what I had learned from Tony, to see New Orleans society in three dimensions.

To tell the truth, my excursions were a disappointment. It was with knowing as it had been with freedom: to be about to be was better than to be.

I had already seen the other side of New Orleans, the bottom side, and could now compare. Because of my father's position the professor of economics not only gave me a high grade in his course but also had me appointed tenement house inspector. Social consciousness was coming into fashion; I became its dubious beneficiary, the cause of justice even more. I was instructed to measure windows, calculate the cubic space of rooms, and, by some obscure mathematical operation, equate them with the number of inmates. The statistical results were, I am afraid, misleading, for some of them were faked, and even honest figures told nothing about humanity. Tulane had already made me suspicious of numerology in education; I was now confirmed when I saw it applied to misery and joy and boredom.

My badge admitted me everywhere, and I went everywhere. My curiosity led me first to the Negroes, to see whether they were different from those I had known in South Carolina. They were not, except in two respects. Many spoke no English, only their corruption of the already corrupt French of their masters, making a third version of that language spoken in the city. (The three were: Eighteenth Century, the speech of upper-class French descendants, commonly called Creoles; Cajun, spoken by the Acadians in the Evangeline country; and Negro, a mixture of the two, softened and slurred.) This Negroid French I had heard spoken before, by our washerwoman, who brought her young son along as interpreter. The surprise, the thing that made the New Orleans Negro different from any I had known, was his sterility. There were few children where previous acquaintance had taught me to expect many. I asked why, and got an answer, from a doctor who had a local reputation as an authority. He said, "If all the Negroes were moved into cities, within two hundred years there would be none left; tuberculosis and syphilis would have wiped them out," and he added, "That's what we ought to do."

Many of the poor lived in beautiful houses, for in New Orleans, as in the South, there was little building for them; they inherited lodgings that had come down in the world. Around Jackson Square, in the French Quarter, and spreading out from there I found Negroes living in rooms under whose high ceilings their grandparents had served as slaves, and little Negroes slid down mahogany banisters and peeked through wrought-iron gates that proved that there had once been taste in New Orleans. Descendants of the owners, of slaves, and houses, had moved away and built for themselves dwellings that were as ugly as these were beautiful, and no one seemed to know the difference. But once in a while, in the midst of this decay, I passed a courtyard or came on a house set way back behind a brick wall, the citadel of some old French family that defied time and change. I almost forgot that I was a democrat.

There were other explorations: into tenements bursting with Italians, among the shanty Irish, as mean in New Orleans as in Boston; and always back to the Negroes, to sit and listen, for once again I was sure they had a secret. I also skirted Storyville, in fear and self-mistrust.

Among my acquaintances was a retired prostitute. While I measured her room, she had sat in the corner and rocked and asked me questions, and, when she got the answers, said, "You're wasting your time, young man. Like everybody who tries to do good, you're making a fool of yourself. Don't you know this is New Orleans?" But when I reassured her she laughed and said, "Well I guess there ain't much difference between us, 'cept I'm out of business now. Know what my business was?" and she told me, and in the telling, told me the story of Storyville.

Some years before, a pious legislator, she said, had introduced and ultimately persuaded the legislature to pass a bill creating a segregated district in New Orleans. One of its boundaries was the railroad tracks. Here her house, of which she eventually became madam, stood facing the passenger station, a convenience to traveling men (drummers) and other out-of-town customers. Her house had been high-toned, none of your dirty cribs. (The cribs were little one-room houses, rows of them, set flush to the sidewalk.) "Why was it called Storyville?" She laughed when I asked. "Of course," she said, "the bill didn't hurt our business, only fixed it so's anybody knew where to find us, and cut down the graft; we didn't have to give the police so much. So we sort of felt grateful to the old geezer and named the district after him."

She was right about New Orleans. If I and a thousand others measured every sagging wall, counted every broken window, nothing would be done about it. She knew her New Orleans.

III

The docks were a pleasant diversion from Tulane. Here at least was action with some kind of purpose. Seagoing ships, which I had never before seen with my eyes, gave me a new idea of quantity, as they discharged bananas by the million, until then a Christmas rarity, raw sugar that took me back in memory to my grandmother's smokehouse in South Carolina, bales of spices enough for a thousand cupboards, sacks of green coffee, peanuts in crokus sacks that had somehow been snagged for the convenience of dock hands. There were smells too and mixtures of smells, tar, jute, cottonseed meal, oakum, fresh pine, some new, some old, and one that was oldest of all, the smell of sweating Negroes; one whiff, and I was home. For, just as a Chicagoan born on the west side among the stockyards may grow to manhood and travel far away and live and learn other smells, but returning feel tears in his eyes at the oldest and dearest of all, so it was with me on the docks of New Orleans; but when I came near, something was wrong: the melody of their speech was the same but the words were unfamiliar. They spoke a patois very like the Gullah dialect of low-country Negroes in South Carolina, and that too I had not understood—not the words.

One day I was watching the stevedores at work, although that is hardly the word to describe Negroes in movement, any movement— an elevator boy is the only Negro I have ever seen at work, strictly speaking. Presently an upriver boat was tied to the dock and, when the gangplank was lowered, first off was a splendid Negro. He must have come a long way, from Memphis or farther, for, while the passengers that followed merely disembarked, he made a practiced entrance and stood waiting for the effect. He had reason, for his getup was a Miami tourist's dream. The stevedores, however, merely looked up and laughed and went on twirling cotton bales. Just to be sure there was no mistake, or to forgive the oversight, he went toward them ready with a greeting, but when he got near enough to hear them speaking he stopped in amazement and mumbled to himself. I could almost hear him say, "Dis ain' right. Sump'n wrong."

The stevedores were to me the city and I was as bewildered as he. These people lived in a different language, strange in its hidden meanings. How different, and why, I was slow to learn. I only knew there was, for me, "sump'n wrong."

If my prejudices had allowed, I could have attached myself to the sporty Negro and learned in a short time what took me long to learn, for the Negro is a convex mirror, reflecting in little the civilization in which he finds himself. The Chicago Negro is Chicago, Harlem New York, Atlanta University is middle-class Atlanta, Tuskegee agrarian Alabama, as the Negro in New Orleans was New Orleans itself. In the surrounding delta country he accepted without question the tenet of the white man's creed that said, "Once a Negro always a Negro." In Natchez he might be as white as his white father; it made no difference in his status. But in New Orleans the article read, "Once a Negro always a Negro—maybe."

"Passing," as it came to be called in the North, was not hazardous among the lower orders. Although the quadroon balls were no longer held and a lady could now give a party without fear of having most of the men guests unexpectedly absent and the rest fidgety until they could get away, the quadroon was still there, a beautiful menace to racial purity. It was for love of her, perhaps, that the legislators would never pass a miscegenation bill. The results were to be seen in every streetcar. The company had complied with the law by putting signs on the back of seats toward the rear; but, having gone that far, it washed its hands of the whole affair and thereafter let conscience or caution decide who should sit where. One of the janitors at Tulane sat behind the sign, his nephew in front, although to my eye there was no difference between them. That could not have happened in Columbia, nor Montgomery, nor anywhere in the South.

In the upper reaches of society the Negro was more firmly excluded, but not completely, if persistent rumor held any truth. It was said that more than one family of secure position, and names were named, had been touched with the tarbrush, but years ago. I remembered this when an English lady boasted to me of her descent from a king's mistress who had died in the gutter, more years ago; and out of my childhood memory came the story of the pious old Methodist woman who said of the crucifixion, it had happened so long ago, please God it wasn't true. But if the touch of the brush was recent, and that alone was in balance, outlawry was sharp and sudden.

Among the girls whom I knew were two dark beauties, daughters of a wealthy man who had come unknown to New Orleans some years before and built a house on St. Charles Avenue. On Sunday nights, the usual calling time, their rooms were filled with young men, for the girls were charming also and their food was good. This went on for a year or more, until one night when I reached the port of call, there was no other visitor, and none came. The next Sunday I went again, and again the girls were alone. I was puzzled and disturbed, and asked where I knew I would get an explanation. I got it and thereafter stayed away. (Who ever said the young are not keepers of conventions?)

Their father, I was told, had been a member of one of the most exclusive Mardi Gras balls, until at a meeting another member had stood up and said, "I won't be in a ball that has a nigger in it." There was consternation, confirmatory in itself of the general uncertainty, and a demand that he name his man. "All right," he said, "I mean him," and pointed to the girls' father, who rose and left and shortly afterward sent in his resignation.

But the story had a happy ending. About a year later a grandmother died and left to each of the girls a hundred thousand dollars, and within three months they were married into two of the oldest families in the city.

But New Orleans was not the South. New Orleans was half-caste, truculent, servile, proud and ashamed. In the French Quarter there were old ladies who had never learned English and watched eagerly for the start of surprise when a granddaughter translated to a visitor that they had never been above Canal Street, and yet who were willing to forget their pride when it was time to marry off this same granddaughter. He might be a rake, even an American rake, if only he had money.

The insularity, or even greed, of the New Orleans French might have been overlooked, had there been a single spark, flash of wit, intuition, grace or poetry, some form of life. There was none; merely a formula of existence, and dullness. They were hard, complacent, tight-packed in their small past. Colonists from other lands suffered some change; Germans, Southerners, even the Italians, made some adjustment to newness, but not the French, not if they could help it. They were an island in New Orleans as New Orleans was an island in the South, and their isolation was not only physical and from America. Things had been happening in France for the past two hundred years, but the New Orleans French were preintellectual, pre-revolutionary; they were even pre-Bourbon, for while they had forgotten nothing, there was some question as to whether they had ever learned anything.

They were an infective blight. Let a green shoot appear, and presently it began to wither. Once in a while a boy went away to college, to Princeton preferably, or, if adventurous and willing to let something happen to his mind, to Harvard. Within three months after graduation and return, he was no different from the output of Tulane.

If the Americans had themselves been healthy, they would have implemented their contempt of the French, but sham this is no better than sham that, and sham that had got there first. All aristocracy, being an antiquated mode, must be touched with pretense. I had seen that in South Carolina, but nothing could have prepared me for an aristocracy founded on pretense.

The casual visitor went back home and told of the breathless gayety of New Orleans. If he had stayed a little while, he might have known that it was the cheerfulness of a sanatorium, where death hides in tubercular laughter.

IV

Parsonage breakfasts were always under a curtain of newspaper. First it was the Columbia *State*, with a palmetto on the masthead, then the Montgomery *Advertiser*, followed by the *Picayune*. My father loved food; he also loved hurry, and while the rest of us were in the midst of the meal he had long polished his off and was now blocking off the light with fluttering pages. When broadcasting came in, it was nothing novel to me; I had always got my news in snatches, but edited, with a snorting "Humph!" or "Goodness gracious!" or "For land's sake!"; sometimes the interjection alone, without explanation. Usually the news came over the top, but when he lowered the paper and looked over it and his glasses, we downed tools and waited, knowing we were going to hear something that was good for us.

One morning, long before we came to New Orleans, he said, "John Andrew, listen to this," and he read from the day's paper that Cecil Rhodes had left a fortune for scholarships at Oxford. "Three hundred pounds a year—let's see, that's about fifteen hundred dollars. My gracious, I wish there had been something like that when I was your age," and he let it soak. Caution kept me silent. "When I was your age," often heard, was an incomplete reproach. I decided that, whatever else, I would not be a Rhodes Scholar.

Nothing more was said and I had forgotten all about Rhodes Scholar

ships, and, for that matter, any scholarship, until the middle of my
second year at Tulane, when the dean sent for me and suggested that
I go to Baton Rouge the next day and take the examinations, "responsions," for entrance to Oxford. At that time all candidates had to pass
responsions before being considered for a Rhodes Scholarship, for the
mother of universities was as yet unwilling to admit that she had any
offspring in America. The chance of passing on such short notice was
meager, even though I might remember enough Greek and Latin from
Webb School, and more meager still of election, for in the continuous
feud between Tulane and Louisiana State University that particular
perquisite had usually gone to the state university. The dean knew this,
but having previously protested, he was unwilling to let the present
election go by default, and I, he thought, was Tulane's most likely
candidate.

I was not eager to go to Baton Rouge, nor to Oxford. Three or four
years more of the dusty road to learning was just what I did not want,
but since I had no objection that could contrive to sound reasonable,
I said yes, I would go. But, once in the game, I decided to play, and
took with me an English textbook in arithmetic, to learn on the train
and that night in the hotel the difference between pounds, shillings,
and pence, for I had been warned that no concessions were made to the
barbarians even in such a small matter as that. There were others
taking the examinations, and when they saw me studying arithmetic,
they laughed. When the ordeal was over, however, they laughed no
more. They had all failed, and they knew it, in arithmetic.

Some months later I was notified that I had passed and should appear
before the committee of selection, again in Baton Rouge, where the
decision would be between me and a graduate of Louisiana State
University held over from the time before.

Again I was reluctant, but the game—and that was all it ever had
been—was now more exciting and I made up my mind to play it
through to the end. At that time the committee of selection was com-

prised of college presidents, that is, politicians, and so I played according to the rules. (This was thirty years ago. Since then merit has become the basis of selection.) First I wrote to John Webb and after that abandoned honor and got letters of recommendation from everyone who could be cornered and persuaded, however sour the looks that met my request—the professors were not cordial—hundreds of letters. The most convincing of them all was written by the mayor of New Orleans, who had never seen me; the next in order of excellence, by me. I had tutored a boy, and when I asked his father to write for me, he had some trouble understanding what I wanted—"Oxford University in Ohio?" he asked—took me to his secretary who in turn took me to a stenographer and suggested that I dictate what I wanted. I gulped, but I did as I was told and was pleased when I read what I had said. It was restrained, but comprehensive. (Later, in comparing notes with my fellow Oxonians, I discovered how restrained. One of them, the greatest rake in the lot, had been described as the "whitest flower of South Carolina young manhood.")

I went to Baton Rouge, shook hands with the committee as they filed in and again shook hands with them some two hours later when they came out and informed me that I had been elected. They had asked me no questions. They had read my letters, and my rival's, and decided on that evidence alone. I felt a little ashamed, but I had one consolation at least: there was, as the Duke of Wellington said of the Knighthood of the Garter, "no damned nonsense of merit about it."

CHAPTER VII

Oxford and Rhodes Scholars

THE THRIFTY TRAVELER TO A FAR COUNTRY IS NOT A DISCOVERER; having read guidebooks and steamship folders and listened to his friends, the learned Columbus will make a voyage of confirmation, and will approve according as he meets with the expected. A British visitor to Switzerland said, "I have seen the Jungfrau and the goiter and I am ready to go home." An American school teacher came upon the bust of Homer in the Capitoline Museum and exclaimed, "Ah Homer, how you do look like yourself." But once in a while the tourist will come properly equipped, with complete ignorance. One compatriot, on first seeing the Forum, said, "Must 'a' had a big fire here."

When I got off the train in Oxford in the autumn of 1911, I was, unfortunately, not completely ignorant. From the cab rank I chose a hansom, for I had seen its picture in my childhood reading of *Chatterbox*, and while the beery cabby stored my luggage on the roof I hopefully waited for him to make a witty remark. He did not, nor did one ever in my presence; he mumbled a question and I answered, "Queens College."

We drove on the wrong side of the cobbled streets through dirty, grimy slums and past what looked like public buildings—post offices, courthouses, and the like—while I craned for the university. I never found it, then or later. How was I to know that Oxford was a state of mind? Presently we stopped in front of one of these buildings that sat flush to the sidewalk and had for an entrance two huge wooden doors flanked by columns of peeling sandstone. The cabby made a noise and began to climb down.

As soon as I was out of the hansom I got my first lesson. The luggage had by then been deposited on the sidewalk, and when I stooped to pick it up an old man rushed out of the entrance, quivering with horror and pouring out apologetic sounds. I understood nothing, except that I was not to touch the luggage; but I did hear the h's dropping and this made up for lack of wit in the cabby. I had often wondered how h-less English would sound, but this was more than that: it was un-h'd. Where the letter belonged a hole of silence was punched. When I knew the old man better—he was the head porter—I liked to stand at the little window of his lodge and hear him punching, but at our first meeting he was teaching me something. Without saying so he was saying that I must never carry my own luggage, leading me into knowledge that would one day come under the general heading of "It isn't done." I did not protest. I humbly allowed his assistant to take the bags and show me to my rooms.

He led me through the front quad, into the back, and to a stairway at whose entrance a sign said my name with seven others. While the luggage was being stored in the tiny bedroom beyond, I took in the coal fire burning in the grate, the furniture, ancient rather than antique, and the sun feebly shining through the windows of the sitting room. "Your scout will be 'ere presently, sir." I heard the words but not the meaning, for I had no notion what a scout was. Left alone, I examined the pantry and the bedroom, and wondered why its windows were barred. Then I sat down on the long settee in front of the fire.

After a blank half hour the door opened and admitted a large mustache, the largest I had ever seen, followed by a small dark indistinguishable man who said, "I'm John, sir, your scout," and I knew what a scout was. "I'll make you some tea, sir." He did, and also let me understand that hereafter I was to make my own, that he would lay my fire, bring breakfast, make up my bed and tidy the sitting room, bring lunch and whatever hot food I should order for tea—all this without saying much, while I drank tea inexpertly. Then John said (I never heard the rest of his name), "You'll be wanting a gyoon, sir." I had not felt the need, did not in fact know what a "gyoon" was, but I said "Yes." "Very good, sir," he said, "I'll fetch you one, sir." He took the tea things and came back bringing a black alpaca garment well along in years, a sort of smock open in front, with two tabs hanging down the back at the shoulders. " 'Ere you are, sir. Dinner will be at 'alf past seven, sir, in the 'all." "Where is that?" I asked. He took me to the window and pointed. "You'll see the other young gentlemen gathering there, sir," he said.

It would be imposing to report that I made resolutions looking to the honor of my benefactor, Cecil Rhodes—I still called him Ceecil—that gratitude brought tears and a firm will to do my best; the truth is, I had not wanted very much to come, and very much did not want to be there. But the fire was pleasant; it was soft coal, which had been a treat in South Carolina, to be used sparingly as kindling for stubborn anthracite. I sat and poked it and presently got up to have a thorough look at my rooms. Then I made my first discovery.

I discovered privacy. I had never had any before, except for moments and those stolen, none such as this, long privacy, stretching out into the future. There were two doors to my sitting room, one the ordinary kind, doorknob and all, the other knobless and solid oak that, once closed, shut out curiosity. I tried it on that first afternoon, "sported my oak" as I should learn to say, and for the first time in my life tasted secure privacy.

Southern life had been crowded life, for everyone. The "Big House," from which every Southerner is, however remotely, descended, was not big enough to hold family and kinsmen and servants, much less allow anyone a corner of his own. But, more than that, the Southerner lived and lives in relation to people, if only in his consciousness. This was different. The room was mine, and I knew no one, nor needed to know any in the way to which I had been accustomed. The doors told me that.

This was my first discovery in England, but there was another that would begin with dinner and within a year come to expression, in a conversation with a visiting American girl. "What do you like best about Oxford?" she asked, and I answered, "It's a man's world. Here women are accepted, if at all, as inferior to men." (She turned her back in anger and we were presently engaged to be married; and were, in time, but that is a story that may not be told.) Oxford was a man's world, as the South was woman's. I had not known it until I spoke the words, but as soon as they were said I was as startled as Cortes.

I had been unable to see the South while I was in it (as for the rest of America, I was as ignorant as any crossroad Confederate veteran); the matter was there, but so was I, and I was part of the matter. To know the South was as impossible as self-knowledge, the Socratic delusion. One cannot be knower and known at the same moment; one can only know what one was, yesterday or an hour or a year ago, but one is already different when knowledge comes. As long as I was the South and the South I, my eyes could not focus—distance was needed for that. I began to understand why the American poet, if he would be articulate, had to get away from home, and also why he loved London or Paris or some remote unheard-of place, or even New York, where he had discovered Maine or the plains of Nebraska. He loved them for his discovery.

When the bugle blew I put on my "gyoon" and went to dinner in the Hall. I had expected dignity and good food, but as I stepped inside the door I was smitten with clatter and haste; and the meal, soup, boiled mutton with caper sauce, boiled sprouts and boiled potatoes, tamped down with boiled pudding, was academic. But the silver was beautiful and old, each piece, and the beer mugs—Queens was famous for its ale brewed on the premises—engraved with the name of the donor. (My fork on this first night was dated 1765 and the mug twenty years earlier.) At the far end of the room, however, there was calm dignity, at the high table, raised a foot or so above the level of the floor. Here the dons sat, ranged around three sides of the table, in imitation, tradition said, of the Last Supper, sat and ate slowly, and would be eating long after the undergraduates had hurried away. On this first night they all looked alike, as like as the portraits on the walls which spanned in years four hundred but were all painted by the same itinerant hand in the eighteenth century. In time I should know some of the dons as individuals: Sayce, the Egyptologist and looking like a mummy; E. M. Walker, reputed to know everything, including the schedule (pronounced "shedule") of all trains to and from Oxford; B. M. Streeter, a mild dyspeptic, a firebrand among the Moderns in the Church, and successor to another, William Temple, the present Archbishop of Canterbury; white-bearded Doctor McGrath, who had wearily retired on full pay from the headship of the college when he was fifty and planned to live to be a hundred, and almost made it; T. W. Allen, Homeric scholar and eater (when it came his week to plan the menu, the high table was crowded), whom I should know well, for he was what we should call my "adviser," but called in Queens a "moral tutor" —"relatively moral, Mr. Rice," he said.

As I was coming out of Hall an American came and introduced himself. He was Elmer Davis, he said, and would I have coffee in his rooms.

Thus began for me three wonderful years of loafing.

The day began with John's knocking on the door of my bedroom and saying, " 'Alf past seven, sir." On the hearth of the sitting room I met my first English breakfast: porridge, filet of sole, bacon and eggs, toast, marmalade, and a pot of something that looked like coffee. I filled myself and went to sleep again. The next day I was invited out to breakfast, the favorite time for entertaining in Oxford, and was fed exactly the same food, and every morning of that term, eight weeks in all, I ate until I had to loosen my belt. (In the second term the belt was gone; I wore braces, which is what the British call suspenders.) I could not understand why I was fed so much until I understood something else, that the English never planned anything but groped their way to comfort, and for comfortable talk, one needed a full stomach.

Lunch, which was followed by action, was scant—bread and cheese, and bolted. Then came the playing field or river, and, when that ordeal was over, more plenteous food at tea, with more talk, until dinner, followed by still more talk.

Privacy, to be had at the closing of a door, talk at the opening; re-treat, and sortie into the realm of ideas, for, excepting ghastly intervals, that was most of the talk—ideas, food for the starved mind. Here was John Webb's classroom again, vast, and all were teachers and all taught; then, bowed under the intolerable weight of thought—the young are serious, inside—privacy, which is to the conscious mind as sleep to the unconscious, a time for knitting.

Loafing was nothing new to me, but this was a new kind, guarded privilege. I could not remember the time when other people were not there or about to be there, and to the onlooker there is no difference between loafing and idleness, which is loafing without content. Hard work was an American virtue, and if one's heart was not in it, one had at least to pretend. Some day, when man becomes enlightened and gets his values straight, loafing will be a universal right, and work a privilege, reserved to those who can prove their case.

But even in Oxford loafing was not for everyone: there were a few, chosen and self-chosen, gaunt scholars who must bring honor to the college or else sink back and become nameless again, and others, driven by merciless ambition—these worked. I had long decided that I would become rich, but respectably, and so, sharing the Southerner's contempt for business, had fortunately elected to be a lawyer. I could hardly have made a better choice, for the School of Jurisprudence ("school" was the equivalent of the American "major"), was the only one in which I could make an even start with the Englishman. I had better sense than to try "Greats," the Oxford word for Classics, in which the native was trained from birth. Also, law was easiest.

For my preliminary examination I was tutored by two dons, one in Roman law, the other in history. At the end of my first tutorial in history, the tutor, a close-clipped tweedy cigarette smoker—the other smoked a pipe and was reasonable—looked at me in wonder and surprise: I was, I think, his first American, and he had not supposed there could be such concentrated ignorance. He said, "I think you will have to take a year for this." I said nothing.

I said nothing because I had nothing to say. All I had was a feeling which told me that I could acquire, for purposes of regurgitation, as much history in six weeks as in six times six. At the end of my third tutorial, while he was still sounding for the bottom of my ignorance, I told him I had decided to take the examination at the end of the term. He was furious and all but called me a fool. I left and never went back, and when I took the examination and passed he was still more furious, and would say to one who knew me, "You know that man Rice? I can't imagine how he ever got by." I could have told him.

Rather, I could tell him now, now that I have the words that were somewhere in the feeling that I should let history alone. It was only a hunch, but it was a good one. I could tell him that I could not learn history, I mean really learn, not parrot, history, because I am an American.

When the Pilgrim Fathers landed, they, and all immigrants since, discontinued the past, turned toward a future that was to be theirs, not their ancestors'. America is unhistoric, even antihistoric. The millions that have poured in, my forefathers and others, dropped their past off the deep end of the dock. They were to be makers rather than learners of history. During my three years in Oxford, persuaded by stones in the corner of the quad that had chilled the bones of scholars for half a thousand years, by old glass, by old ways, my roots began to grow again and history to make some sense; but the taproot remained as it was, cut off.

My first examiners found this out, to their amusement. One of the five, seated on the opposite side of the felt-covered table, handed me a piece of Latin and asked me to translate. It was something about Thomas à Becket's quarrel with his king, and went smoothly until I got to the point where he took something into his hand. I called it a stick. The examiner smiled and said, "No, you don't mean that, not 'stick'." I said, "That's the only meaning I know for the word. Doesn't it mean that?" "Yes, of course, but not here, not in this connection." Then, when I stuck to stick, he tried to help me out, "No, not stick. What is it that a bishop carries in his hand?" I said, "I don't know. I never saw a bishop in my life." (An American bishop, being Non-conformist and therefore not the real thing, carried nothing in his hand, except perhaps a sheroot.) They all laughed, and he said, "That will be all, thank you," and, as I got up, "The word, Mr. Rice, is 'crozier'," and they all laughed again. I do not say that they passed me because they were amused, or because I seemed unlikely ever to learn; but I know it was not because I knew any history.

In June, 1914, about two and a half years later, I sat before another group of examiners, who received and passed me with the same grace. In the meantime I had learned a little law, which I soon forgot, but one thing I did learn, the one thing that I brought back to America: it was not necessary to treat undergraduates as infants, a bit of wisdom that would, when I became a teacher, get me into endless trouble, with my colleagues.

At first it looked otherwise. We were incarcerated. At an hour in the evening, eight or nine according to the season, the "gate," the wooden door that was the only entrance to the college, was locked, and graduated fines were assessed against later entrants, until midnight, when none could enter. Iron bars were set in all outside windows, and surrounding walls, twelve feet or more in height, were topped with spikes that turned in the hand, for they were in consecutive sets of four strung along iron bars. Every college had its perilous ways in, but they were used only by the very amorous or the very drunk. The rest of us knew that, from midnight on, we were locked in prison.

That was the way it seemed, but in time a kind of wisdom appeared. From the closing of the gate the college became a self-contained community. During the day one might wander, but monks could not be trusted in the dark. Inside the walls we might do as we pleased, loaf, drink, gamble, all the things that could be done within celibacy; but there was one thing we might not do, hence the bars. A celibate is hypersensitive to his maleness, and night is an underscore. (It is, I suspect, this constant awareness that is the why of celibacy in a priesthood. The priest will not be fruitful, but his confessed flock, if their spirits flag, will catch fire from him.) For most of us celibacy was only temporary, but it needed heavy insurance.

Until we were locked up for the night the university proctors walked the streets to guard us, two of them, followed by swift-footed college servants, known as "bulldogs," or "bullers." (The wordbound Oxonian, incapable of slang, broke out in a rash of -er words: brekker for breakfast; fresher (freshman); rugger (rugby football), as well as the more familiar soccer; divvers (Divinity Moderations), the required examination in the Bible; rollers, roll call, morning notice to a college official of one's presence, and its variant, dirty rollers, for which one need not be completely dressed; and even Pragger Wagger, for the Prince of Wales, who at the time was in Magdalen College.) These bullers knew every shady spot and lady in the town and were a terror to the impecunious amorist, to whom, when caught, punishment came swift.

There was, on the other hand, no incarceration of the mind. Nowhere else, except at Harvard, have I known such a spirit of free inquiry, and as to Harvard it is only a visitor's impression. In Germany, where I spent a summer before coming to Oxford, and went often thereafter, the student was free in all action except the one that means most, action of the mind. That was the difference between Oxford and Heidelberg, a difference of padlocks. But at the time, and for long after, the world outside England, particularly America, believed that there was intellectual freedom in Germany, as if a door closed to thinking anywhere will not in time be followed by other closings, and twisted thinking not twist all thought.

But, wonderful as it was to think and say what one pleased, after a while came a teasing question. What was the spirit of free inquiry worth, if it did not turn in upon action? Was it only a game, harmless for youth and old men encysted in pedagogy, but not to be taken seriously when it came to doing things? I have heard it said by an American father that he would consider a son worthless who was not a radical while young, and know him worthless if he still was a radical in middle life. Was this what the British meant?

There was evidence in the talk heard over tea, in the common room, in the boathouse, everywhere. Whatever the words that bounced along on the top, the undertone, the sustaining bass, was one insistent note. "Get on," it said, "get on and get up." I never met an Englishman who did not propose to be well paid for what he should do. Wit and tongue were being sharpened, not to the glory of God, not even to the glory of man, nor the Empire, but to help one get on and get up. This was not the pursuit of truth; this was truth-chasing, to be left off when something serious showed up.

Oxford was, in fact, a vocational school, very good, but still vocational. That accounted for the connection between what happened to a man there and what happened afterwards; that made a first class in the final honor examinations obligatory, or certainly a good second.

(The examinees were put into four classes.) One man who lived on my stair fainted when he came out of the building where he had written his last paper. He would, he knew, get at best a third, which meant, as he said, that he would be a third-class man all his life. The church, politics, law, the civil service, all offered a high price for brains. Oxford was therefore no place for the stupid young man on the make, who was ignored, nor for the man chary of brain in the larger interest— he was despised. Mind, and the willingness to use the mind, there must be.

Beyond that one ran into fog. Asquith, then prime minister, had been Balliol's most brilliant scholar, and Asquith said that he had decided when he was nine years old that women should not have the vote. Sir John Simon had been his equal in mind and Sir John would find Laval congenial. Philip Kerr, afterwards Lord Lothian, was a member of the Cliveden set, until he changed his brilliant mind. I asked him, the one time I had more than polite greetings with him, why the British would not grant independence to India. He stopped further question with a question: "You want markets too, don't you?" Oxonians used to say, "If you want to know what Aristotle said, go to Cambridge; if you want to know what he meant, to Oxford." That might account for Stanley Baldwin, but how account for the others?

Ronald Knox gave me a clue. He had been an undergraduate at Balliol and left a pleasant memory when he became a priest and propagandist for the Catholic faith. Toward the end of my first year a controversy flared in the Established Church over the action of the Bishop of Kikuyu in Africa, who had taken communion with Non-conformist missionaries. This, it seemed, was a violation of one of the tenets of the Church, and there followed a terrific outcry—literally terrific, to me. I, being a simple American, thought such heated talk would surely bring on civil war; but when that became the only possible outcome, the British found another. The whole matter was referred to the Archbishop of Canterbury for adjudication, and quiet was restored. A year and a half later His Grace issued his report, running to many pages, which Ronny Knox reviewed, saying, "The Archbishop has just reported on the matter of Kikuyu. God, he says, is indubitably pleased with what happened at Kikuyu, and unquestionably it must not happen again."

Compromise is good, inherent in the idea of democracy, and England, I had been told, was a democracy. But democracy is only a means, an easy way for people to get what they want. What did the British want? At what point had compromise stopped, where had they drawn the line and said, "Inside this space is what we want, what all of us want." Words would not tell me, I knew; sermons, Uncle Ellie's oratory, commencement exercises—all these made me distrust words. I was listening for meaning, catching a note here and there.

There was the joke about women's suffrage with its recurrent theme; the silence of my hostess while her husband spoke, and her daughter's saying of a rude guest, "O but I'm not as good as he is; I'm a woman." There were three women's colleges in Oxford, but no woman could get a degree, and there were dons whose indecencies, turned on when women were present at their lectures, were recited with glee.

One night I sat and listened to a roomful of men telling stories. If a session lasts long enough for relaxation to be complete, stories and their way of telling reveal the natures of the tellers. This, and others, began with one or two stories salted with humor, but humor was soon pushed aside and in its stead came streams of eructed filth. On other occasions the tellers were decent fellows, courteous, considerate, a little stiff but kind underneath, civilized; but now, as the central theme emerged, eyes became beady, mouths wet, and the fingers of one hand pulled at the fingers of the other in nervous disgust and delight.

In Germany, it had been no shock to find women by definition—the only way they can be—inferior to men; I had supposed the English would be different. They were not, however, except that, having a better sense of form, they usually put more grace into the expression. (Also, as in Germany, they paid a toll, not so openly perhaps, but still they paid. When I first read Horace, I had innocently thought that his poems to beautiful boys were in the same class as the slit lips of Africans, until a seasoned Orleanist assured me that it was not quaintness nor ancient history. In South Carolina a term of endearment to children was "a little bugger," but in England it was not used of children, or in mixed company.)

The poor scholar who lived at the top of my stair had been given a "leaving" scholarship by his school, which with his stipend from the college, gave him a stingy living. He was treated with distant courtesy by his fellows, with none at all by John, the scout. He had his foot on the rung, but that was as far as he ever got, for his third class thrust him down again, to live, as the prayer book said, "content with the station in life to which it had pleased God to call him."

I began to see why the porter had been flustered on that first afternoon when I picked up my luggage. I must not carry anything in my hand—luggage, a tennis racket, a plate of food, anything—if it might appear that I was serving rather than served. I was an American and therefore of course queer; but I was also an undergraduate, for the time being a gentleman.

Scribes in medieval law courts wrote records in a script unreadable by any except those to whom the secret of the twists and curls had been taught in youth, and thus preserved to their descendants succession to place. The invention of printing, prelude to democracy, had destroyed that monopoly; but speech remained to their spiritual offspring—speech, inflection, tone. The Canadian was safe; his accent might be American, or, if his parents had been of the best, and careful, he might even pass; but the New Zealander, not being fortunate as to parentage, or almost certainly as to grandparentage, was put down as a Cockney, a state of misery from which there was no resurrection in this life.

Knowledge of Latin and Greek bore no demonstrable relation to fitness for position in the church, the law courts, army and navy, the civil service; but lack of knowledge was a bar, and the ancient languages were taught to the secure young.

Then there was reverence for poverty, lying deep in rich and poor alike, acceptance of poverty as somehow good. Every village church offered testimony, with its marble memorials to long-dead benefactors who left something, never very much, to "the poor of the parish." The nose collected evidence, in the stinking fish shops of Camden Town in London, in Southwark; but Oxford itself gave examples enough, with its smelly tenements; and the eyes, in scraggy teeth, yellow skin, the hungry look, and scrawny children who would one day be called up to fight a second world war and be found as unfit as their fathers.

But inequality was not static, not for the individual, if he had stamina or ruthlessness enough to rise out of his class. The door was open, if he pushed hard, and was willing to forget his origin, and his originators. The greatest snob in Oxford was, by birth, the son of a greengrocer, by effort and an eye to chance, president of Magdalen College. There was a sort of ironic propriety in the Prince of Wales's being his charge. The university was one of the doors, the church another; that was why neither was the center of religion; they were only means.

This recruiting from the class below and at the same time keeping the class itself there as an outward symbol of inner acceptance of the rightness of inequality, this use of the two institutions as recruiting officers while old bells and ancient walls called them something else— these and all other shorings waked in me my ancestors. America might not know what equality meant—who could, until men found it?—but America had taken the first step. We, my ancestors and I, had rejected the idea of inequality. The English accepted it, and called it good.

II

There was some feeling in Oxford that Cecil Rhodes should have chosen a more conventional way of showing admiration for his univer-sity. He had left fifty thousand pounds, as I recall, to his college, Oriel, to spend as the dons might choose, and ten thousand pounds as endow-ment of the high table, for he knew that they liked to feed themselves, if not the undergraduate, well. But there his unquestionable beneficence —and, some thought, benevolence—had ceased: all the rest of a great sum had gone to the founding of the Rhodes Scholarships, which, carrying a stipend of three hundred pounds a year, would, he hoped, draw from the colonies and America the future leaders of the English-speaking, and therefore the whole, world.

Heads were shaken, and have been shaking since, throughout the world that was to be led, while among the dons, by the account, there was consternation. They felt toward colonials as one does toward dis-tant relatives about to pay a visit, but Americans most of them had never seen and, from what they had heard, never wished to see. The principal of Corpus Christi, Grundy by name, refused to admit any to his college, having been told, as he was glad to explain, that some American tourists had once entered the rooms of an undergraduate at Magdalen and through the window had fed sugar from the absent tenant's sugar bowl to the deer in the parks.

They were a strange ingrown inbred lot, the dons. They spent their lives securely immured from the world, of which they knew little more than what they chose to read. They might have learned some-thing from the young whom they professed to teach, but they had never learned how to learn that way, for the young learn mainly from action, while they could only reflect; but, since they were withheld from action, theirs was reflection once removed, reflection upon the reflection of others—which is, I believe, called philosophy. In such an existence the mind, cut off from any will to action, may be spun in any direction by chance encounter with a new thought. Hence the enormity of the fed sugar.

Some twelve years ago the Rhodes Trustees proposed to do something about the dons, send them out into the world toward the horizon, and thus repair the oversight of the founder; so they announced that traveling fellowships, good for a hundred pounds a month for six months or longer, would be awarded to a specified number of dons yearly, and applications were invited, the only stipulation being that the traveling should be done outside the British Isles. (This was to be part of the broadening process.) I happened to be in the London office of Philip Kerr (Lord Lothian), general secretary to the Rhodes Trust, on the day of the deadline for applications. He told me that he had hurried home from America in his eagerness to read them, but when he asked his secretary to bring in the lot, she smiled. There was only one. Some time afterward, however, another came in, with a request that an exception be made in the applicant's case and he be allowed to remain in Oxford.

It was no wonder, then, that the first Rhodes Scholars were a perturbation. What would they be like? Nobody knew, and when the dons read the credentials of the appointees, of which each college would choose a certain number, they knew even less, for in their reading they had never met a letter of recommendation written by an American.

Spooner, who shares with Colonel Buncombe inclusion in the dictionary on account of his manner of speaking, was head of New College at the time the first Rhodes Scholars applied for admission, and was remembered for a comment made then. When he had read to the assembled dons the letters of the first candidate, he looked up and said in his high squeaky voice, "Well, gentlemen, I don't know anything to do but to take this young man. He seems to be a cross between Jesus Christ and Goliath."

By the time I reached Oxford the dons had learned how to read the letters. Jim Watkins, of Michigan, asked the head of his college whether he might have, from among his papers, a certificate that he had graduated from an American college. The withered old gentleman looked them through, mumbling quotations as he went along, "sterling character," "leader of men," "Christian gentleman," "superb athlete"—"what was it you wanted, Mr. Watkins?" Jim said, "A statement that I am a graduate of an American college." "Ah," said the dean, "that at any rate is a matter of fact."

There were among us a few Goliaths and also a few of what the British called "Christers"; the rest were, if not the cream of American colleges and universities, mostly the top of the bottle. Among us were two or three who avoided and were soon avoided by their fellow Americans, for they thought of themselves as emissaries from the United States to the British Empire. They were usually not to be seen on Saturday nights, when the American Club met for refreshment, needed by most of us, for it was not easy to live in Oxford.

It was not easy, but there were compensations: relative freedom from worry about money, something new to most of us, for, while not exactly poor, we had known worry at home; the feeling that one had time of one's own; freedom to work or not to work, and lectures to be omitted without remorse; but perhaps the best thing of all was that we came to know each other as we might not at home. It is possible to see people as individuals when they are outside their own country. The Harvard man found occasional good in the Yale man, though he was inclined to stick to his opinion of the Princetonian, but besides, he lived on the same stairway with a Midwesterner or found himself in the same tutorial with a Southerner. This did not always make for tolerance, but at least tolerance had a chance.

To all of us the English, being now convinced that we would not wreck the place, were quietly but deeply indifferent. Some called it tolerance, and praised it, and would praise it when they came back home, and there would be talk of union; it was indifference.

Life for the English had long ago found its forms—forms, not formulae—large and generous perhaps, even open, not closed, but forms all the same, and the word conformity for once had full meaning. Whatever action by aliens conformed, went unnoticed—which happens in any society; whatever did not conform also went unnoticed, and this it was that set the English off from any other people. They turned the same unseeing eyes toward the Americans laughing overloud as toward the cannibal hopping about his pot. It was neither approval nor disapproval; it was indifference.

This was in the Roman imperial tradition. In Oxford the history of the Roman Empire had meaning, and it was this rather than adventitious philosophy that drew the best minds into "Greats." They proposed to learn how it should, and should not, be done. One lesson they learned was to keep their interest narrow and to ignore what did not contribute thereto. But it was not the sort of ignoring that we met with in America, discomfort, chasm of silence, the averted eye, any reproof. They simply did not care.

There was, however, discomfort among some of us—that is, at first, before we knew what it meant. Afterwards, when we got the point of their indifference, we began to enjoy a kind of freedom such as we had not known, the kind that Southern Negroes know, the benefit of inferiority. If we misbehaved, we knew that it would be put down, if put down at all, to our origin. If, however, we chose, and we usually did, we might lose ourselves in the general fog of good behavior, that is to say, English. But he was a foolish man who thought that when he was behaving he was being English.

There were two kinds of Rhodes Scholars: those who were taken in by the English, and those who were not. (It goes without saying that the English were equally indifferent to both.) The handkerchief stuffed up the left sleeve could be the sign; if worn unconcernedly, you had your imitation Englishman; but if it was a playful gesture, a recession into likeness for the befuddling of tourists, then you might also expect, when its wearer spoke, his native speech, tinged, if at all, quite con-

sciously. Speech was a certain clue, for its matrix was cast in childhood and no amount of chiseling, however delicate, could get off all
the rough spots or change its form. Some tried hard, only to learn in
the end a kind of boogie-woogie English, underneath whose modulated
treble, imitative to the quarter tone, the bass from Pennsylvania or Ohio
or points west thumped doggedly along.

It could have been funny, if it had stopped there; but some Rhodes
Scholars went about misunderstanding the English in a serious way.
They were to be found of an afternoon in the drawing room of Dr.,
afterwards Sir George, Parkin, general secretary to the Rhodes Trust,
who took up residence in Oxford from time to time and explained to
those who would listen the high purpose of the Rhodes Scholarships.
Dr. Parkin was himself not an Englishman, except by profession. Dr.
Parkin was by birth a Canadian, but having early slept in the light of
the imperial moon, he was, as Uncle Remus said of an uppity Negro,
"mo' samer dan white folks," and was as zealous as my old-maid Methodist aunt turned Episcopalian. It is only fair to say, however, that in the
opinion of some of us Dr. Parkin had extended his misunderstanding
of the English to include Cecil Rhodes, whose words furnished insuffi-
cient evidence to his oracle. Even the casual reader of Rhodes's life
suspects that he had a larger interest than preserving the Empire, but
Dr. Parkin was not a casual reader, of Rhodes or anyone else. At any
rate, there was no doubt in Dr. Parkin that he knew and we should be
taught to know, our duty. One could not even question. At the first
hint of infidelity, the tea grew cold in his cup and the offender resolved
never to start that again.

III

When the first Rhodes Scholars went to Oxford in 1904 there was a
question in America. At that time scholars in the technical sense were
saving their pennies in order to go to Germany, where scholarship in
the same technical sense was an article of export. The method of their

scholarship was something an American could put his teeth into, this getting at truth through facts and facts alone, welcome release from the heavy hand of the theologian, to whom education in this country was still mortgaged, and for whom the poet alone was a match. But poets were not frequent and could not be made, while scholars could, and Germany was the place; and until such time as the American graduate school could get into mass production, a degree from Berlin or Leipzig was a safe investment. It is difficult now to recall the then abject attitude toward German scholarship; many an American professor died happy having won immortality in a German footnote.

Oxford was backward; Oxford clung, it was thought, to the poet's method. Cambridge was the place, or so the story ran; in Cambridge science was ascendent. This was not, however, a scientific statement, for, in the beginning words of an Oxford don's prayer, "paradoxical as it may seem, O Lord," poets were coming out of Cambridge and scientists out of Oxford. And yet the honest apologist had to acknowledge that, measured by the German standard, both were in fact backward.

There was another inconsequential thing that turned the verdict against Oxford. At the end of three years the degree granted was B.A., while the same number of years put in at a German university brought a Ph.D.

The question in America was, what would Oxford do to the Rhodes Scholars? No one seems to have put the question another way, what would returning Rhodes Scholars do to America? The two belong together, and their answers, which range from "nothing" to "plenty." Some ten years ago a Mrs. Millin wrote a biography of Cecil Rhodes in which she called the scholars "decent fellows." This was taken as an insult and letters were written to the London *Times*; nor did her defense bring forgiveness. She explained what she meant by "decent fellows": just that, too decent. Rhodes himself was, by implication, not "decent," and had not established the scholarships for men to whom decency would be a check to action. In general the record tends to give Mrs.

Millin some support. The range of action among my fellows is not startling: there have been several ambassadors and congressmen, there are now some twenty college presidents, and so far as I know there is not a single Rhodes Scholar at present in gaol.

In Queens there was one who was brilliant, and another who would be a surprise, Edwin Hubbel, now a famous astronomer. He was, when I knew him, a disconsolate law student with a gnawing vice, love of mathematics; but he, as I, wanted to be rich, and kept his love secret. One day, or night, over a beer or so, I asked him my one question: his eyes filled with tears and he confessed his love. (There is something strange in America, where, for all the freedom, a man is restrained from doing what he wants to do.) Hubbel left Oxford and the next time I saw him was between trains in Louisville, where he was teaching in high school, sneaking up on his beloved. When some years later I saw him in Chicago, a graduate student, he had found himself out, and let himself go.

The one brilliant man in Queens was Elmer Davis. When Elmer Davis smoked a cigarette he held it stiffly between his forefingers and pulled, not at it, but away from it. There was something of this pulling away in everything he did. Whenever I went into his room, he was usually sitting braced in the corner of the sofa, reading Tacitus, learning to be himself a commentator, although he thought at the time that he would be a teacher, and even from Tacitus he pulled away, cocking his head back at a sharp angle. Whenever he and I went girl hunting —nice-girl hunting, for he was even more puritan than I, Midwest puritan, which is without compromise—the same thing happened. The more attractive the girl, and he had as good taste in girls as he had in words, the more he pulled away. If, at the end of ten minutes I saw him relaxed, with his head in the perpendicular, I knew the verdict was indifference and we might as well get going. If, however, he held stiffly away and, even when there was laughter, did not duck his head and hide his eyes behind his heavy brows, I knew he was in for a fever.

Most people liked him, but he never believed it. It seemed incredible to him that any should like or admire one so ignorant as he, for he, as none I have ever known, was aware of his periphery of ignorance. Others might stand with their backs to their ignorance, but he faced it squarely, and hated it, hated it as deeply as he hated its twin, stupidity. Some time after I left Oxford I ran across a saying of Isaac D'Israeli's, that "ignorance is a mutilation of the mind," and I thought of Elmer Davis braced to meet the enemy. As a consequence he was the most erudite American at Oxford. But there was another result, not uncommon among Midwesterners: he propitiated ignorance, tried to fool it into believing that he loved it; only with him, it was a ruse, whereas with many it became a real affinity.

In New College, which had been new some four hundred years before, there was another American who would give his own answer to the question. This was Christopher Morley. The world was Morley's oyster and he had the choice of two knives for its opening, the one sharp-edged and dangerous, to himself as well as others, the other dull and sure. There is evidence of the scalpel, somewhere hidden away—not lost, I hope—in the minute books of the American Club. While he was secretary the meetings were like Episcopal services during Lent: the house was crowded through the reading of the lesson and thereafter hastily empty. No one who heard him there could have believed that, forced to choose between the two knives, satire and sentimentality, he would put away the sharp and use the dull; but he did, until Kitty Foyle came along.

In the same book of minutes is the early staccato prose of Elmer Davis, and among other records, if they still exist, another kind. He belonged to a club called, I think, "The Midwives," whose members would, they said, be writers, and for practice began a novel to which each in turn contributed a chapter. But, as it grew in volume, ambition

also grew, and Elmer realized that he might be required to help pay
the expense of publication. It was not published. On the night when
he read his chapter he invited me to be a listener. Out of the fervid
nonsense I recall only one phrase that could have been admitted to
print, "the interlocked lambent tongues of the lovers."

He was a small-town boy, a small-college boy, and a small-state boy,
for Indiana is spiritually small, as a border state is apt to be. When he
left Oxford he had already decided not to go back home but, after stubbornly refusing to take a teaching job at small pay, to stay in New York,
make or break; and he did, though it meant selling magazines from
door to door in the beginning. There were, I think, two things working
here: the balm of anonymity, and fear of poverty; for, just as he feared
ignorance in the world of ideas, so he feared poverty, which is a kind
of ignorance in the thing-world. For a long time I wondered whether
it would happen to him as to many Rhodes Scholars, whether he would
finally come to love money for its own sake and continue to enjoy
anonymity, a fine cloak for this corruption. But fear of poverty is not the
same as love of money, and I might have known that; and anonymity,
in measure, gives a man a chance to grow in his own, which may not
be the small, way. In the interval, however, he wrote a lot of trash,
and that itself can be a corruption; but every now and then there was
a glint, one unexpectedly in one of his novels, *Strange Woman*—the
rest were unreadable—more in articles and essays. His dissection of
Bishop Manning, which was entitled "Portrait of a Cleric," remains the
best piece of satirical writing ever done in America. But he had not
yet found his form. The novel was too sprawling, the essay too committal, and poetry, that is, the writing of verse, was blocked in him by
the danger of personal exposure.

Radio gave him the form. It was talk, and he talks better than he
writes; furthermore it was talk against a blank wall, to his ideal listener,
whom he seldom found in conversation. It also was concise, succinct,
sharp, with clear-cut edges, the medium for the modern Tacitus. Most

news commentators try to give their listener a bath in fifteen minutes, but when the time is up they have barely got the soap on the rag. Elmer Davis brings him out clean and fresh-smelling, on the dot. Having mastered the art of saying something in fifteen minutes, he went on to the sterner form of putting twenty-four hours into five minutes, a prose sonnet, and when he says, "And that's the news to this moment," one may sigh contentment, for it is so. But there is something more than that: there is a use of time to punctuate time, stopping it for the moment to put the point. It is as if war, famine, and pestilence pause at 8:55 for him to give the report of their doings and one feels that, while promptly at nine o'clock they will be at it again, in the meanwhile, for five minutes, nothing has happened, nothing in the world.

When the history of America's last twenty-five years comes to be written, a chapter will be required with the title "The Influence of a Misunderstanding of Oxford on American Education."

Oxford University is a federation of independent, self-governed colleges, each with its separate staff, from head to buttery clerk, and there is no absentee control by a board of trustees—a wasteful kind of administration, perhaps, but the British think freedom is worth a high price—whereas the model of the American university is the department store. But Harvard and Yale wanted to look something like Oxford, or thought they did when an American millionaire, nostalgic for a past that was never his, poured out money to fulfill their wish. Buildings were put up and called, by Yale, "colleges," and, more discreetly "houses," at Harvard. There the resemblance ends, for Yale's collegiate Gothic blushes at the imposture. There is no way to imitate freedom.

Elsewhere, however, there has been an honest attempt to impart some of the reality of Oxford, springing from the memory that the mind of the undergraduate was there respected.

St. John's College, in Annapolis, is a vocational school, without a vocation. With a curriculum straight out of medieval Oxford, it trains its students, not for the church, as Oxford then did, and not for office in or under an oligarchy, but for something pleasantly vague: to be artists in the art of thinking, Neo-Thomist dialecticians, lawyers without law.

Some seventy or eighty years ago a few Oxford dons, waking from the sleep that had deadened the university since the early eighteenth century, established the "Honour Schools," special curricula for specially brilliant students, while the rest were left to dawdle their way through the "Pass Schools." Balliol College, under the driving of Jowett, who translated Plato into evangelical English, soon became the model, and at the turn of the century every college was squeezing the pass men to death by requiring all, or most, of their undergraduates to read for "honours." (They reappeared, however, in the class lists, as "thirds" or "fourths.") There were two unforeseen results: little or no attention was paid to anything that was not a subject for examination—Samuel Morison, the biographer of Columbus, left a professorship in Oxford because of a lack of interest in colonial history—and, worse, the average don became a slogging plug of a coach, competing with his fellows for a high record of "firsts."

Many Rhodes Scholars, sickened by the neglect of intelligence in college and university, tried some form of "honours," with doubtful success; Frank Aydelotte, the only man I have ever known with energy equal to my father's, made a thorough test at Swarthmore.

He was born and reared in a small town that had got stranded on the edge of a coal field in central Indiana. His father had been owner of a small woolen mill where honest blankets were woven on ancient machinery and dyed by hand in vats, until new ways and machines had driven him from business; but not from life, the life he loved, of going down to the courthouse square once or twice a day and sitting silent with his friends, and to Masonic Lodge once a week. When I first knew him he was postmaster, a job to which he was appointed because the politicians found themselves in the curious predicament of having to name an honorable man. He had taken to his new assignment the same silent decency that had made it impossible for him to sell a shoddy blanket, the same decency, more vocal, that, passed to his son, rendered him incapable of selling shoddy education. Frank Aydelotte's mother was descended from the English by way of Canada, and, although she had lived all her life in America, she was homeless here, and more homeless in the blighted little town which kept her husband inexplicably content; inexplicably, because she had a brilliant wasted mind.

Four years in the town high school supplied Aydelotte with the meaningless information required for entrance to the state university. In the same high-school class was a student of life untouched by ideas, who would one day graduate from a denominational college and thereby prepare himself to sit at a desk in Hollywood and, as Czar of the Movies, draw the line of decency on speech and leg. Historians will be put to it to explain how the same town produced the two, the one to reach the crown of his career in a D.C.L. *honoris causa* from Oxford, the other in a magnanimous decision to let Fatty Arbuckle back into the movies, because, as he said, his father had once given him a Bible with the inscription, "To Master Willie Hayes, in the hope that he will always do the right thing . . ."—a hope of wide ambiguity.

Indiana University was, by the evidence, like other state universities, different from the high school in having a larger stock of information to dispense, and like in its unconcern with meaning. Four years more of information left Frank Aydelotte's mind untouched, except in one respect, and that important, for it enlightened his subsequent life. Among his instructors was a young Harvard graduate who admired Ruskin, and Ruskin led to Matthew Arnold, and Arnold in turn to Newman, and all together led to Oxford, where he would go and find them, all.

To love her, an eighteenth-century poet said of his girl, was a liberal education. That was Frank Aydelotte's liberal education, love of Oxford, pure chivalry, with never a thought to the old ways that made her and kept her what she was; and to love was to defend, her and her nation.

Swarthmore gave him his chance, a nondescript Quaker college on its way nowhere and therefore incapable of resistance to Newman's idea of a university. (What that frightened little man would have thought of his idea plunked down in a coeducational college, invites laughter.)

At first most of the teachers were skeptical, but any faculty is helpless against an energetic innovator, for even the most callous members are semiconscious of secret sin; they know that they are not much good and that what they are doing will bear no scrutiny. At last all came in and, once in, enjoyed the applause, first of their president, and then, as the news spread, of the outside world, which until then had hardly been aware of their existence; and so it went for some ten years. At the end of that time the faculty had learned how to do it. The vernal advent of the examiners from other institutions no longer frightened them, for they now knew how to prepare their students for examinations, and they were on the third or fourth or fifth repetition of their seminars, from which they once had learned but which they were now content to teach. They had learned how to do it and had gone to sleep again.

Frank Aydelotte had not gone to sleep, but he was stopped. Irony had smilingly bound his hands with the thongs of success. He might have broken the bonds and started over again—but no, he could not have done that, not even if he had admitted doubt, not at Swarthmore; the faculty would have murdered him in their sleep.

It was on Frank Aydelotte's front porch in Swarthmore that Black Mountain College had its beginning—not out of acceptance of Oxford: out of rejection. Or had I too misunderstood?

CHAPTER VIII

Sam Avery and the University of Nebraska

SAM AVERY HAD A NOSE LIKE THE NECK OF A WHISKEY BOTTLE. IT jutted out and downward straight from between his eyes, and then, when it was about to be too long, bulged suddenly and rounded into the size of a golf ball. It was as if it had been poured into a mold; where the bulge began there was a clearly marked depression that kept the same angle even at the joining of the smooth-shaven upper lip. His glasses loosely straddled the bridge, always tipped lower on the right, and never cleaned until he could no longer see.

I remember his nose because he used it. Most people do not; or, if they do, surreptitiously, as though there were something shameful about smelling, and whatever odors came their way must approach and be received athwart. Sam Avery, when he was at ease, was as frank as a dog, with the difference that he freely used the fingers of his right hand to bring the smells to him. But this was only when he was completely at ease; in public he indulged with caution, quickly putting hand to nose when he thought no one was looking, while in quiet talk he let himself go and sniffed long and lovingly. When the tale was beginning he dug his forefinger into his ear and took a moderate sniff, but as the tension increased—not the tempo; that was in reverse; the more excited and exciting he was, the slower he spoke, drawing his listener to a hearing intolerably acute—he slipped his hand inside his coat and to his armpit and came out with a real refresher. "We-e-ell," he would say, sniffing hungrily, "what do you suppose he was up to?" and out would come the point of the story, a trick foiled, a link in a long chain of action, and always a weakness exposed, for he had unabashed disrespect for humanity. "Ninety-nine out of a hundred who come in this office," he said to me more than once, "come because they want something. The reason I like to have you come is that you know you won't get it."

He had been born and reared on a Nebraska farm and was the first member of his family to go to college, which meant a lot to him and to them; for it was the first step up and out. But it had for him another, adverse, meaning: it meant that the earth was no longer underneath, to catch him if he fell; he was on his own and must live by his wits, or, if he chose the slower way and less profitable, by his brains; cattle in the pasture, corn in the barn, the loft full of hay and the cellar of root crops, all were transmitted now into money, money in the bank. He was not stingy; he was cautious, careful, apprehensive when it came to money, a characteristic that often came bluntly out when he was appraising some petitioner. "How much does he want?" might be the first question. But even so he had in him some generosity, as much as any farm boy come to town.

He had gone as an undergraduate to the little town of Crete, about thirty miles from Lincoln, where Doane College had been founded some years before by Congregationalists from Yale, at the time when Americans were beginning to believe in education as they had once believed in God, but still hoped that the beliefs might be reconciled. The college had fared well for a while, until Yale, which has always been a chart of the American spirit, and perhaps therefore called democratic, turned to the worship of success. In Avery's youth, however, the college was not yet left stranded, and probably offered him as good training as he might have had at the godless state university. After graduation he taught for several years in high schools and then went to Lincoln, and from Lincoln to Heidelberg and a doctorate. Except for these few years in a German laboratory he lived his entire life in his native Middle West. Nor, for that matter, had Heidelberg made any difference: he had gone there for chemistry and got chemistry, and nothing else.

He served his apprenticeship in the chemistry department in the University of Idaho, "the best school of academic politics I have ever seen; if you could save your neck in that place you were something. I remember one of my students, a girl, saying at the end of my first year, 'It's fun to watch you profs squirm. All during the year you keep us on pins. Now it's your turn, when you're afraid you'll get fired.' " He never forgot the lesson, nor the feeling he had when he learned it, nor its meaning to others as well as himself, for he was almost fanatic about tenure. He would fight in every way he knew, and his technique was wide and varied, to prevent the dismissal of the most worthless professor.

The University of Nebraska had started even with others in the Midwest and until the turn of the century and later had not fallen behind, but the state was poor and in time good men were sieved out, leaving behind incompetents, misfits, the intellectually lazy, and trash. When I was appointed in 1919, along with ten or eleven others, it was the first time in ten years that anyone not a graduate of the university had been taken onto the staff. As a rule a man will not admit to his department anyone then or likely to become superior to himself, and most of the heads of departments had followed the rule, with the result that nearly every young man on the faculty was already a permanent fixture; certainly no other university would ever want him.

The university did not want me, as a person: it wanted some one to teach Classics, and since the salary was small, and the head of the department had put off filling this vacancy until late summer, I was casually appointed at the end of a fifteen-minute interview with him. At the time I was in the University of Chicago, where I had gone after leaving Webb School, for I had the notion, which now seems foolish, that I should prefer teaching older students. I was to find, then and later, that while university students were older in years, they were in no other way, only more hardened. I had another notion, that a graduate school would mean freedom to learn in one's own way, a school for scholars rather than, as it was, for technicians. I was therefore glad to leave, and glad to go west, for I had some notions about the West too.

Sam Avery had come to Lincoln when the subsidence of the university was well on, and, using and improving the arts he had learned at Idaho, emerged as a candidate for the chancellorship when that office fell vacant in 1908. The regents, a body of five men elected from the state as trustees, set out to find a new head, hopeful at first of a distinguished scholar; but after a long quest they gave up and appointed Avery. No one, not even the regents, could ever explain how it had happened, and at the inaugural dinner the chairman of the board apologized, in the presence of the honored guest, assuring faculty, alumni, and friends that they had made a careful search but had been unable to find the man they wanted, and so had appointed the new chancellor, whom he was now delighted to introduce. No one could explain, except Sam Avery, and he never did; but he knew. It had, in fact, been quite simple. He had merely been and kept on being a candidate. Whenever the regents met, whatever might happen to other names, his was always there, until at last he had worn them down to acquiescence. He let it out to me once, obliquely, when he was urging me to put my name down for some traveling fellowship or other. I demurred. I was no scholar. I had no reputation. "Don't be a fool, Rice," he said, "you don't need to be; all you need to be is a candidate. How do you think people are chosen? By merit?"

I too had asked for an explanation of his incumbency the first time I saw him. My companion pointed to an ill-dressed, slouchy man of about fifty and said, "That is your chancellor." I stared. This was not the careless dress of an Oxford don or any absent-minded scholar. Care had gone into the selection of this baggy suit and cheap shoes, care and frugality, as I should learn. "Yes," my companion said, "that is our chancellor," and he told me of the inaugural dinner, and the completely blank look on Avery's face at his odd introduction, and the equally blank speech that he gave.

Some time after that I heard him make a speech and, as I anticipated, he said nothing. But there was something unusual in the speech. I had heard enough college presidents to know he would say nothing, but he was different from all the rest, who had said nothing about scholarship and character and all the other things about which they say nothing, while Sam Avery said nothing about nothing. When he sat down at the end of ten minutes, I found myself applauding an artist. He had reduced the official speech to its final absurdity, a thing no stupid man could do. In the eight years that I was at Nebraska I heard him make many speeches, and the result was always the same. I remember, as the highest point of his skill, a speech he was called on to make at the inauguration of a new curriculum in the Arts College. The committee in charge had laid the mine carefully; this time they would blow him out of his cave; so all the speeches led up to his. But when he finished I looked at the conspirators and smiled. He had done it again, brilliantly. Every word he spoke taken alone made sense, but all together none at all. He sat down and smiled to himself; and presently, when no one was looking, I saw his hand stealing up to his nose.

The first time I saw him close up, I began to recognize a kind of gritty shrewdness. He was chairman of the state committee on Rhodes Scholarships, of which I was a member, delegated to arange the meeting with him. "How long will it take?" he asked. "We should like the whole day," I said. He drew his mouth down toward the left and laughed. "Good Lord," he said, "I never spend more than fifteen minutes over appointing a professor. But all right. You just let me know when, and I'll take the day off."

Besides him there were three of us on the committee, all returned

Rhodes Scholars, and at every point he deferred to us, asking few questions and appearing abstracted and inattentive. But when the last candidate had left the room he said, "Well, I don't think much of the lot," and he said why, finishing off each in a sentence or two. "He'll make a pretty good dean," he said of the least promising; "sort of soft," of another, and was right; and so through the list. "They all look like second-raters to me," and we agreed; "but not third-raters, not bad enough to turn all of them down," and we agreed again. Then, after a moment of silence he said, "Tell you what. If we must pick a second-rater, let's not pick anybody from this campus. It'll save explanation." We chose a second-rater, and broke up in the early afternoon. I sat with him on that committee at all their meetings for eight years, and it always happened the same way; a sort of catalysis, as became a chemist. But in all that time he never revealed, even by a shade of tone, his opinion of the whole idea of the scholarships, which I knew. He was against them, with deep feeling.

When I first suspected feeling in him, I was puzzled; here was passion where I had expected none, and members of the faculty confirmed my early opinion: "Cold as a fish," they said. But they were wrong and I was wrong. Time taught me that there was passion, deep and hard, in him; the passion, passions, of the Middle West, of accomplishment; and, more deep, of frustration, of the road taken and its rewards, but also of another road, an older road that his ancestors had traveled and to other rewards.

Until some time in my third year I had never talked to him alone, and except for these glimpses in committee meeting, had not seen him as a man, only as an official. But one day, by chance, I saw them both together, and finally the man. I had just finished lunch and was sitting in the faculty room, a space of concrete basement with steam pipes overhead, and the dean of the Arts College and I were talking, he in the corner, I facing him with my back to the crowded room. At first there had been general noise among my colleagues, but, as he and I warmed to the theme, all began to listen. My thesis was that numbers rather than quality determined the status of a department, and, when the dean denied, I quoted a statement by a university official. "Who said that?" he asked. I answered, "Does it make any difference who said it?" He insisted that it did, that it was not the official point of view, and pressed me again to say who it was; for, as I found out afterwards, he thought he knew and wanted to nail his man publicly. At last I said, "Well, if you must know, it was the chancellor."

There was silence, not only dead but of death itself, and instant petrifaction. The face of the dean, and of others whom I could see, set in consternation, as if a moving film had been suddenly stopped. Then from behind me came a question: "Who told you that, Rice?" It was the voice of Avery. I turned and said, "I can't tell you. I was told in confidence." He said, "I have no recollection of having said any such thing." "You may not," I said, "but you said it. I have no reason to doubt the man who told me."

When I had spoken the room came to life again and then was empty of my colleagues, who left me alone with Avery. He said, "If you haven't anything to do, come over to my office." We left the emptied room, and as we passed some of my hushed fellows on the stair they looked at me with the expression one sees on the faces of visitors to the stockyards in Chicago at the passing of doomed cattle.

When we got to his office he said nothing more of the controverted point; he spoke instead of inconsequential things. But I knew what he was doing: he was telling me that my colleagues were fools to think him so mean; and he did more than that, he told me how they came to think that way. He told me a story. "My first teaching job," he said, "was in a high school, and the laziest pupil I had was the son of the president of the school board. He wanted to go to college and knew that if he flunked my course he couldn't. With the rest of the teachers he was safe; they wouldn't flunk him for fear of his old man, but I was new and he couldn't be sure what I would do. So, when it came to the exam he looked at the questions for a while and then asked to be excused. I let him go but I slipped out after him and followed, going quiet so he wouldn't hear, to the toilet. When I heard him close the inner door I tiptoed in and looked over the partition and saw him copying the answers out of the textbook. I didn't say anything, but when I graded the papers I gave him a zero." He paused, as I would often see him do, before he finished the story. "I had in my pocket at the time," he went on, and smiled, "a contract to teach somewhere else the next year."

He never, as long as I knew him, said, "This is what I believe and this not." The process was inductive and gauged to the reception of the pupil, for that was what I soon became. Every man carries around inside himself two pictures, patterns, ideas, one of the human being as he is, one as he ought to be. I was always getting mine mixed, Avery never, and by the time I knew him he had so long been guided by the is rather than the ought to be, that the is had almost disappeared. But a man has also his own personal is and ought to be, and here again we were different. Whatever of the is of humanity made him uncomfortable, he quietly ignored, or he became suddenly stubborn. He would not join any kind of organization in the town, nor pretend to like football, alumni meetings, "lap suppers,"—the common mode of entertainment in Lincoln—educational conferences; and professional piety froze his face stiff.

He never went to church, nor approved of zealous church people; but I remember one time when he used them brilliantly. He knew that a stand for is also a stand against, but that those you have been against have longer memories than those you have been for, and, if you are ever got, they will be the ones to get you; he was consequently most pleased when he was the means of bringing antagonists together in such a way as to escape the charge of partisanship while at the same time gaining some advantage for himself—a sort of hidden fee for his services. The zone of operations on this occasion was the football field, and the antagonists on the one side the football alumni, as was to be expected, while on the other were, of all people, the ministers of the town.

A delegation approached him one day to inform him of what he already knew but had hoped that they did not, that one of the coaches was a heavy drinker, "disgraceful" they said, and asked what he proposed to do about it. He replied, with wily calm, that he proposed to learn whether it was true. The football alumni, having meanwhile heard of the other delegation, sent one of their own, uttering threats, for the coach was good and also a favorite among them, his drinking companions. He gave them the same blank look, and answer. Then he sent for the coach and put to him the question that had been put to him, what was he going to do about it, and the coach, who was a decent fellow, promised to reform, and in a spectacular way. He would, he said, not only stop drinking but would even join the church and teach a Sunday-school class. This was more than Avery would have required of any penitent, but he took the gift and paid the preachers off, in their own coin, reminding them of the virtue of forgiveness. They went away shaking their heads, for they would have preferred punishment. The alumni applauded, and laughed, for they never supposed their coach intended to be so foolishly extreme. They would see to it that he did not again go onto the field tottering, and that restraint was enough to ask of any man.

But the coach had meant what he said. He joined the church, took a Sunday-school class and became a boys' hero, sat every Sunday in the same pew, and never touched a drop. The preacher of his church, pleased at the sudden increase in the number of young worshipers, became the coach's champion among his fellows and placated them; and he, as well as they, now became open admirers of Avery.

The next year, however, the coach began and continued to lose games, and wound up badly on the down side. (Avery once said to me that the perfect football team was the one that was winner of half the games, never more, and not less, than half. "I can sleep nights, then," he said.) This time the alumni demanded the head of their former darling, whose failure to win had now made him completely uncongenial. But this time, as before, the coach had champions; he might not win football games for the university but he was winning souls for Christ. When Avery told me how he had saved the coach's neck, "for the time being, at least," I asked what he would do next year, for the alumni were still thirsty. "I don't know," he said, "I guess I'll have to trust the Lord to help me out somehow," and laughed at the aptness of the prayer. The Lord did help: in the spring the coach suddenly discovered that he had tuberculosis and resigned.

The story of the coach and a hundred others, were told me in a bare room Avery had furnished—if two great chairs, a table, and a lamp can be called furnishings—on the top floor of his house. I came by special invitation, delivered in his drawling voice over the telephone. "What you doing tonight?" he would say. "Come on down," and I went and sat and listened. Occasionally I spoke, but usually to supply surmise or information toward completing the moment's speculation, for most of his talk was of things past, seldom pending. He never asked, "What would you do?"; often, "What would you have done?" but I knew this for what it was, merely the introduction to some unexpected turn. Once in a while, however, I had some bit of information that made a link in the tale, some small point that had worried him because, without it, the beginning was not one with the end. When I produced it, he laughed as he fitted it in as a child will laugh when the stubborn toy train at last moves. "So that was it," he would say, and sniff his fingers with delight.

One evening he said, "Some of these nights when I'm lying awake wondering how I'll get by next time"—and looked at me to see how I would take it. I took it unflinching. I was discovering something I had never known before, something that Methodism had never taught me: that a human act is a human being acting, and that what he is, colors, tones, even transmutes, what he does. But this was only part of a more important discovery, the discovery of a kind of human being new to me. Poets I had known, artists, dreamers, men who were what I wanted to be and could not, and I had known others, mean men, grubs, and despised them. Avery neither admired nor despised any one; hated, yes, a few intensely, but looked at the rest with an eye of a chemist.

I have never heard of a scholar who would not cease pursuing truth if he could catch a university presidency. Avery had been a good research chemist, but on election to the chancellorship he had walked out of his laboratory and never set foot in it again; nor would, except in the last outwitting of his enemies. But he had taken his method along.

This was what was new to me. A man was to him a group of elements that acted and reacted—a literal word in his mouth—in a known or at least knowable way. There must have been a time when he was learning, or was this a new kind of poet? In either case, by the time I knew him he had all the formulae. But they were not simple. Sometimes it took him as much as two hours to complete the statement, but in the end it was complete, everything accounted for, no intrusion of accident —action and reaction. That was why he was delighted when I fished the missing phial out of my pocket and added it to the mixture. But the formulae were not, for all their range, inclusive. Some people contrived to act queer and unpredictable in spite of data. There was an elusive unknown, abhorrent to a scientist. It was as if the manufacturer had sent him an impure ingredient. If he disliked the man, he wished him out of the way; if he liked him, he shook his head, and, using the known in him, did the best he could to counteract the unknown.

When he telephoned me at night, it promised pleasant hours; but if he sent a messenger to my office, it usually meant trouble. I could always tell as I stood on his threshold. If he said, "Come in, Rice," and pointed to a chair, I could breathe, but when he closed the door behind me, my throat tightened. Life in a state university cannot be greatly different from living in a jungle.

One day a message came with an added note of emergency: would I come, please, and at once. This time I knew the door would close behind me, but even that knowledge was hardly preparation for the look of heavy anger on his face as he banged the door shut and burst out at me, "What's this I hear about you now? What do you mean by doing such a thing?" I answered, "What? What have I been doing?" for a quick cast of memory hauled up no clue. "What do you mean by accusing so-and-so of bribery?" he almost shouted, naming one of the deans. "When?" I replied. "This morning," he said, "after faculty meeting." Then I knew what he meant and I laughed. "It's no laughing matter," he said, looking straight at me. "Wait till you hear what I said," and I told him what it was. The dean had proposed that an honorary degree be conferred upon a man who was so widely respected that, when he was nominated, many wondered by what oversight the gesture had not been made before. There was consequently no sluggish approval nor the usual muttering under breath of caustic questions. As we crowded out of the meeting I found myself beside the nominator, with whom I was on terms of amiable hostility, for I liked the man but not his job, and said, "Well, what did you get out of it?" whereupon he, instead of taking it as it was meant, a sort of inverted compliment, grew furious and said, "You go too far, young man."

When I finished my story, Avery said, "Very funny, but not as funny as you thought," and when I looked a question, "You see, Rice, he did get something out of it," and when I gaped, added, "A little matter of a couple of scholarships for his college. That's all," and at last he laughed, but at, not with me. Then, when he had his fill of my discomfiture, he said, "Why don't you keep your mouth shut, Rice? If you would just keep it shut for, say, six months or a year, I could raise your salary. You know I can't do it now, the way you talk. Of course, folks would say, 'Wonder what's the matter with Rice? Don't hear anything from him any more,' but what would you care? You could buy yourself a car and take your family out in the country on Sundays and you could live in a better house." I said nothing and we were both silent for a while. Then he dismissed it with, "Well, think about it, anyway," and with an apology, "I just thought I'd mention it. You know, when a man has been a college head for ten years, he is either a martinet or a grandmother." This time we both smiled, for we knew he was neither.

He was called both. Every time new regents were to be elected candidates were put up on a one-plank platform, to get rid of Avery, because he was too high-handed or because he was not enough, and every time at least one was elected. Then, when he came roaring down to Lincoln to carry out the will of the people, faculty and town waited, in hope or fear. The outcome was always the same. While the new regent was making investigations of his own, that is, listening to gossip —and there is no place like a university town for that—Avery was silent. He too was waiting, until his executioners should begin to get cross-current reports of what was wrong. When that had happened, and there was complete confusion, his first move was to confirm what the investigator now knew, that running a university was not a simple act. The rest was easy. Gratitude followed hostility, and on its heels admiration. One year the new regent looked like a real danger, for he was a graduate of an Eastern college and sought advice, not from known politicians, but from cultivated gentlemen on the faculty and in the town—his own sort. This was something new; but the end was not. When about three months had passed, I met Avery on the campus one morning and said, "How's it going with the new regent?" He smiled sweetly and said, "Well, Rice, I won't say I've got him in my pocket. He's not an ideal regent," and I laughed for I knew that he meant "not yet." He had said once, when we were talking about regents, "Now you know, Rice, the ideal regent—don't get 'em very often—is the one that sleeps all during the meeting, until it comes time to vote. Then he wakes up and says, 'What does the chancellor recommend?' "

The regents were the titular governing body of the university elected by popular vote from five districts in the state. They served without pay, except travel expenses, and most of them without qualification. They were, as trustees everywhere, part of the hidden government of America, there to see to it that things did not get out of line. At one time two were bankers, one a football alumnus, and two businessmen; that was the usual proportion. The businessmen were the least circumspect in their behavior. One of them suddenly left town in anticipation of the sheriff. When he was gone Avery told me about him, how, under threat, he had forced a member of the staff to mortgage his home and lend, that is, give, him the money; of other deals; and how at last he had come to him and demanded a thousand dollars. "I didn't elect him, you know," was his reply when I was speechless, and he went on to expose the natures of other regents, one a coxcomb banker from Omaha, another who padded his expense accounts by getting a member of the faculty who "owned" him to drive him—at my colleague's expense—on journeys for which the university paid. When he was speaking of another who was widely distrusted, I asked, "Why is he such a puritan? He doesn't look like one," for his face was the face of a drunkard. "Oh well, Rice, you know how it is. When he was young he was a hell-raiser, but when his sons were growing up he got afraid that they would be like him, so he reformed." "What happened to the sons?" I asked. He laughed and said, "They turned out just like their old man."

Who, or what, actually governed the university, I never knew for sure. Avery often disclosed the strings that made this or that regent jump, but whether they all came together in one hand, or whose, he did not say, perhaps because he always talked with me of people whom we both knew, or he may himself not have known. "My job is," he said, "to keep them off my neck—and yours." But, for that matter, who governs Harvard? It may be, for all I know, someone whose office is two flights up on a back alley.

The other, biennial, threat came from the legislature, for not only was the appropriation to be got through somehow, but also Avery, as well as the university, was liable to investigation. Usually it happened with the committee as with the new regent, but one year its members were violent and refused to consult him. Rather, they chose to begin with the assumption that he was not money-honest. They could not have made a greater mistake, for he was scrupulous, so careful that he even stocked his own stamps for his personal letters, never using those bought by the university. The committee looked and of course found nothing, and they were not nice in their methods. When they had been going on several days, I said to him, "So, I understand you are being investigated." "Yes, Rice," he said, "I am," and then he waited a moment and went on. "You and I could tell them where to look, couldn't we?"

Another, and perpetual, annoyance was the regent who was "owned" by some member of the faculty or administration. "He's a Buck regent," or "Didn't you know? He's Sealock's," and so in turn through a list of four or five, the full number of the board, every one of whom was owned by someone or was held in joint ownership. Avery's method was to set them against one another and thereby cancel out their claims, but sometimes this failed; the regent remained faithful until his owner got what he wanted.

Avery made the best of it, and sometimes his best was brilliant. He was not vindictive nor malevolent. He simply did not propose to allow such things to be done, and set about quietly toward their undoing. The head of one department, whom I shall call Dr. Lend, learned too late that owning a regent might prove unprofitable in the long run, and the run in his case was quite long, and disastrous in proportion to its length.

On every faculty there are members who want some position that will entitle them to be called by a name other than professor. "Dean" is the favorite title, but anything will do, just so it carries distinction. Dr. Lend's regent persuaded the board to elect him to "an administrative position," duties and title unspecified. After considerable search Dr. Lend chose for his title "Provost," and then set about to learn what the duties of a provost were. He asked me, after my first six months, what I thought a provost should do, but I was as ignorant as he. I did, however, suggest that in one instance his explorations were leading him into potential danger, with more of prophecy in me than either of us knew. I found him making a calculation of costs of instruction, by which it appeared that a student in Greek came to about twenty-five dollars while one in education cost less than two dollars. "You'd better be careful," I said; "if a committee from the legislature sees your figures, we both may be out of jobs," for he still kept one Greek class while I had the rest as well as some Latin. "Can you hope to prove to a legislator that Greek is twelve times as valuable as education?" For the one time in our association he took my advice and kept the figures secret.

He also asked Avery from time to time what he thought a provost should be doing, but Avery, knowing it would be a long game, was slow in applying his method. His first offering was small and harmless. He asked Dr. Lend to check the university clocks to see whether they synchronized. The provost found to his delight that they did not, but, since it took a short time to get them together, he was soon back for more suggestions. The next road was longer. Would Dr. Lend like to make a comparative study of grades? He would, and did, with startling results. Conspicuous was a class of more than fifty members in educational measurements whose average grade was about ninety. Another was an average of more than ninety-five among two hundred or more students, taught by Dr. Fling, who was proud to have spent his life studying a single day in the French Revolution, and came in for paragraphs of loving reference in Willa Cather's One of Ours. When Dr. Fling saw the figures he snorted, "That only shows that

I am a better teacher than the rest of you," but he did not forget the implied criticism; nor did others, for there were other exposures.

With this beginning Avery went on to suggest that the provost revise the catalogue, with the special task of cutting down the length of description of some of the courses. Since the longer the description the slimmer the content, disaffection spread, for by this time whatever affection had been, never very much, was dry as tinder.

Then Avery made his first explosive mixture of chemicals: he turned over to the provost the job of making up the salary budget for the whole university. Dr. Lend now took the opportunity to pay off scores and reward friends, until the university was in a state of rebellion and Avery was obliged to resume the making of the budget.

One might have supposed that the provost would see what was happening and grow wary; but no. Athletics, Avery said, needed reforming. Would the provost undertake that? Dr. Lend moved in on the athletic department, drew the university out of the Missouri conference, in order to please the Omaha alumni by having a game in their town, and, when that proved a fiasco, began to hear demands for his head. Once again Avery rescued him.

Dr. Lend grew restless with nothing to do, and was therefore glad to become censor of university publications, which included the annual edited by the students. By this time the provost was getting nervous, for the alumni were not satisfied to have let him escape, and he now used the device, itself a sign of panic, of courting the favor of the students. "I trust you boys," he said, "not to print anything that you shouldn't. Don't bother to show me. I know I can trust you. Besides I'm not very well." When the annual was published anger flared throughout the state, for some of the pictures were, by any standard, scandalous. There were threats of horsewhippings by fathers and brothers and loud demands to know who was responsible. Then the regents took it up; they proposed to abolish the job of provost, and some of them wanted to abolish the provost along with it, and Dr. Lend's one regent was helpless.

When the clamor was at its height, Avery stepped in and, before faculty, who were also demanding blood, and regents, plead for clemency. "Dr. Lend," he said, "is a sick man," which was certainly true now, for he had at last realized whom he had to thank for his predicament. But that was not the worst of it: he also had to thank Avery for getting him out of it. He came limping back to the department, cursing, and hoping no one would know how much it cost to teach a student Greek.

In the midst of action Avery spoke never more than a sentence or two, but when it was over he would retrace every step, account for every link, until the whole story was told. Dr. Lend died shortly after his last adventure, and Avery spent many hours pulling him apart and putting him together again while I sat and listened. There was no trace of malice in the account; it was as if he had been a doctor reporting an interesting case. He did not even say, "Men ought not to be like that." There was no indignation, no expressed wish to have them otherwise.

He was consistently the scientist, however, the observer of humanity with a measuring eye, in that he did not include himself in the chemical process. Scientists, I have observed, seldom apply their doctrines to themselves, herein being somewhat like preachers. One of my colleagues was in the habit of saying that "thinking was nothing but the brain giving off CO_2." I said I was quite ready to believe that of some kinds of thinking, and he was offended. Psychologists in particular, faced with the necessity of turning either themselves or others inside out, are grateful for the presence of others, as one of my humanist colleagues was grateful to the Greek dramatists for leaving behind so many examples of syntax. Man the machine, or man the bottle of chemicals—this was their dogma, when applied to others.

One however, a former professor of biology, was consistent. He had retired from teaching in order, as he said, to carry on his researches in private, and presently his secretary sued him for breach of promise. He vehemently defended himself and plead with the jury to let him off, on the ground that he was merely a machine, that every act was predetermined, that there was no such thing as the will, that whatever he had done he had done because he couldn't help it. The jury found for the secretary, presumably on the same ground. His retirement had been due in part to this propensity of his, but it was about the only thing short of insanity that could compel retirement, and even insanity was not immediately enough. In one year three members of the faculty were sent to the state asylum for the insane. One of my friends in town asked me, "How do you know up at the university that the time has come to put a professor away?"

Alexander Meiklejohn used to say that the difference between a freshman and a sophomore was that the freshman expected something to happen; not at Nebraska, not at the end of six weeks. They came eager enough, and intelligent, but they also came without the wit to defeat the system, of which their high schools had made them a part. Wherever the university reached down into the schools, it blighted them, and stunted their students, the best native intelligence I have ever seen. I do not know other western states so well, but I know that, if the intelligence of Nebraska students had been trained to its best, they could easily have made over America.

They had in them, many of them and some of the faculty, the toughness that had created the West, the spirit of the second great migration, and being tough and intelligent and ignorant, they, more than any students in America, would have known the meaning of an education in and for democracy. But they got neither. The curriculum was like a cafeteria table, except in the proportion of unpalatable dishes. One thing was as good as another; that was what they were told. They found out for themselves that one thing was no better than another. When they realized that the university was not superior to high school, but in some respects inferior, they turned away to things which they could do and from which they could learn, extracurricular activities (the word is never used of matters curricular).

With their intelligence thus neutralized, they became culture beds of a virus that had been in the blood of their fathers and grandfathers, but had lain dormant as long as they had to create and re-create their life. Lincoln and the university, both themselves virulent, brought out the deep infection. The disease was the cult of respectability.

The most obvious aspect was the social life of the university, that is, fraternity life, for there was no other. In no servant class, not even the Butlers' Ball in New York, has there ever been such ruthless snobbery. No one could tell for sure how a boy or girl got elected, but, once in, the line was drawn and stayed down for life. The Lincoln *Journal* kept a file of student names, and the society editor might scout birth and breeding, but the Greek letters had better be there.

The town was the same. Emily Post was their bible. When *Main Street* was published, they read it with the delight of self-recognition, but that was all they recognized. When I suggested that there was another meaning, they silenced me and banned its mention in my presence.

Middletown might have been written of Lincoln, and Lincoln would have been proud, as Middletown was. The houses were respectable, by those who respected such houses. Many of them were "Tudor-bethan," a name coined by the "realtor" Harvey Rathbone to describe his curiosities. Lincoln was an imitation of a city, the city of Omaha, as Omaha was of Chicago, and Chicago of New York; and Lincolnians were imitation city-men.

Before I crossed the Mississippi, which I swore, the Lord forgiving, I would never cross again but once, I had been reading *The New Republic* and *The Nation* and thought I was going to the home of liberalism. I never found it. The revolt of the West, led first by Bryan and in the time of my story by the Nonpartisan League, was nothing but opportunism. When La Follette was running for President, he was about to carry the state by at least thirty thousand; but it rained, and the crop was good, and the vote was Republican. At the beginning of the campaign eight of us, all members of the faculty, met one night to hear a paper on the candidates; when it had been read and we had talked, we took a straw vote and seven were for La Follette. But when the election came, after the rain, I was the only one to stay by my choice; and, as I soon learned, at my peril. One of the men who was present that night came to me and said that there was a rumor going round that I had voted for La Follette. He would not ask me whether it was true, but, if I would just keep quiet, he and others would deny it. That was the liberalism of my Midwest.

In any society the highest class has no aspirations. I had known that in South Carolina, and in England, where the aristocracy, having arrived at the top, had put aside all idea of improvement, content to remain as they were. Only one other class, the lowest, was so content, while all in between were concerned with improvement. These, the middle classes, and there are about three, had emerged dominant in the nineteenth century and had taken as their own invention the idea of progress, words to be heard in their churches—Methodist, Baptist, and, more faintly, Presbyterian, for Calvinism was a logical block, while the Unitarian creed had progress as an article of faith. (I am using the word "class" in the Greek sense of economic; professors of the newest science would naturally require something like socio-politico-economico-.) Progress meant climbing, becoming like the class immediately above. This too I had seen before, but it was here that Nebraska was a puzzle. In the South the upper middle class, enriched by the sale of sheets and pillowcases, tobacco, patent medicines, and Coca-Cola, had set about, without complete success, to become the aristocracy, and had taken the remains of the landed, now landless or land-poor, aristocracy for model. This gave a sort of imitation grace to their living.

But in Nebraska the corresponding class had little or no grace, even imitative. How was I to account for this?

The explanation, here offered with apology, to go some way toward avoiding the inevitable charge of snobbery, lay, I think, in the nature of the pioneer in the West. He was lower- or, at best, middle-middle-class, and the thing that part of him wanted to be was upper-middle-class; but only part—there was another part, which had braced him to face without cringing the rigors of his new life, the remainder of eighteenth-century individualism that, in its first step toward freedom, wanted isolation, both spiritual and physical. The West promised this, and kept the promise; but after a while security and comfort came, and the spirit of the pioneer, having nothing more to do, weakened and was lost in the stream of imitation, what I have called the cult of respectability. It was here, then, that the new aristocracy of the South and the new aristocracy of the West were different: they had imitated different classes. In the South the middle class has become aristocratic, in their fashion; in the West the aristocracy was middle-class, and there remained, without aspiration.

Not all Nebraskans were infected. In some the pioneer remained alive, and they despised the university, knowing that it too was part of the cult of respectability—an imitation university. Some rebelled and, as soon as they could, hurried away, to be buried in time in the cities of the East; others, a few these, remained and were defeated.

Hartley Alexander, philosopher and poet, was one. He had been born and reared in Nebraska, son of a horse trader, and hater of horse trading all his days. In his search for something better he had spent four years in the university, and found it, in one man—there is always at least one man in every university—a Doctor Wolfe, whom I never knew except through his students, for he had died some years before. (But that was test enough; is, in fact, the final test of a teacher. The real teacher is the real aristocrat; his pedigree stretches back to the beginning of time.) Hartley had gone away and become a learned man, and then, returning, found at the head of his university another horse trader.

He could never see Avery any other way, while to Avery he was a wayward, and therefore dangerous, chemical mixture. When I knew them, all communication had long broken down. Hartley gave, and Avery felt, contempt. The mention of either name aroused in the other deep and violent anger, and I soon learned to keep my boat out of those waters. Avery saw a future no different from the present—intolerable affront to a dreamer.

Whenever I talked with Avery I was careful to stay out of the future. (For that matter, when I talked with any university official, for Avery had chosen them with care. The dean of the Arts College, Herman G. James, now at last president of a college in Ohio, said it, when I was proposing some change, "But Rice, we can't afford to be that much better than the rest of the country.") Hartley lived in the future, rather in two futures, his own, that would never be, and another that might, if the present had its way, and this he hated as intensely as if it had already arrived. Here I felt more at home with him, and we damned heartily together. One of the pleasures of belonging to the human race is that you do belong; you are not alone; there is somebody who thinks the way you do. This was my pleasure in knowing Hartley.

His students and mine were often the same, and, because he and I sometimes said the same things, I was accused of stealing his ideas, and it was useless for me to plead coincidence for his students thought him a saint. Once it was completely useless, and yet it was pure coincidence, for he and I had never talked about this particular thing. I said at nine o'clock one morning that every American baby should be given a B.A. degree at birth, that those weighing ten pounds or over should get a *summa cum laude*, the eight-pounders *magna*, and all the rest plain *cum laude*. I do not tell this because it was brilliant—others, as I afterwards discovered, had said the same thing—but Hartley's addition was. That afternoon a student said to me, "You've been stealing again," and told me that at eleven o'clock that morning Hartley had said it word for word, with, however, one more class, and this was the touch: that all babies of six pounds and under should be given teachers' certificates.

It was in Hartley's home that I became a conspirator. There were four of us who met at night in a carefully shaded room, for we knew that if we were discovered before the plot matured, none of us would be safe. All of us, except possibly one, the brother of the editor of the Lincoln *Journal*, were immediately vulnerable, Hartley because of his known recalcitrance, another who was a graduate of Cambridge and therefore as suspect as I, and I knew that not even Avery's kindly feelings would remain kindly if he should find us out. The purpose of the conspiracy was to raise faculty salaries to somewhere near living level. The reason we met in the dark of the night was that the regents regarded the faculty as hired help, who should be grateful to them for such living as we had and would quickly punish us if we questioned their benevolence.

Our conspiracy was successful, but it was not forgotten that Hartley had been ringleader and within a few years he was gone from the university, forced out by a trick. He had been "consulted"—that was the word used—by a regent who came, he said, to talk frankly and ask for frank answers about the state of the university. At the end of a pleasant conversation with the emissary Hartley was requested to write out the substance of his recommendations. He, who was without guile and could not even recognize it in others, did as he was bid, only to learn that his letter was presented to the board as an ultimatum.

He left the university, at the end of eighteen years, a native son whose love could not be questioned; and when he was gone, it was as if he had never been. I knew that I too would be going soon.

Before the chance came Avery got ill and retired. But, as a last gesture, he played his last hand with outrageous skill. The hounds were on his heels, even before his illness, but with its coming they were closing in, and his enemies were already enjoying the prospective kill. Then he moved, and left them speechless. He offered his resignation to the board, to take effect two years thereafter, and at the same time let it be understood that he would like to return as professor to his laboratory, at a salary which he would leave to the generosity of the board. They, grateful at getting out of a tight spot, for the clamor for Avery's removal was still in their ears, granted his request, in full; and he repaid them shortly afterwards by asking for an indefinite leave of absence.

When the friends of the university had recovered from this stroke, they began to look for a successor, and it was then that I learned that, in my seven years, I had learned almost nothing of the ways by which the university was controlled. The light came one evening in a hotel room, where I was drinking Red Cloud liquor with a lawyer from that town and a reporter of the Omaha *Herald*. As the raw stuff went round—it was still prohibition—we grew hopeful of a better day, and began to cast about for someone to take Avery's place. The reporter named Meiklejohn, who had recently been dismissed from Amherst for having ideas about education. "Who's he?" the lawyer asked, and we told him. "Well," he said, "who's the man to see?" and the reporter named a man of whom I had never heard, a wealthy contractor. "If he says O.K. it's O.K.," he said. "Then it ought to be easy," the lawyer said. "How can we fix him?" "Fix him?" the reporter exclaimed, coming down hard on him; "Fix him? Hell, he's a fixer himself."

We gave up. We were, as well as the university, fixed, for as acting chancellor the regents had already appointed the dean of the school of agriculture. "Yep," the reporter said, "and he'll probably get the job." The lawyer was incensed, for by that time the liquor had him in love with education. "That man? My God, how can he be head of a university? He sharpens plows."

With Hartley gone, and Avery, and the new plow working diligently, plowing under the good there remained, I was ready to take, and took, the first offer that came, from the New Jersey College for Women.

Sam Avery had never talked about himself. He was the catalyst; he made things happen to others while nothing happened to him. But when I went to see him for the last time he had been in the hands of the doctors for some three months, and he talked about nothing but himself. Not sniffing now, his hands lying along the arms of the chair, lifeless, or at moments taut with fear, he gave me a clinical report, what this doctor had said, what that, in endless detail and reiteration. I tried to draw him down some of the old trails; it was useless. He did not listen to me; he was listening to the doctors. I tried another road. It was completely useless. He did not even look at me; he was looking into the near future, seeing something he had never seen before: the crazy chemistry of death.

CHAPTER IX

Rollins Was Holt

I HAD HEARD AND READ SOMETHING OF ROLLINS COLLEGE, ALL OF IT A little questionable, and had seen pictures in the rotogravures, one in particular that invited speculation, of Corra Harris surrounded by carefree students. This, the caption said, was the class in "Evil," the only one of its kind in the world, a statement that was easy of acceptance. Also from time to time I came across references to another innovation, the Professorship of Books, the only one in the world. I would have the fortune to know the Professor of Books and learn new uses to which books could be put, and sit by the side of the prospective Professor of Fishing and Hunting on a dock at Winter Park while he fed speckled perch from his bait bucket; he caught none, for he used a deep-sea rod with a forty-pound test line, whereas the only way to catch those tricky bait stealers was to angle for them with a feather-weight rod; within a few minutes the perch were practically sitting on top of the water, waiting for the next cast. Corra Harris I never saw—the class had met only once, to have the picture taken—but I was willing to believe of her that she knew no evil. But these pleasantries waited in the future; meanwhile I made two other experiments.

The first was in a kind of laboratory new to me, a dispensary of information. The New Jersey College for Women had been founded by an energetic butter-and-egg woman, literally, for she had taken over her deceased husband's business and made a small fortune before becoming dean; and remained at that level, for the pill doctors were too many, and too much, for the few teachers—there are always a few, in every college—who were interested in education. I learned one thing there, however; I learned, from the dean, that some colleges are founded out of hatred or contempt for professors. She took me back to that day when her professor of English had returned her theme penciled with disdain. It was as if she had just come out of the room, met me, and poured out her scorn of him and his kind, forgetting for the moment, or not caring, that I too was one. But I did not learn my lesson well enough, as I should have reason to recall when I went to Rollins, and also after.

My second experiment was made partly through accident, chance curiosity as to the significance of some marginal manuscript notes in a copy of an eighteenth-century book, and partly through avoidance of an obligation to write a doctoral dissertation and lift myself into decent professional standing. At any rate, for whatever reason or unreason, I was sent to England on a Guggenheim Fellowship in 1929 and there made my only experiment in research. For fifteen months I was a detective, and liked it. For the most part it was drudgery, and I remembered Paul Shorey's quotation from a Chicago paper, "The detective worked hard all day and got nothing but tired," but there were moments of discovery—moments in which, behind the immediate discovery, was another: that I was living in another century, and my own. Jonathan Swift was my author and Swift was one half of the eighteenth century—Doctor Johnson was the other—and Swift was half, or more than half, of me. The trouble was, that I was both of them—minimum editions—and they were enemies.

Research is the report of what one has found out rather than of what one knows. The area of exploration is outside oneself, and, if not already dead, must be deadened; for, just as the herbalist cannot recognize a living specimen but must have it first pressed and dried, so the psychologist, who might, of all the scientists, report what he knows inside himself, prepares his specimen by expressing life. I knew, at the end of my stay in England, that, whatever I should do, I could not spend my life apart from life.

Conviction came to me on top of the bus on which I rode from Hampstead Heath to Bloomsbury. I found myself making notes, not on Swift, but on plays I should like to write, paragraphs in search of a book, and stray sentences of recollection.

It is a long and costly process, discovering what one must do by discovering what one must not do. In my last year as an Oxford undergraduate I knew I would never be a lawyer, and when a letter came offering me a place in Webb School, my answer was ready. That was in 1914. The same thing happened in 1930. I had gone to England the year before in doubt as to whether I should ever teach again, but when a letter came from Hamilton Holt, asking whether I should be interested in Rollins College, the answer again was ready. I had gone and left my girl, but when she crooked her finger, I came running.

I first saw Holt in the railway station of Stoke Poges, where we had arranged to meet; but I did not see him at first. I walked through the station looking for him and out beyond, passing on my way a man whose head seemed familiar, and, as one will search in memory and find a likeness, I found myself saying, "That man has a head shaped exactly like Sawney Webb's." I came back into the station and he rose and asked my name.

His eyes were not like Sawney's; they were blue and deeper set, and more friendly; but his mouth was hard-cut. Here was a puzzle, the eyes saying one thing, the mouth denying. His speech gave no clue; it was dry and very Yankee; but the words were gracious, and, if one came armed, disarming. It was always so, throughout the three years I knew him, except at the end, when eyes and mouth and speech at last were like.

I arrived in Winter Park in the latter half of September in 1930.

I had almost forgotten how hot and muggy that climate could be, and, as it had been growing hotter as I drove down, by the time I climbed out and went into the administration building I looked and felt like a tramp. I was received like one, by Holt's secretary, who let me understand that something better was expected of professors. Her manner was rigidly correct; it was the tone of her voice that told me. But I did not hear. I was glad to be there, and forgot what I had learned on my first boat trip, that, if you want to know what the captain is like, the manners of the cabin boy will tell you.

As I came away from the anteroom of Holt's office—I had not seen him; his secretary said he was out—I noticed on the next door a sign in large letters which read "Publicity Office." I thought, "Well, at least there is frankness here," and thought no more, at the time.

A few days later came the first ominous notes—there would be many —without invitation, for I had learned that the way to find out was to ask no questions. There was, "Rollins is Holt and Holt is Rollins," spoken in the impersonal tone of common use, as one says "Good morning." Well at least, I reflected, it would not be butter-and-egg. Then, while I was standing at the library desk, a man passed and the assistant said to me, "There's a 'G.P.' for you," and I went homeward wondering what a "G.P." might be. In the night it came to me, what it must be, "Great Personality," for Holt had used those words. This was pretty bad, worse than "Rollins is Holt"; but I was wrong. The radio, a college outlet, corrected me. The voice said, "I should like to introduce to our radio audience, friends of the college, our newest Golden Personality," and I heard my name.

I was not alone in honor, however; I soon knew that every member of the faculty was by definition a "G.P.," spoken with awe or derision. The Orlando paper solemnly printed the list, and pictures, of the latest Golden Personalities. (In my last year, when Holt had discovered the meaning of hydra, and had dismissed another teacher and then another, the Golden Personalities came in for caustic reference in this paper. A reporter, no friend to the college, brought a story in late at night when the watchdogs were gone or asleep, and wrote for it the headline, "Rollins Goes Off Gold Standard.")

The third warning came from Holt's secretary, within the first few weeks. The name of a colleague was mentioned and she drew me into a corner and breathed, "He is an unbeliever." Holt had said to me in England, after a long conversation in which, if he had been any judge of men, he had full opportunity to discover that I was not the kind of man he wanted, "I think it's about time I had a liberal on my faculty. I haven't got one now." My unbeliever colleague was on the faculty at the time. In one of the many articles written about the college by Holt I found the statement, "I wouldn't have an agnostic on my faculty." There was something wrong here.

The students, about four hundred of them, had been drawn from all over the country, by promises. Rollins was, publicity said, the latest thing in education, conducted under the "conference plan," that was, classes meeting for two hours. The teachers, also drawn by promises, would have freedom to teach as they pleased. But again there was something wrong. The students complained that most of the teachers were no better than their high-school instructors, and that two hours with bores was at least an hour too much. The teachers had grounds for complaint. Two hours on end with students, most of them there for a good time—had they not been promised freedom?—was a drudge, and when Holt thought of "putting Socrates on the eight-hour day" they brooded over the uncomplimentary end of the phrase. Besides, the curriculum might have been copied from Amherst. When I met my first classes, I was amazed to find so many taking Latin and Greek, until I learned that, not having had either in high school, one of these languages was required for graduation. This was not the latest thing in education; it was about the oldest.

There was another confusion that began to appear in November. Until then the houses along Interlaken, the town's Park Avenue, had remained closed, but now one over-length Lincoln and another rolled along at a solicitous pace, with their clear windows, like the windows of a hearse, giving one a full view of untroubled calm within, white hair and white blank faces. How, I reflected, was a liberal college to live in the midst of this? I would soon find out.

Along the same avenue sat all the churches of the town, except one, the Catholic, and at one end of it there would be built within two years a more pretentious Rollins Chapel. These churches soon gave me part of the answer which the chapel would in time complete.

About the middle of my first year noisy announcement was made of a coming religious conference. Years of sitting in hostile silence on hard pews had, I knew, unfitted me to take part in such an enterprise, which I supposed was intended to promote the cause of religion rather than publicity—such was my innocence—and I therefore planned to stay away. The day before the first meeting, however, one of my colleagues asked me if I would come to a reception being given for the invited conferees, among them Dr. Everett Clinchy, secretary of the Committee of Jews and Christians; Dr. Henry Bradley, who had preceded my father at St. Louis and subsequently been driven out of the Methodist and into the Congregational Church by Bishop Warren Candler; Rabbi Lazeron of Baltimore; Rabbi Newman of Chicago; and several others. I said I would, and did, but when I got there it was not a reception but a meeting to decide on the agenda of the conference. When I discovered this I got up to leave but my colleague and some of the guests insisted that I stay, perhaps I might make some suggestions. I made none, and would have escaped trouble, if toward the end someone had not turned to me and put the direct question. "I have only one suggestion," I said, "and that is that you make doubt respectable." At that both Rabbis immediately invited me to sit at the conference table, and others, Clinchy among them; but, with some regard to decency, I refused. Would I then ask questions from the floor? I made the foolish promise.

The first public meeting was given over to the usual felicitations; the second got down to business and died at the end of the hour. The subject was "The Place of the Church in the Modern World" and it began to look as if the title was intended to be ironic. At that point I kept my promise. I said, "I live in Winter Park, and I should like to ask a question that has to do with the church in Winter Park, and with those of us who live here." By the time I came to the end of my sentence, white heads, about two-thirds of the audience, began to mount and turn toward me. "But before I ask my question," I went on, "I should like to explain the method of thinking that requires the question to be put in this particular way. It could be asked in other ways, but by the method I am going to use, in thinking about anything, I try to see what everything else would be like if that thing were absent. It is only a method, nothing more. I should like that to be understood, and also just what the method is. Is it clear, what the method is?" Apparently it was. "Now," I said, "I am ready to put my question. Here it is: if I should come along Interlaken Avenue tomorrow, Sunday, morning, and, instead of the churches, I should find green grass growing, what difference would it make, and to whom?" Two preachers leapt to their feet. One said that the Boy Scouts met in the basement of his church; the other, a visitor from Cleveland, gave a long indignant account of how his church had provided an indigent with enough money to buy a ticket to the West Coast. . . . When they had sat down, I said, "So far as I know there is no one in Winter Park in immediate need of deportation to the West. Now that I understand to whom it would make a difference, I should like to hear an answer to the first part of my question."

I never got it, in words, but the answer was plain. Within three years, using piety as a spearhead, these white-haired frightened people had moved into Rollins College and thereafter barred all heretical questions. A rich woman from Boston gave money for a chapel, had it designed by Ralph Adams Cram, and placed a bronze plaque at the entrance, which said that it was erected to the glory of God—this in small letters—and to the memory of—in huge letters—somebody Knowles. There was the answer.

What was the college? Was that self-worship too? Holt had come to Rollins some years before on the invitation of Irving Bacheller, a member of its board of trustees. The college was dead but unburied, for somehow the deader an institution is, the more certain it is of continued existence. The presidency was vacant and Holt needed something to do; *The Independent*—he had married into the editorship—had been merged with another periodical, and the League of Nations, for which he had afterwards lectured, was no longer profitable. He had come out of Yale dissatisfied—often said, "I never learned anything at Yale," a statement that had more than the one meaning he gave to it—had tried Columbia and found it no different; he was like thousands of other college graduates, and like some in that he was resentful. Rollins gave him his chance.

Some one, Emerson I think, said that every institution was the lengthened shadow of a man. He might as well have said, a cloak to wear, a decoration, to catch the eye and keep it from the wearer; bootstraps, for increasing one's height; a screen to hide the thing he was; a dream, and a hope, dim, but still hope—hope for his own salvation. Rollins was all of these, and Rollins was Holt and Holt was Rollins.

I sometimes longed for Avery's hard clear ruthless mind, wished that he might be there to separate for me the chemicals, put them in test tubes for me to see. I found them in time, most of them I think; Avery would have done the job quickly, pointed to the row of test tubes and said, "There's your man." But even so something would have been left over, something that defied inclusion, a stray chemical not to be found in Avery's list. Holt was a mixture of many things; Holt was also a very lovable man.

He was driven in unpredictable turn by ambition, sentimentality, charity, Yankee shrewdness, pride, humility, and childlike wonder;

but somewhere nearby was always ambition. He wanted to be a success—Sawney Webb again—having come out of Yale, if it can be said that anyone ever comes out of Yale, in the success days, success as ponderable as a load of bricks (a member of the class of '94—his—came to the twenty-fifth reunion in a Packard, or else stayed away) or, if not ponderable, success certainly measurable. A man may be an autobiographer in one sentence. Holt was, in more than one sentence, but the most complete was spoken at the height of the uproar during my last year, when the issue was, for him, still in doubt. "Everything I have ever done," he said, "has been a failure. I was a failure at Yale and at Columbia; *The Independent* was a failure"—Henry Ward Beecher had also once been editor—"then I campaigned for the League of Nations, and that was a failure; now it is Rollins"—and, pausing, he waited for expostulation, and got it. But he was not sure. His face, for once, was grim while he was being called a great man.

Doctor Johnson said of a contemporary, "He would be a great man if he but knew how to go about it." Holt also did not know how. Greatness is in truth seeking, never truth making, and Holt was a journalist. He believed, and practice had beguiled him, that if he said a thing three times and nobody called him a liar, he had spoken truth. Even facts could be twisted, if one was expert. This came out in an amusing and harmless way in a controversy over the Professorship of Books, the only one in the world. A small librarian lady wrote to say that she had been Professor of Books in her Midwest college for thirty years. That was for the moment a stumper but Holt came back with the statement that, anyway, his was the first Emersonian Professor of Books. Like master like man, the Professor of Books was himself a truth maker. He had once been a salesman for Rand-McNally, and more recently, just before coming to Rollins, advance agent for Billy Sunday, and therefore as well prepared as any journalist. He had, he said, once been a printer and could not "keep his fingers out of ink," and had therefore established the *Angel Alley Press*, whose name was taken from an adopted printer ancestor of the eighteenth century. There was no press; but it had been said, and no one contradicted, and so there was.

I tried to see Holt with Avery's eyes; it was useless. Here was perpetual change, everything moving in some sort of unintelligible relation to everything else. It was not that he was unprincipled; he was too principled. No human being could keep so many principles at peace with one another. When he had dismissed me, someone asked him, "How can you do that?" His answer was, "Sometimes you have to throw away your principles and do the right thing." . . . Freedom of speech offended the white heads of Winter Park, and it was from white heads, nodding toward the grave, that he must get gifts of propitiation. Using freedom of speech, I said that I thought fraternities had no place in the college. He heard me courteously and appointed me chairman of a committee to state the case against them, and at the same time continued to invite new chapters. (One of my colleagues warned me earlier that, if I would be secure, I must stand in with the fraternities and sororities, particularly sororities, and had named those on which he himself could count.) . . . Freedom of worship did not also mean freedom not to worship, if the chapel was empty of students on a warm day that invited to the beach. . . . Freedom of action was all very well if it meant restraint, which it did not. There was the inevitable baby, concealed by the expectant mother until concealment was no longer possible. Holt called her sisters together and told them that, unless they went virginal to the marriage couch, they could never hope to be happy. Some of them laughed scornfully and said, "Well, I guess that fixes at least a third of us." The girl and her lover were married, and the following summer at the Rollins reunion, on Holt's birthday, the child was held up to be admired by the crowd that had gathered at his home in Connecticut. . . . He said to me, when the storm was gathering, "It's all right to upset students, Rice, but can't you do it gently?" After he had dismissed me, and before he had finally ordered me off the campus and given me twenty-four hours to remove my belongings, he came into my classroom and asked to speak with me in the adjoining office. He wanted to know if it was I who had written to the Association of University Professors telling of my dismissal, and when I told him "No" he asked what I was teaching. When I had explained that, while the conclusions about human life were the same in all ages, each generation had to find new premises, and I was looking for new premises, he put his hand on my shoulder and said, "Rice, you're a teacher after my own heart," and he meant it. . . . There was outspoken objection to the building of a chapel. He said to me, when he was assured that I had not "attacked" the chapel, "But it cost three hundred thousand dollars and we've got to do something with it." A man milliner, one of the fancy preachers from Park Avenue, was asked at another meeting in Holt's home what should be done with the chapel. He said to the students, "You root for the football team; I don't see why you're unwilling to root for Jesus." There was silence, but he felt contempt in the room—such men always fear the pointed finger—looked angrily at me and asked, "Well, what's wrong with that?" I said, "I was only noticing the expression on the face of the girl who is sitting at your feet." He turned to her and said, "Ah! I see I am among purists." Holt was puzzled and confused, but he remembered.

Many students passed the harsh judgment of youth. During my first term Holt was speaking to the students and faculty in assembly and, as I could see, was troubled. Suddenly it came out, as it will when a man is filled with sorrow: a close relative had just died, and, although he was speaking of something else, the thing that was most in him came tumbling out. He stopped speechless and reached for a handkerchief to wipe the tears. As we were coming out of the room, two seniors passed and one said to the other, "Well, the old boy pulled all the stops again."

But Holt was not a hypocrite. He merely had different sets of eyes for seeing different kinds of things, and sets of feelings for feelings. He said it all to me once in another autobiographical sentence: "Rice, I've been a liberal all my life and you've got me on the other side and I don't know how it happened."

He had been too, on paper. While he was editor of *The Independent* he had spoken for every liberal cause. But an editor communicates to, not with; what he says does not meet the test of action, for, if there is any action at all, it is not his. If the editor is also journalist, and most of them are, there is a disability added: he assumes that his readers have no memory, and therefore what he said yesterday has no necessary relation to what he says today. An editorship is a chair of irresponsibility, and if an editor calls himself liberal he sits on a throne of irresponsibility, for liberalism is compromise, and compromise without action, merely in thought and expression, can have no center. The liberal editor is a homeo-allopathic doctor with leanings toward faith-healing and chiropractic.

Sometimes it was funny. A colleague who had been there longer than I said to me when I was fuming, "I used to feel the same way. Sometimes I thought I couldn't stand it another day until one day I suddenly found myself saying to myself, 'Look here: you've been a student of comedy all your life and now you've got before your eyes the greatest comedy imaginable, and you don't see it.'"

Sometimes it was not funny. One of the most respected men on the faculty, in the college for his character and in the town for his dyed conservatism, had been a classmate of Holt's at Yale and subscribed to the same creed of success. But in spite of this, in spite of the fact that we agreed upon almost nothing, I liked Ralph Lounsbury for the toughness that was in him; for there was toughness, and, if he was not polarized by some word, toughness to the bitter end; as I should see, and also see his bitter end. When I was dismissed he thought injustice had been done, and tried to persuade Holt—"Hammie" he called him with affection—to reverse his decision, and almost succeeded; but when he had failed, he went in and fought his friend, for his friend's good. At one point Holt called thirteen recalcitrant members of the faculty into his office and handed them slips of paper to sign, pledges that the administration would be supported whatever it did. Ralph took one look at him and said, "Look, Hammie, you don't want to do anything like this. If you take my advice you'll collect these and not let anybody else see them." Holt went meekly around the circle doing as he was bid, collected the unsigned pledges, and put them into his desk. Ralph came away thinking he still had a chance to win; but he was wrong. After college had closed, having long before received a letter of appointment for the following year, he now received another, of summary dismissal. I was sitting on the porch, with others, talking over what had happened—I had lost, as the Devil said when he had lost Heaven, but all was not lost—when Ralph came with the letter in his hand. I shall not forget the look on his face.

Sometimes there was a mixture, for which tragicomedy would be the nearest, though too strong a word. Avery once said to me. "I guess all of you hate me—well, just a little anyway—for I've got power of life and death over you." He had, and Holt had, the power of economic death, the only kind of death that the modern world, until the coming of Hitler, would allow in the hands of an individual, and to be known as a "trouble-maker" in the academic world is certain death. Someone reminded Holt of this; he answered, "The American people won't let a man like Rice starve." He met my wife and said, "I'm sorry this happened." She said, "So am I, and I think you have made a mistake." "Do you?" he asked, and it was a real question. "Would you like to talk to me about it?" A time was appointed and when she got there and asked him what his charges were, the first was, "Your husband was seen whispering in the chapel," and then, mixing serious and silly, I had destroyed the faith of students, and walked very slow.

Holt asked me to come to his office, one Monday, graciously and giving me no hint of his intention, and when I sat down said, "I have decided that it would be better if you would withdraw from the college." I said, no, I would not, and he was nonplussed, for, as I later learned, he had made the same request often but had never received such a response. He insisted, and offered to write letters of recommendation, which, as I pointed out, would hardly hold much value; but I continued to refuse, and we left it there. Rumor spread, and then confirmation, and the first skirmish was on. By the following Friday he had, by all reports, relented, and I was to see him on Saturday morning; but on Friday night he had dinner with Irving Bacheller and the donor of the chapel, and when I stepped into his office the next day his face was grim. He said, "Have you anything to say before I give you my decision?" I did not say what I thought, that he had given it on Monday; I only said, "No, except that I think you are wrong." Then he said, "My decision is that you shall not return next year." This was my second dismissal, but there were more ahead, five in all, until at last a committee of investigation was sent in by the American Association of University Professors.

It would be tedious to retell a story that has already been told in a report by the Association and a rejoinder published by Rollins, nor could I hope to recapture, except by a long retelling, the changes and shifts of mood and feeling that came over Rollins and Winter Park, for in time both were inextricably involved. Most of it would not, in fact, be interesting, for there is something essentially adolescent about college doings. But there were some things that are, I think, part of all human living, conflicts that grow out of a meeting of alien forms. Every society has some meaningless forms, with their appropriate rituals, left over from a time when both had meaning—the vermiform appendices of life—and they cause no great trouble for a while, if they are not too numerous and if most members of the society hold them quietly. Once they become too numerous, so numerous that they shut off the emergence of new forms, the civilization that is weighted with them finally collapses; if, however, they are not so numerous nor so widely held as to stop new growth, there is constant threat of civil war. The white heads clung desperately to theirs. My question about the churches on Interlaken Avenue was quoted as far north as Maine, where Winter Park's winter visitors became summer visitors—rather, I should say, my question was translated. A professor at Rollins had said that the churches should be torn down and green grass planted. If that had ever happened, whatever the parentage of the thought, I think many of the old people would have gone quickly to their graves; for when forms lose meaning and die, they die inside people, and to take them away is only to reveal death, of container as well as form. But there were also young people in Rollins—some of the young stay young— who were seeking new forms for what they thought were new meanings. The meanings were not new, if they were good, and they would find that out in time, when they began to learn from the past, but to be accepted they needed new forms and new rituals. There was the conflict, not of age with youth as measured by the calendar, but of age with agelessness, and the old may be as ageless as the young.

Holt asked me, on the occasion of one of my dismissals, "Rice, why do people hate you so?" I said, "I have often wondered, and I think I know the answer. They know that, if I had the making of a world, they would not be in it. They take that thought as a desire on my part to destroy them. I don't, as a matter of fact, want to destroy anybody, but I suppose the very thought is a kind of destruction, and I can't blame them for hating."

I did not know there were so many haters until the day of the hearing came. The committee sat on one side of a long table, I and two colleague champions, Ralph Lounsbury and Frederick Georgia, both of whom would be dismissed for their advocacy, on the other; and at the end sat Holt, flanked by two underlings, and almost hidden by the pile of papers in front of him. When the issue was finally joined, when I had appealed to the Association, and been dismissed for the fifth time, a message had been sent out over campus and town that "anyone who has anything against Rice"—those were the words—should come to the administration building and make an affidavit. The pile of papers were the affidavits.

Not all of them were signed by people who hated me; a good many were by men and women who hated themselves. For some of the former I had respect—I was their enemy, the enemy of their life and way of life—but for the others my feelings were different. Some, who had once been my friends, had been forced to make a miserable choice. I knew that. One of them came to me and said that his sympathies were entirely with me, but he could do nothing, for he had a wife and two children. Another was a great gossip, and had been compelled to put his gossip into the form of an affidavit; when he was called in to read it, one of the few witnesses who were called in person, he read, though the words would hardly come out of his mouth. I have seen men die before, but nature's death is a decent thing.

I saw another thing in that room, a thing I should not want to see again. I saw a man decide to lie. It all happened in time too short to measure. There was the question, sudden comprehension of its meaning and consequence, panic, and then the decision. The face is a wonderful, intricate, thing: muscles, flat surfaces, curves and lines, moving eyelids and lips that speak without a word, all held together in a harmony of tension, even in a face of settled evil. But when the blow came swift and sudden, my accuser's face fell apart completely. Cheek denied eyelid, nose, lip, the mouth was no man's mouth, there was even no sign of breath—the lungs had heard—and the eyes withdrew and disappeared.

It was not all like that; only momentary depths while Holt sat and read his affidavits, refusing to give the name of any signer. After I had recovered from the first shock, I began to find out how I felt. Holt was determined to destroy me. There was no doubt about that, even if I had been willing to misread the look on his face, whose cruel mouth was now matched by cruel eyes. They read affidavits attesting to my incompetence as a teacher; my impiety: I had "attacked" the chapel. I said "No." Well, hadn't I called the Christmas service obscene? Yes, I had, and with, I submitted, good cause. Cram had designed a chapel that was Catholic in every detail; and form, I said, requires form. You can't put on a vaudeville show, pink spotlight, stunt singing, a choirmaster standing with his back to the altar, in a Catholic chapel without incurring the charge of obscenity . . . My bathing trunks, white, and no shirt—this in fifty affidavits. (These two charges would follow me to Black Mountain, transmuted into atheism and nudism) . . . I had been told by Holt that after two years I should be on permanent tenure, which meant that I could be removed only if cause could be shown. He was asked about tenure and said he wasnt sure. His dean was, sure that I had no such assurance, and set about to persuade Holt. They debated, but Holt would not say he had not; he held back, until, when he was crowded to the wall, I pulled a letter out of my pocket. That settled it, for it was written and signed by Holt . . . The next affidavit hinted at immorality, which means in the vocabulary of the academy, only one thing. Did Holt intend to make that charge? He said certainly not . . . On the walls of my classroom were, a colleague swore, indecent pictures. Would I explain? I would. They were calendars got from the drug store, one an Indian maid, another entitled "Sincerity," a third a mother and child. I had put them up to tease the class into an opinion about art; had protested that I liked them, and therefore they were art, until, at the end of the week, when someone had asked, "Now tell us what you really think," I had said, "I think they are indecent." My colleague had heard, and reported. His wife, who had supervision of a cottage on the shore rented for the faculty by the college, spoke out of knowledge. She made affidavit that I had left fish scales in the sink . . . I had said, said another affidavit, that a chisel was one of the most beautiful things in the world. This time the chairman did not ask me to explain. He said, "Plato said the same thing of an ash can." "Did he?" asked Holt, ready to please with a question. "Why?" "Perfect mating of form and function—will you please read on, Mr. President," and Holt read on, through the day and into the night, eleven hours in all; on and on, the trivial with the grave, all in no order, a blunderbuss load of hate.

When we came out of the room, after the last hoarse affidavit had been read, the chairman of the committee, Professor Olin Lovejoy of Johns Hopkins, asked whether I would be willing to accept dismissal, if thereby Holt could be got to guarantee security to my colleagues who were still on the faculty. I said yes. It meant, I knew, that I would not teach again, and I was sorry on that account, for teaching was to me like a bottle of whiskey to a dipsomaniac; but just because it was like that, I thought it might be better to do something else. And yet, for all my telling myself that I would now be a writer, as if one should say, "I'll get religion," my spirits were low. I could, using success for a measuring stick, now match Holt failure for failure. It was enough.

The next day, however, the terms were changed. Holt refused to make any concessions. "If I hire a cook," he said, "I don't call in a committee of cooks to decide whether I shall fire him." With these words my name became a mere symbol. Thenceforth I was spectator while Holt fought about a third of the faculty, tussled with students, and continued to defy the committee. When it was over, that is, when the end of the academic year brought cessation, enough resignations had been added to dismissals to account for, as I recall, somewhere near a fourth of the faculty. Holt spoke our obituary: "The trouble is, I like the ones that are going better than those that are staying."

When I went to tell him good-by, he was gracious again; all the hate was gone from his face, except from the hard lines around the mouth. When we had exchanged regrets, it spoke: "This thing has cost me at least fifty thousand dollars."

I have known only two completely free men. One was a neighbor in Lincoln, an expert accountant who had retired and was living with his father, on his father's Civil War pension. He spent his time reading, and inspecting Lincoln, on which he gave one a free report. There was nothing, of good or evil in the town, that he did not know. The other was my landlord in Winter Park. He spent his waking life in his back yard, which faced my porch, seated in front of his garage with children and dogs and cats, who were waiting for him every morning and stood around in admiring circle until he sat down for the business of the day. If no visitor came, he simply sat, but on invitation he filled the hour with talk, as a man will for whom an empty day lies ahead. He told me all I needed to know about Winter Park and its people, handing out with calm impartiality the good and the bad—until Holt's name was mentioned, when his face became charged with anger. I never knew exactly why, because he mentioned only one slight, a likely cause, put upon him by a member of Holt's family, who had come to fetch the car, parked at the time in the garage, and said to him when it would not start, "Crank my car." "Lady," he said, "I don't crank my own car." That was all, and that was not enough. But when at last I was leaving, he told me my whole story, plotted the curve with precision, and ended by saying, "I couldn't tell you. I saw you liked the man."

CHAPTER X

Black Mountain

BLACK MOUNTAIN WAS BORN ON THE WRONG SIDE OF THE BLANKET. An agent of the Carnegie Foundation told me that, about two years after we, some twenty students and eight teachers, had gone up on the mountain to create, or in the hope of creating, a new kind of college. The year before, when I was innocent of the ways of foundations, I had appealed to him for help and he had given me cause to believe that a small grant was just around the corner; but when I turned that corner, there had been apparently a misunderstanding: it was to be the next. He conveyed his regrets to me in a personal letter, which I, still innocent, accepted for what it said; but when corner beckoned to corner and the letters degenerated to mimeographed sheets, I began to feel, as indeed I was, a little foolish. He received me, however, with diminished cordiality, and said, when I pressed him for an answer, "Nobody told you to jump into the water," hastily adding, when he saw my face, "Of course it was a fine thing for you to do, but all the same. . . ." I did not hear the conclusion of the sentence; I had already stopped my ears, a thing I had learned in church.

When I looked up at last he was gazing out of the windows and talking about art, what a wonderful thing it was. We had said that, in Black Mountain, art should be at the center, and he was speaking to that theme with approval, lest I depart thinking him rude. Then, musing, he underscored our illegitimacy: "It's such a pity," he said, "there's no objective test for the appreciation of art."

The agents of the General Education Board were more consistently cordial and skillfully evasive. Some of them, being young and still interested in education, listened, but when it appeared that what we proposed to do at Black Mountain could not submit to scientific direction nor yield scientific results, there was little hope; and none when I said that if we were granted money, we would spend it as wisely as we knew and give an accounting, that that was all we could honestly promise. But I remember them with respect, for they were as forthright as men in their predicament could be.

If they had not been so polite, I might have demonstrated, using them themselves as examples, that it was impossible to direct human action above the level of bricklaying, and that the more minute the specifications, the more carefully drawn the plans, graphs, tables, charts, of what was to be, the less it would be, until at last it was nothing, except inertia.

Carnegie and Rockefeller were the two greatest buccaneers of their day, ruthless, unscrupulous, insatiable. When either decided to board a ship, a second later he was in action, slashing, mauling, scuttling, anything to win. On the first day of creation in America man had started to work on the land, had subdued it, pegged it to his use; on the second, their day, man set to work on man, with the same dogged will. At the end of that day—it is over now, I think—they were named the foremost pirates in history. But they wanted another name; they knew that in time their piracy would be forgiven, for it had been only a game and no one had lost, and they would be forgotten. But artists are unwilling to be forgotten, and they found a new way to be remembered. That was what they hoped.

Men had burdened the earth with pyramids, temples, whole cities, in the vain hope that the earth would remember; that failing, they had put their trust in Heaven, filled the treasuries of the church, but at the end of a hundred years, while prayers for their souls might still be mumbled, their names were forgotten. But these men, Carnegie and Rockefeller, and their brother Rhodes in South Africa, knew that a piece of carved granite was nothing to be respected. Had not oil spurted from cemeteries and dishonored the dead? An old lady in North Carolina told me that she had bought a burial lot and endowed its upkeep; she would, she said, rest in peace, knowing that she would lie in consecrated ground "as long as the earth spins on its axis." They, these artists of the second day, would not be so foolish. They would create, not build, a new kind of memorial, within humanity, a memorial that should itself be a creator, creating and re-creating on into time. That was their hope.

Old men see far, even to the gates of the other world; but when the eyes are fixed on the horizon, they are blind to the table, the plate, the glass standing by the plate. If Carnegie or Rockefeller had seen the soft ordered hand that filled the glass, the correct sleeve-length of the braided arm, had caught the implication of the ritual, "Will there be anything more, sir?"—if either had taken one good square look at his butler, he might have stayed his hope.

Butler, secretary, both live in an ordered way in an ordered world. They like to sleep sound of nights. Theirs is the managerial mind. Man, to them, is a problem in mechanics. Find the formula. Take no chances. Is it proposed to scuttle a ship? Appoint a committee, with paid secretary, to study and digest—the manager is a busy man— the history of scuttling; another on methods, another to hear the claim of different schools; call in the treasurer, to learn the sum set aside for scuttling. Above all and in all, be cautious; impatience is out of order. . . . "Man overboard, you say? Who told him to jump?"

As a matter of fact, I had not jumped; neither fallen nor been pushed. I slid in, very gently. When the Rollins affair was over, I resolved not to try teaching any more. I had learned my lesson. I would do something else, unspecified. There was no place for me, I now knew, in any established school or college. That was my decision, and I stuck to it for a long time.

One night, in the spring of 1933, Frederick Georgia took me in his car out to the edge of town and we parked among the pines. "What are you going to do?" he asked. "I don't know," I said, "write, I suppose." "Write what?" he asked. "Plays," I said. Then he, more practical than I, asked me a question I had not thought of, "How're you going to live in the meantime?" I said, "I don't know." After silence he said, "What about starting that college we've been talking about?" We had often talked about that college, he and I and half a dozen others, and sometimes students too, as small boys will cease the serious business of play, sit by the wall, kick the dust and say, "When I get to be a man . . ." Thus will grown men dream in the moonlight.

Some students began to ask the same question. "We came here," they said, "thinking this was it";—students dream too—"now this is a flop. What are we going to do?" I asked, "What'll we use for money?" and we laughed. One, a girl, came alone and said, "I've lost my scholarship here. I was warned I would if I supported you. Now what'll I do?" I had no answer.

Then came the sudden blow that struck down Georgia and Lounsbury, both appointed for the following year and now peremptorily dismissed. This was getting serious, and the question more insistent, "How about a new college?"

I hung back. Bob Wunsch, a teacher of dramatics, said, "I know just the place," and he named it, Blue Ridge, a great building in the mountains of North Carolina near Asheville, used summers by the Y.M.C.A., vacant in winter. By this time Georgia was in dead earnest. He had misread my silence and came one day with a definite proposal, that we should go in his car and look at the place.

"What shall we call it?" someone asked on the way. I said, "New College." We agreed, and called it by that name—any other would have done, for I was sure there would be no college—and joked about it until we got into the mountains near Waynesville, when Georgia suddenly stopped the car and said, "I want to show you something."

He backed some fifty feet and there was a sign pointing to a side road and saying, "New College." I, now free from the danger of an affidavit, said, "Well I'll be damned," so simply does prophecy slip from the tongue.

New College, we afterwards learned, had been established a year or so before, as one of the branch stores of the Sears, Roebuck of learning, Columbia University, to be quickly abolished within a few years, when it got in the way of a man's ambition.

Blue Ridge was perfect. Set halfway up in the bend of a mountain, it looked out over an endless chain of peaks. Here was peace. Here was also central heating against the cold of winter, blankets, sheets, dishes, flatware, enough for a dozen colleges, all at a moderate rental, and besides these the one guarantee of civilization, a perfect chef, Jack, a Negro, and the only authentic gentleman on the staff of Black Mountain College—still a notion—and a perfect assistant chef, his wife Ruby. They would, these two, within the coming years, put us all to shame with the grace of their life, and at last, as Negroes can, rebuke, and yet not rebuke me, with kindly silence.

From Blue Ridge we drove to Swarthmore, where we sat on my brother-in-law Aydelotte's porch and talked. He said it was worth trying—the "what the hell" spirit of the West coming out again—and then, "Don't have a board of trustees." There was more talk and questions. How many students could we count on? Georgia thought seventy-five; calculation, so many head at so much a head—why, we wouldn't need any money. This was getting serious indeed.

Still I held back. There were doubts, many unstated, one specific. My wife had long wanted me to get, and stay, out of teaching; this was my chance. Would she be willing to go in, to try once more a thing in which she had no faith? There was also doubt as to whether the revolutionaries could survive the revolution—they often did not—whether we were agreed, really agreed, inside. I was tired, too, of people's troubles, mine and others'. I wanted peace, but, perverse, something within peace that was a denial—action, proof, to know that I was right; but not in the spirit of the braggart. I wanted to know.

At last my wife made the decision: she would come in. "Wholeheartedly?" "Yes, wholeheartedly." Then I too agreed, but I was troubled.

That was a wild summer. I traveled all over the East, talking to students, arguing restrainedly with parents, explaining what the college was to be when I did not know, interviewing the merely curious, and being interviewed, and encouraged, by the merely curious. At the end of a month my son Frank, who was chauffeur, washed the dust of thirteen states off the car. Meanwhile prospects went down and down. Parents were furious. Didn't we know we were in the midst of a depression? "How," I asked, "was a professor to know?" and won no friends by my retort. Frantic telegrams came from teachers who had left or been dismissed from Rollins. Were we sure that the college would open in September? With them we were honest, but to the world we turned brazen faces: "Sure," we said, "absolutely."

We were not; but, with the promise of fifteen students, I went to see a wealthy man who had taught at Rollins and left the year before, and asked him and his wife to underwrite the college up to a limit of ten thousand dollars. The money would be used, I said, not for salaries, and not at all except to get us through the year. Others raised the sum to fifteen thousand, on the same terms. One of the men who came with us from Rollins, Theodore Dreier, was descended from a millionaire and had money in his bones, and I knew I could count on him to keep us from spending it needlessly. (He did. At the end of the first year we offered to return forty per cent of the underwriting to our patrons, who were so astonished that they gave it to us, and it carried the college through the second year.)

Misgivings, hunches, the vague sense that something is not right without the wit to say what it is—these had stayed with me all summer. When I stepped through the door into the main hall, I began to know why: on a door at the left, in letters big enough to be seen a hundred feet, was a sign which read "PRESIDENT." We had agreed, during the summer, that Georgia should be head of the college for its first year, with title to be chosen, but only titular, to meet the laws of incorporation. This was to be a new kind of college, which was in fact the oldest kind, a *communitas*, and, to mark its difference from other academic institutions, we would avoid the conventional forms as well as realities. The board of trustees would be the faculty, and called by an old name, the Board of Fellows; while the head would not in fact be head at all. But the sign said otherwise.

The huge building, which had been full of people when we first saw it, was now empty and bare, with great cracks in the walls and sagging ceilings. The hallway, with splintered flooring, seemed miles long, and gave back no hope as I walked its length to the stairs at the end and up the steps to a second—there was still a third—and to my bedroom in the wing. The students would live along the long hallways, girls on the second floor, boys on the third, their bedrooms at the far end, and studies, with faculty studies interspersed, at the near.

I went into my bedroom, closed the door, and sat down in a rickety chair. Some day, perhaps, a clever scientist will be able to pick my thoughts off the walls of that room, record them on a film, and translate through his cold lips the history of a man's soul. It will be, as he will demonstrate, not mine, not anybody's; it will be the record of every sentient man; not a work of art, a hodgepodge rather: comedy, tragedy, tragicomedy, farce in plenty, simple blundering that those words do not include, and hope and joy too—everything.

That night when we gathered for dinner in a room off the kitchen, in a smaller building behind—Georgia, his wife, and two children; Ralph Lounsbury and his wife; Theodore Dreier and Barbara; one or two others, new teachers—we did not look at each other nor speak beyond the ritual. Jack and Ruby alone, seen through the door moving about the stove in quiet dignity, were sure of themselves.

The next day the students arrived and hope picked up. In the afternoon we gathered on the wide front porch of the barnlike building which still, true to the Southern tradition, denied its nature with great columns that held up nothing but a flimsy roof, as if to keep their heads from getting wet. Georgia rapped on his chair for silence.

There are moments that call for poetry, or complete silence. Here we were, a small band of fools against the wise world, setting out to conquer that world and give "wise" another meaning. We had, by an instinct as old as man, gone up on a mountain, there to make our living sacrifice. We would conquer or die. One could almost hear the old words, the old wrong words. The wise, the really wise, know, have always known, that they are wrong, that the order is wrong, and the "or" is wrong. "Die and conquer," those are the words and the order. Humility, the wise have said, is the beginning of life. We had no humility, not a tittle.

That was why, I think, there was no poetry and no silence. Georgia unconsciously did the right and appropriate thing. At the first meeting of a college that was to start the revolution in American education the first speaker called was the permanent caretaker, who would explain fire precautions.

I sat where I could see Ralph Lounsbury's face. I had not seen him for some two months, and in that time he had become an old man. When the meeting was breaking up he drew me aside and said, "What am I going to do?" I said, "What do you mean? Teach, of course, history and political science." "I didn't mean that," he said, and his eyes became red with distress, and when he spoke again his voice was broken, "I didn't mean that. I mean, here I am over sixty and without a job—this is no job, really." "Of course it isn't, not yet," I said, "but wait." "I can't wait," he said, and the words would hardly come out. "I'm an old man without a job. I'm a failure." There was the word again, Hammie Holt's word, Yale's word, the word of millions of Americans. "Nonsense," I said, "you fought and you lost. That's not failure."

But it was no use. Every time he had a chance he said it again, until the time came when he could say nothing. Some six weeks after college opened he had a stroke and died a few days later. The last thing he said to me before his illness, which stopped his speech, was "What will people say, John? I'm a failure."

He was soon forgotten. The living cannot afford to remember the dead, for what can life learn from death? That was what we thought.

We changed the title from "President" to "Rector," and we changed a lot of other things, but we did not change ourselves nor each other, we teachers. You cannot change middle-aged men; they have to change themselves, and middle-aged teachers cannot change themselves.

Teaching is a secondary art. A man is a good teacher if he is a better something else; for teaching is communication, and his better something else is the storehouse of the things he will communicate. I have never known a master in any field who was not also a master teacher; but to be a master teacher in Black Mountain one had to be a master man. In other places education was part of the day and part of the man; in Black Mountain it was round the clock and all of a man. There was no escape. Three meals together, passing in the hall, meeting in classes, meeting everywhere, a man taught by the way he walked, by the sound of his voice, by every movement. That was what it was intended to be, the fulfillment of an old idea, the education of the whole man: by a whole man.

None of us were whole, man or woman. Western civilization does not produce whole men and women. (Unless we can learn, we shall be destroyed; of that I am convinced.) We were man, youth, child, infant, and just plain foetus. For a while, under the spell of novelty, the creed was not questioned, except at moments; but soon foetus began to cry that it had been left behind, then infant, and child, and the rest.

I used to say, "This is a school for giants." I meant that every one of us should grow to the giant that it was in him to be; not some one else's giant, but his own. Few are by nature dwarfs, however many may have been dwarfed. Few are by nature stupid; most of the rest are stupefied. That was what I believed. That is what I believe.

At the end of the first year we were a community of some thirty-five or forty, with one new student in prospect for the coming year. But we decided to go on, for we were still a community in spirit, although the great division was beginning. Georgia—and I say it without disrespect: a man is what he is—wanted a conventional college, and others wanted one too, slightly different from his, but still conventional. The students, nearly all, did not, nor did some of the faculty.

At the beginning of the second year I was made rector. This was in 1934, twenty years since I had first entered my classroom at Webb School. In the interval I had learned some things that fitted me for the position, which I was to hold for four years, but I had learned and perfected one thing that unfitted me: I had learned the technique of opposition; that is, of irresponsibility, for criticism without chance or obligation to act is irresponsible. Whether in graduate school or in classroom, I had opposed not only the administration—every professor does that—but also my colleagues. But the spirit of opposition was older than that, beginning in a Methodist parsonage and cultivated in Methodist pews, and then in school and college. In all that time I had known only one teacher, John Webb, whom I was willing to call master, only one whom I did not in some measure despise—poor preparation for what I now undertook.

It is not my intention here to tell the story of Black Mountain College. That would require a volume; it would also require a steadier hand than I now have to probe among the tender tissues, others' and mine, to find the truth; and even if I should find it, I know that it would be only the story of my six years, not any others'. It began in doubt, rose to high hope, and ended in despair. No one word can describe more than a moment in a man's life, much less six years, but when I climbed in my car and drove away from the college, alone, for the last time, at that moment the word was "failure"—not Hammie Holt's, stilled applause, nor Ralph Lounsbury's, being out of a job—not these nor any meanings of the word that can be set against "success."

During these last three years I have read the history of Brook Farm, of New Harmony, and other communities, and I have laughed, and squirmed, many times; but I was glad that I had not read them before: I would never have gone near Black Mountain. That would have been a loss greater than the final loss, great as that was. I learned many things.

I learned, for one thing, the need of law, an abstract, intellectual, bridle to hold passion when intelligence fails. Black Mountain was a pure democracy. Jefferson, and my other coevals, would have shuddered at a community that was usually lawful and fairly peaceful, but at times completely lawless. That was when everyone was frightened. The English, in their blundering intelligent way, had found the answer: not a college, but many; a community of colleges, a *universitas*; perhaps they would not all be fools at once.

We had a constitution, of course, but when it came to the test it was torn up. The college was seeking a level of comfort, which meant comfort for the majority. In the history of communities the only stop to that movement had been a religious sanction. We had none. Our sanction, we said, was intelligence. But human intelligence, a nice balance between intellect and feeling, is a young thing, younger even than human love. Sometimes intelligence took leave.

Other colleges, we knew, existed as ends in themselves. (They are, says the law, "nonprofit" organizations, but that law is a liar. They are as much run for profit, to their runners, as the General Electric.) Black Mountain, we said, would be a means; the end was the individual. That sounded well, but I was not satisfied. I knew that the life span of an idea in a college was at most ten years; that at the end of that time, or earlier, the institution sank back into mere existence. I asked John Dewey about that. He reassured me; said, "As long as you keep your eye on the individual, that won't happen." I went away asking myself, "But who is to see to it that the college keep its eye on the individual?"

I got an ironic answer, in time. Meanwhile we bought a piece of property, and from the moment of signing the papers the change began. Hutchins of Chicago said, and I am glad to record it as our only point of agreement, that colleges should be in tents. Blue Ridge was our tent; renting it, we would fold together. But once we had a place of our own, the center shifted gradually, until, when the test came a few years later, the institution won, not the individual. There was my answer.

We did not know, at the time we took over the new property, Lake Eden—another ironic note—that it would become the center, else we might have had the hardihood to refrain. But three years of gradual increase in the student body, carefully selected by students and faculty, and no diminution, we thought, in the spiritual strength of the college, made it seem that the time had come to think of moving out of our tent. Ted Dreier, the best kind of college treasurer, because he believed that money should be spent on education, had, with wise frugality, accumulated enough for a down payment, but it took all our reserves. From that time forth, our backlog was no longer in the economic structure; it was in nonproductive land.

We knew that land was nonproductive, for we had gone through and come through the "back to the land" neurosis, whose bible, among us, was Borsodi's *Flight from the City*, the title itself neurotic. We would, we said, run the Blue Ridge farm and feed ourselves; but farming is not an amateur game, and when we found that farm help would work for a dollar a day and feed themselves, hope began to chill. But it was Borsodi himself who turned on the refrigeration. Some of the students visited him on the farm to which he had fled from the city, but they found more talk than farming, and when, the following morning, the milkman, indistinguishable from his city brother, left bottles on the step, they were ready themselves to flee, and did. When they came back to college they were sheepishly silent.

Lake Eden made us checkbook—or, as they say in the peach country, telephone-farmers. Nor was there any way we could become economically independent. We were obliged to live on charity, small gifts begged here and there. We were on the wrong side of the economic tracks. Money is the language of the thing-world; we would talk small. The simple life—that old myth—was the answer. One of its advocates came back from a summer in Mexico and praised the native Indians, who lived on a handful of grain a day. Then, without a smile, he resumed ordering his weekly ration of pumpernickel shipped from a bakery on Long Island. I visited Berea College in Kentucky, where industry was developed, but I found that its insecure base was charity too. Antioch looked hopeful, until Arthur Morgan told me he spent most of the year on wheels, begging.

I was no good at raising money, for reasons that must by now be clear. Holt loved money and its possessors. That made it easy. Aydelotte did not love money or its possessors as such, but he made them believe that what he proposed was what they had intended all along. When I walked into the room of a rich man I said, without opening my mouth, "You've got no business with all that money. Now shell out." It never worked.

Of all the rich men, and I met a good many in my begging, there was only one who was not himself his wealth. He was Samuel Fels of Philadelphia. He received me in his summer home in Maine as if it was he who was asking a favor, and there was something about the way he placed my chair before the broad window that said, "This chair and this room and the view are not me." But what he said in words was "Now tell me, please, Mr. Rice, what it is you are doing." I told him, and when I had finished he said, "I have quite a lot of money, Mr. Rice, and I want to use it for something. I want to use it, if I can find the way, so that a man won't come home at night to his wife and family worried for fear he may lose his job. I don't think people ought to be afraid. I don't think fear does people any good and I'd like to use my money to take some fear away, to make a beginning at least of getting rid of fear. Now while you were talking I was listening to see if what you are doing will help what I want to do, to make a man not worry about his job, and I don't see how it will, not directly. Do you?" I said, "No, Mr. Fels, and if I had your money I might want to do the same thing." He said, "Thank you, Mr. Rice. It was very kind of you to come and see me."

Black Mountain was to be education for democracy. The college was not, we said, an end; it was a means. Such a dichotomy of life is moral irresponsibility; some of us knew that, some did not. Here was another division. If it was to be education for democracy, if that was its end, that must also be its means: it must be education in democracy. I used to fool myself by saying that Black Mountain was different from every other community in that its end was not happiness, at any rate not happiness there in the college. I said that its end, its job, was to send people out into a wide democracy. But this was not true, as to the faculty. We stayed in our small democracy: I see now that, with some exceptions, everybody who has had the experience of such a small democracy, everybody, should get out into the beginning democracy that is America. Afterwards, from its graduates, faculty and students, a few of the wise and the good should return and teach, by their living, that old age may be a noble thing—a lesson that America needs to learn; for American democracy is young, but youthfully young, and must learn to be agelessly young.

That college education in America is not education in democracy needs no demonstration. Its model is European and, in the universities, continental European. Black Mountain, which began in the hope of being American, also became European.

It happened in two ways. Rather, it came from one center, the unconscious habits of man. People think they want something new and different, think they want freedom, but what they really want is the old things changed enough to make them feel comfortable. This is apparent now, in the year 1942, in the talk about war aims. The governments in exile, and the exiles, want the old order again, changed a little here and there, but still the old; and the governments not yet in exile want the same thing. So we, the dwellers on the mountain, even the voluntary exiles, wanted a college that was Princeton or Haverford or Oxford, with a new coat of paint.

When Thomas Mann speaks about democracy, I do not listen. I have read his books, and I know what he wants, another sick Europe. One of my colleagues at Black Mountain said that Hitler was an entirely different kind of human being from himself. I had heard the same sort of thing before, even in England, where the skivvy was, they told me, unlike her mistress. I did not believe it, much as I might like to believe that I myself am an entirely different kind of human being from Hitler. It would be a great comfort to believe that.

The center of the curriculum, we said, would be art. The democratic man, we said, must be an artist. The integrity, we said, of the democratic man was the integrity of the artist, an integrity of relationship. The history of man had been the struggle between man and his environment, that is, the corporation of his fellows; sometimes one was winner, sometimes the other. When the individual won, he found himself the individualist, when the corporation, a polyp. That was the struggle then on in Europe, now in the whole world. Sometimes, however, the corporation won without great struggle, by persuasion. Would not man become like his fellows? That would make it easier all round. Many accepted that easy way, and became "adjusted." But still they were not satisfied. Still they did not have integrity.

The flaw was as old as Cain and Abel. It was a fight. It was either—or, and one of them had to win, to absorb the integrity of the other. But the integrity of the artist was not a fight, not sprung from hate and distrust. It was a creation, this integrity of the artist, a creation by him and his environment. The artist, we said, was not a competitor. He competed only with himself. His struggle was inside, not against his fellows, but against his own ignorance and clumsiness. The painting was his integrity, the score, the words of a play, and, at last, understanding, the will and the skill to do with his fellows, with the corporation, what he had done with paints and sounds: the integrity that was a relationship between himself and the corporation. But just as the painter must learn to paint, starting with ignorance and clumsiness, so this new artist, this creator of integrity between himself and his fellows, must know and know how, must have knowledge and skill. Also, just as the artist would not paint his picture with muddy colors, so this artist must see clear colors in humanity; and must himself be clear color, for he too was his fellow artist's color, sound, form, the material of his art. But, different from pigment, bow, granite, not used up in the use; rather, made more of what he would be, a note within the symphony, the clearer for having been written; giving up, and asked to give up, nothing of himself. That was the integrity of the artist as artist. That should be the integrity of man as man.

The trouble was, that there was not anyone calling himself an artist who was an artist. They were not in love with art; they were in love with themselves, and being in love with themselves, alone, they loved only what they themselves did. When one has lived with them and come to know them well in their daily living, it is easy to understand how some psychologists call art a neurosis. Their ruthlessness might be forgiven, if it were used to defend and protect art; but it does nothing of the kind; it is self-defense, and at the same time a plea for pity. Their private stomach-ache becomes the tragedy of the world.

Writers, painters, musicians, all were the same: peddlers, each crying his own wares and crying down his fellow peddlers. Their associations, whether meeting in tower or basement, have no unity; it is the unity of the Union League Club.

It would be funny, if it were funny; but to live, day after day, with these spiritual porcupines is no fun. The students knew; they knew inside themselves that they must live as artists in relation to their art; but when they came to me and asked me to name a particular artist who lived that way, I had to confess to myself that I knew none. The best I could do, by way of answer, was to put a screen before my fellow fumblers, and point to their practice in the classroom. But that was no good and I knew it; and the students knew it. The young, the real young, have not yet discovered that they have a stake in not seeing the truth.

There were, besides the artists, the merely discontent. They too had withdrawn from living and, professing literature or science or philosophy or whatever, made up a system which they called "life." But there was no life in it, for no one could live that way. There is no such thing as a system of life, for life, without the quote, is a process, a way, a method. It is not an experiment.

They came to Black Mountain, the unhappy, the disillusioned, the misunderstood—there is no such person—and at first thought they had reached the promised land; not knowing, for to them the Bible was out of date—primitive literature—that the only man who ever reached the promised land was a Moses, and he never got there. The promised land, and he found it on another mountain, was inside himself.

They, pretenders to art and other malcontents, were one side of the fallacy of adjustment. They could not adjust themselves to the world and the pig-headed world refused to adjust itself to them, so they retired from living and went in for "life." One, a professor of philosophy, retold that, when Hitler was rising to power, he had closed the door of his Berlin study and read Aristotle, in the original.

Besides the permanent staff of seekers after happiness, there were the visitors. They tagged themselves when they walked in the door—

sometimes earlier. There was one sure way to tell whether the latest was interested in the co-operative movement; he always parked his car in the middle of the driveway. Two came, a couple well along in years, to live as well as talk "the philosophy of love," and begged to be allowed to stay. The lady apostle gave her skeptical attention to a class of mine, and stood it in semisilence until I said that, like it or not, hate was in all of us. Within two weeks she came as near as a lady can to spitting when she passed me in the hallway.

There were other visitors, however, who knew what it was about. John Dewey was one, the only man I have ever known who was completely fit and fitted to live in a democracy. He sat and said nothing; but something happened when he was there. For two weeks, on one visit, he came every day to a class of mine, and I suffered torture, for I was in difficulties and could not find my way out. I was no longer pretending to teach. I had said, and I meant it, that my classes were for my own instruction; if the students got anything, that was their luck, but not my intention. Dewey's presence was a terrible test, a daily invitation to pull some of the old rabbits out of the old hat, but I knew he would recognize both, if the rest did not; so, for at least one reason, I went my way of exploring, getting tangled in the brush and longing for the lunch bell to release me. It happened the same way every day: the hopeful start and then the tangle. He said nothing until one day I confessed that I didn't know what I was talking about, that there was a question I wanted to ask but I didn't know what it was. "Could you tell us," he asked, "in what area the question lies?" I tried and failed. On the way to lunch he said, "You might have said this," and there it all was. He had respect for the process of learning.

He had it because he had respect for people. John Webb and John Dewey are the only men I have known who never questioned the individual's right to be alive. They took that for granted, and began from there.

Another who understood the intention of the college, or perhaps I should say, of the dream, was Dewey's friend, Albert Barnes of Merion, who questioned every man's right to be alive and usually found against the plaintiff. Every night he invited some of us to his room before dinner and measured out with the care of a pharmacist drinks of beautiful whiskey. John Dewey was always there and, following the Socratic tradition, drank with the rest until Barnes said, "Now, John, you've had enough. One more and you'd be drunk," but he was wrong, for Dewey, upholding the tradition, could stay beyond the rest and lift the last glass with a steady hand. Sometimes, in my imagination, I invited my father, who revered Dewey, to come and see him in low company.

The students took, and took to, Dewey as simply as if he had been the corner grocer. They did not know he was a great man, not even those from Progressive Schools, which, I was pleased to discover, having perverted his philosophy, yet had the decency not to have mentioned his name. To a regional meeting of the Progressive Education Association in Atlanta I took Dewey unannounced. The students who went along were a little flustered at his reception, but were soon at ease— he saw everything, as I found out, and reassured them by cutting an important luncheon, going to a beer parlor with them, and being old shoe again.

There were other visitors, "a citizen of the world," oriental philosophers fresh out of the occident, devotees of "The Dance" (the ultimate dehydration of art); disciples of Confucius and heralds of confusion, vegetarians and single-taxers (two in one); reformers, that is, creators of a world in their own image, intellectuals a little on the sparse side when it came to intelligence; labor leaders, trained for their mission by four years of Harvard, graduates of the Union Theological Seminary, yearners all—these and many others. They had only one thing in common: disgust of themselves transmitted into disgust of the world.

They rejected the college in time, as completely as the Foundations had: they had come looking for experiment and found experience.

There was not enough love in Black Mountain, and when there is not enough love there will be not enough affection. Here we were on the mountain about to make a new society, withdrawn partly through hate but mostly through the desire for affection, and we lacked the one thing that can create affection, love. The older people needed love, the younger, affection, out of which love has a chance to grow. It came, of course—love—to both old and young, but fierce and dangerous, unmollified by affection. There were spurious substitutions, sentimentality and its inversion, cynicism, which throve in the cold air. At one time or another every member of the staff was a candidate for expulsion, nominated by students, mainly out of habit, but also by colleagues. One of them, if he had prevailed, would have been left alone on the mountain, so often did he decide that someone had to go, and come to me with a whispered name.

Walter Locke, my old friend from Lincoln, now editor of the Dayton *News,* came and saw and understood. We went for a walk and, halfway down the mountain, he stopped me in my tracks with a question: "What are you going to do, Rice, when the intriguer comes?" He was there at the time, but I then thought him harmless; had told him bluntly that if his spirit should ever come to prevail in the college no decent person could stay there. If there had been enough love there would have been enough affection, and he would have remained harmless.

If I were listing requirements for another Black Mountain, first would be at least four couples held together by resolute love, by love in which the conflicts were resolved into equality. There would be no requirement as to age, only that they should be really one, two equal halves that were one. I used to say, when Black Mountain was only a small thought, that I should never have in a college for teacher anyone who was unhappily married or unhappily unmarried. We had both kinds, but, in all the six years, only one couple who met the test; and they, a year after I left, were required to leave.

We were, without intending to become or calling ourselves, a big family; or, if you choose, a tribe. An anthropologist, if he had also been magician, would have learned much; but he would have needed magic to make himself invisible, else he too would have become entangled; as the Freudians, who nodded confirmation and quoted the master's lingo until they were snubbed or jilted, when they returned to their Anglo-Saxon. Here again affection was needed, to prevent and heal the· hurts. I, without intending to be, was the father: confessor, Oedipus's, Christus, and just plain ordinary. I knew too much; for I let people talk themselves out. But, while they loved to spill, they hated to have spilled, and came to hate the listener. All of us, I as well as they, might some day have become individuals, artists with the artist's integrity; but meanwhile we were individualists and dreaded to leave some part of ourselves out of our control, and that is what confession, in frank speech, does. When the individualist tells one something intimate about himself, it is as if he left behind an arm or leg, and thereby lost his integrity. Wise men know this and decline the limb; I did not. My four loving couples could have prevented the concentration. Sometimes members of the faculty were angry with me for as much as six weeks. I did not mind, so long as there were not too many at once. But in the end there were. The majority of the men had been unhappy in childhood and hated their fathers. I knew that, as I was to know what it meant.

Modern man is looking for a savior, someone to save him from his individualism. But he cannot find him, for he insists upon the terms of his own salvation. He wants, and needs, to be saved, but he must be, he says, just as he was before. He is like the fifth-century Athenian, all brain and little heart. He has this choice: to retreat, as the Germans have, to slavery, from which another Christ may come to rescue him—

that was what the early Christian was, slave made into man—or else, by pushing his individualism as far as it will go, he may come to realize, as Socrates tried to teach him, and failed—Socrates was, after all, an Athenian, as Christ was a Jew—the limits of sheer thinking, and, unafraid, look about him and see his fellows all in the same predicament, speak to them with his heart as well as his mind, acknowledge that they as well as he are both thinker and lover, and, losing nothing of himself, find all of himself within all humanity. If he does, if he has the will to go on, he will discover that he needs no leader, that he is in himself both leader and follower. Christ, calling himself son and brother, refused to be leader, kept saying "not me but the Father," and Socrates saying the same thing in the Athenian way, together warned man against exclusion, against either—or as a way of thought and feeling; plead with him to be both and to leave nothing out, to be whole: to be the Christian Socrates, Socratic Christ.

One day in the late autumn of 1936 I was coming out of the music cottage when a student said, "There is someone here to see you." It was in those simple meaningless words that nemesis was announced. He was tall and very handsome, and taut, so taut that even his greeting was forced out from clenched teeth. "I am Louis Adamic," he said.

He came looking for a leader, a quest that he has since had the wisdom to forego, having learned that the only proper leader for mankind is not a man but a cause. Meanwhile I should be made into one, and others in turn—Harry Bridges, John L. Lewis, Arthur Morgan—all of them, and I, with one thing in common, violence of spirit. But Louis is a real American: he learns as he goes.

He had come, he said, because Henry Allen Moe, secretary to the Guggenheim Foundation, had told him to come, but he would stay only an hour. Here was, then, a convergence of what had made and would make America, I, an old stock, Moe, son of an immigrant, and Louis the immigrant.

We had tea, he and I and the students—he was the first writer with a name to come our way—and his wife Stella. I had met Stella before; rather, been given a glimpse of her through Louis's *Native's Return*, but only a glimpse, for artist husbands are jealous. They, in their individualism, like to think that they are God, creating out of nothing; but show me a man—writer, painter, composer, any artist—and, if he approaches his goal, I shall look for the woman. She may not be there, she may be only a dream, as van Gogh's woman was, or a dozen half women, as with D. H. Lawrence; or, if she is there, she may stand out of sight smiling to herself while her man proclaims his independence.

America may yet be made great by its women, when once we have finally freed ourselves from Europe and found what we mean by equality. For, without design, America is in the midst of the greatest experiment yet undertaken, the experiment—experience rather—that will put woman in her place, by the side of man as an equal.

Men are poets, women are scientists. But women are poets too. They create, but they know, as men do not, the limits of creation. They work, as men will not, within the context of nature. It is no accident that pragmatism was stated first in America. The humanists, being men, have made a mess of things. The scientists, being men, have made a greater mess. It is time now for the scientific poet, the poetic scientist. It is time for the woman.

I have known well the wives of two artists, and they are like in that they know better than their husbands what the artist in husband is trying to do. Socrates went to the poets and asked them what they were up to, and how they did it. He should have asked their wives. When Stella Adamic reads a manuscript, she knows what the writer meant to say, better than he knows himself. She has often said to me, when we were talking about some book, "John, if he had only done this. Here was his book and he didn't see it," and there it was.

After tea, on that first day, Louis said he must be getting along. I said he should stay the night. He stayed, and other nights, until there were two weeks of them, and then two months. I remember the nights, for it was then that I had to work. Louis took a cottage in the village and came up at night with a list of questions, to be answered by me before the next night. What was the college trying to do, and how? That was the burden, and I spent many late hours trying to answer. At the end of that time he sent to *Harper's Magazine* a manuscript which was published under the title of "Education on a Mountain." In the same issue Bernard De Voto, who had been born in Utah and hated the word community as intensely as I the Methodist Church, let loose a blast in the "Editor's Easy Chair," which was, for once, not that.

But before the manuscript was sent to the magazine, it was read before a general meeting of the college. It said, "You have a leader and here he is," the wrongest thing that could have been said. Louis did not say, "The leader is everything," though he might as well. He paid tribute to others, some by name, others by implication, but the damage was done. I, without knowing what I was doing, had kept the secret, had let every one, from the greenest freshman to the oldest and best teacher, believe that he was it; had tried deliberately to make the college what I thought a democracy should be, and I was on the way to succeeding. But I was also hungry for recognition, for praise. Webb School, Nebraska, N.J.C., Rollins, all had called me a fool and were glad when I was gone. I knew that discipleship, while maybe, almost certainly, necessary for a time, was in the end wrong, and not only for what it did to the disciple. And yet, when I foresaw my name in print, saw the words "great teacher," I became not even a teacher.

There were protests, in the meeting and afterward, but I paid no attention. The protestants became, not my best friends but my dearest enemies. I stood out for publication, and had stopping reasons: the college had, without inviting it, been written about and pictured, but only in part, and that was not enough. In spite of praise, we could not get enough students to pay expenses, and the prospect for the coming year was no better. This, I argued, would make the college.

It did. Louis's piece was republished in the *Reader's Digest* and we were flooded with letters for months; even at the end of three years they were still coming, at the last from sailors who were catching up on their reading and from inmates of prisons, who saw in the college the thing they wanted.

But it was to be my undoing. Not yet, however. I had to come full circle, from nothing back to nothing, and now I was on the farther rim. Louis had quoted me. I began to quote myself, sure sign of decay. I would wait and let my fellows catch up. They did.

There are moments in a man's life when everything comes suddenly into focus. This may happen when he is on the mountain; then he will find that he has wings, but he will not ask who gave them to him; that question must wait. It also may happen, and does happen, when he is down in the valley, when he will indulge in what the Catholics in their wisdom call the "sin of remorse," and look for a cause, the one thing that was the cause, alike of his soaring and his wingless state. "There must have been one thing that caused this," he will say to himself, and try to find that thing. It is useless, this quest; for life is a texture, a context, in which all thoughts and colors are at once cause and effect. "I have always been lonely," a man will say to himself, and find the beginning of his loneliness in one moment; but it will not be the beginning that he will find, it will be recognition. When he is happy, that is, when he is whole, he asks no questions; they come when he is divided, within himself and within time, between the now and the then. I could make a catalogue of ills, beginning with the alien drugget on the floor of a Methodist parsonage and ending never, but it would be foolish, needing for completion a like catalogue of goods, which I cannot make, for happiness leaves no scars.

In the spring of 1938 I went, on the insistence of my colleagues, to Charleston, a place unvisited by the philosopher who said that all things change. I rented a cottage on the beach, where, alone or in the companionship of George Grice, a liberated South Carolinian, I found anew the meaning of an old expression, "to the marrow of my bones." I was that tired. But the restless sea does something to me: it takes away my restlessness. The endless marshes, too, do something. When I was living in Florida I spent entire days sitting, fishing rod in hand, waiting, not for a strike, though a strike was welcome excitement, but for peace. I chose a spot for anchoring my boat, a spot that gave no evidence that man had ever been there, or ever been. The wild ducks flew over and clattered the mangrove shoots with their wings, and the pelicans called me a fool; but the marshes said it made no difference, and I believed them. So the marshes had spoken to Sidney Lanier, and so they spoke to me in the back reaches of Charleston's Folly Beach. I began to see, but slowly and with reluctance, that I must live apart from people, for their good and mine. A teacher should bring peace. That was what I began to see.

Later, about the first of May, I drove in my car to Milford, in New Jersey, to the home of Louis and Stella. There I sat until Louis said, with peremptory impatience, "Look here, John, you've got to do something. You can't just sit." I was tempted to retort, "Oh can't I? I've been sitting all my life," but I knew that was not the moment. I asked, instead, "What shall I do?" He was waiting for that. "Write," he said. "What?" I asked. "Anything, just so you write. Haven't you got anything to say?" "Yes," I said, "but I've said it all a thousand times." That was the beginning of the argument, but I was halfhearted; I knew how it would end.

I had not merely sat all those years: I had sat and talked, but talking is not writing. I took paper and pencil and went upstairs to become a writer. At the end of a week I had completed the first chapter of this book, some eight typewritten pages. When I showed them to Louis he read and said, "Pretty good notes. Now write it." Stella, a different kind of disciplinarian, read the completed chapter and said, "Look,

John, this is what you are trying to do." How did she know? I don't know how she knew, any more than I know how Keats knew what a stubble field meant.

The story of the next two years must await its telling until tempers have cooled and hearts healed. Athens, a pure democracy, had a device. Black Mountain, a pure democracy, used it, but the name was changed to "leave of absence." Ostracism, by any name, I reminded myself, was very old, but so is heartache, even older.

Man on the mountain knows all the answers; man in the valley knows none. I am writing this on a warm day in April in the year 1942, sitting in a steamer chair on the terrace of a log cabin in northern New Jersey. A mountain, small, but large enough for the name, rises behind me, and the valley runs down below, its little stream just visible through the bare trees. I am half way down, and half way up.

If I had my life to live over again, if I had to, and there were no choice—if there were, I should beg to be excused—but if the answer should be, "No, you must choose," I should choose to be a hardware merchant in Nebraska, where rust corrupts not, and thieves do not break through and steal. I still think a chisel is the most beautiful thing in the world.

But that would be for my later years, say past forty. For the rest, I should choose to be born in South Carolina in the eighteenth century. That would have to be in Charleston, for the rest is nineteenth, but I should be content, provided I should not be born a gentleman; and, if there is any justice, even a sense of fitness, I should not. For father I should want again a man of God.

I should choose the eighteenth century for its violence, yet touched with grace; for its near escape from Catholicism, while keeping the catholic view, everything in one and one in everything, without the impost of piety; for its long, clockless days; for its child's world for children; for its passionate belief that the world would be better, perhaps tomorrow;

for old ladies who were queens compared to whom Victoria was a scullery maid; for curds, fresh cane syrup, cracklings hot out of the pot, rain on the roof and the roof of split shingles, quilts, mud chimneys cracked from the heat of light 'ood knots, muzzle-loaders, calico, firecrackers at Christmas, puppies; for its simple faith in simple words, justice, freedom, happiness; and belief in the rights of man, and faith in man.

AFTERWORD

Too Much Socrates, Not Enough Jesus

William Craig Rice

It should come as no surprise to readers of *I Came Out of the Eighteenth Century* that John Andrew Rice's unstinting candor came at great cost to him in his professional and personal life. Yet that candor also appears to have kept him remarkably honest about the deeds and details of his life—and his shortcomings—when he set out to write his autobiography, a genre not always given to strict verity. There are few corrections to record in matters of known or proven fact, as Katherine Chaddock Reynolds notes in her well-researched biography, *Visions and Vanities: John Andrew Rice of Black Mountain College,* published by Louisiana State University Press in 1998. Even so, objections and complaints were raised when Rice's memoir appeared in print. One objection proved fatal to the book's future—and, it seems fair to say, contributed to the loss of a trenchant voice in American life.

Some objections to the book were trivial, or seem so today. The Rollins College faculty member who held the "Professorship of Books" protested Rice's lampooning of his position and belittling his accomplishments as a journalist and publisher. A second Rollins colleague disputed Rice's claim that her class on "Evil" had met but once, to have a picture taken. William R. ("Son Will") Webb challenged the portrait of his father, Old Sawney, noting among other things that Rice's students at the Webb School had fared poorly in algebra. William H. Smith, a cousin on Rice's mother Annabelle's side of the family, asserted that John Andrew could not have been born in the "middle bedroom" at Tanglewood Plantation because there was no such room. Having visited Tanglewood, I can testify that the cousin was right: the original upstairs floor plan of this Greek Revival structure consists of quadrants marking off four bedrooms along a center hall breezeway. But Rice was also right: one bedroom leads to a rear wing added later, and this was known by family as "the middle bedroom."

But one protest was powerful enough to cause the suppression of *I Came Out of the Eighteenth Century* by the publisher, Harper and Brothers. Hamilton Holt, president of Rollins College and the central figure in the ninth chapter, had his attorney notify Harper of an imminent libel suit. Rice urged a fight all the way to court if necessary, noting that success was augured by the censure of Rollins College by the American Association of University Professors following Rice's termination and his vindication in the AAUP's published report on the case. One author of the report was Arthur O. Lovejoy of Johns Hopkins University, cofounder with John Dewey of the AAUP and a towering academic figure of the era. If the AAUP report could be seen a precedent, it was favorable. (Dewey would go on to become Rice's close friend and serve on the advisory board of Black Mountain College.)

In retrospect, the publisher's timidity seems out of character. Harper and its namesake magazine had a record of facing down threats, as recounted in *The House of Harper,* by Eugene Exman (1967), who describes senior editor Eugene F. Saxton's courage in a standoff with a conservative advertiser. In fact, Rice had handily rebutted a libel threat by his aforementioned Smith cousin. In a "Protest" letter in *Harper's Magazine* in 1939, after a chapter of *I Came Out of the Eighteenth Century* was published there, Smith challenged Rice's claim that their uncle, U.S. Senator Ellison Durant ("Cotton Ed") Smith of South Carolina, trumpeted "the white man's sacred right to lynch." Rice insisted that he had "made no willful mis-statements of fact." In his published "Reply," he observed that if his cousin had been in the Senate gallery on April 16, 1935, he would have heard their uncle unambiguously defending lynching—and he quoted at damning length from the *Congressional Record.* Cousin Smith's lawsuit never came to pass.

The publisher's timidity seems even stranger given that the firm had laid an important stake in *I Came Out of the Eighteenth Century*. It had run the first five chapters in monthly editions of *Harper's Magazine* from November 1938 to January 1942, then launched the book in November 1942. The firm had chosen it for its Harper 125th Anniversary Prize. Rice's autobiography had garnered critical acclaim in large-circulation newspapers, including two reviews in the *New York Times,* and in the dominant newsweeklies of the era. *Time* characterized Rice as "a stormy petrel [and] brilliant critic"; *Newsweek* called him "a skilled and deadly writer." The book drew praise in influential periodicals, including *Commonweal, The New Yorker,* and *The New Republic,* where Malcolm Cowley, one the foremost critics of his day, declared that "Mr. Rice writes superbly," especially "in the first brilliant chapters of *I Came Out of the Eighteenth Century.*" Harriet Sampson commended the book to the readers of *The Nation:* "The judges of the Harper Award have done well to indicate the literary value of this desperately honest attempt at self-analysis. A gift of perception, so acute that it notices whether the whole face tells the same story as the eyes, is joined to a gift for words. One can well believe that oratory was a perfected art in the South. It is here again, vigorous, persuasive, and epigrammatic." The book received approving notices in academic quarterlies as well—for example, in *Phylon,* published at the historically black Clark Atlanta University, and in *The Journal of Negro History.*

Nevertheless Harper and Brothers capitulated to Holt and discontinued sales of the second printing only seven months after book's auspicious debut. (A family story I cannot verify is that the sudden illness and death of Eugene F. Saxton left the book without its most effective in-house champion against Holt's threats.) The volume dropped from sight, in time becoming an item for rare book collectors.

In the intervening years, there have been few discussions, treatments, or notices of the book—an unhappy consequence given its literary distinction and historical significance. Such attention as it has received has come from historians of Black Mountain College. Rice had not intended to write about Black Mountain, evidently for fear of harming the nascent college, but he agreed to do so at the insistence of Harper's editors. In this final chapter,

Rice adopts a markedly different style, as reviewers at the time observed. He becomes uncharacteristically restrained, largely omitting unpleasant details and the names of friends and adversaries, but also invokes a well-nigh visionary vocabulary as he articulates the institution's purposes.

Given the spare history that Rice provides in the final chapter, a few facts and observations may be in order for readers unacquainted with Black Mountain College. In 1933–34, the academic year following his firing by Hamilton Holt, Rice and his compatriots from Rollins founded the college in western North Carolina, not far from Asheville. It was to become the first American college—and seemingly the last—to place the creative arts fully on par with the liberal arts and offer intensive study in both realms for all students. It would exercise complete self-government, without a board of trustees—establishing education for democracy by practicing democracy in education. Black Mountain College rarely numbered more than a hundred souls, but during its twenty-four years (1933–57) it gave shelter to a stunning roster of artistic and intellectual pioneers, most before they achieved fame. When it opened in the autumn of 1933, Rice heeded the urging of friends in New York and provided the first safe harbor in the United States for German artists and academicians fleeing Hitler's Third Reich. A short list of faculty and students includes painters Josef Albers, Jacob Lawrence, Willem de Kooning, and Robert Rauschenberg, ceramicist Karen Carnes, poets Robert Creeley and Charles Olson, dancer Merce Cunningham, writer Francine du Plessix Gray, inventor Buckminster Fuller, mathematician Max Dehn, architect Walter Gropius, critics Clement Greenberg and Alfred Kazin, film director Arthur Penn, and composers Lou Harrison and Roger Sessions. Many of these figures came to Black Mountain after Rice's years, but he was credited by Olson and others with establishing a congenial environment for innovators and mavericks. Yet even at the college that embodied his vision, Rice proved too troublesome a presence; after only seven years, he was forced out in 1940. In the 1937–38 academic year, he had begun convening writing seminars, to which he contributed early drafts of the first chapters of *I Came Out of the Eighteenth Century*. Without realizing it, he had started his second career as an author.

The suppression of his first book, five years in the making, came as a grievous loss to John Andrew Rice, especially after the disappointment of Black Mountain. It also deprived general readers of American autobiography of a distinctive voice during a period of literary and cultural ferment in the South. In a 1920 essay entitled "The Sahara of the Bozart," H. L. Mencken, the iconoclastic Sage of Baltimore, had derided the region below the Mason-Dixon Line as a cultural wasteland. (Although Rice referred to Mencken as "born and bred in limbo," he enjoyed Mencken's writings in *The Smart Set* and shared the journalist's irreligion in general and lively distaste for Puritanism in particular.) As the scholar Fred Hobson has written, southern writers soon took up the gauntlet that Mencken had thrown down. Their greatest achievements came in fiction—William Faulkner, Ralph Ellison, Flannery O'Connor—but memoirists contributed as well. William Alexander Percy's *Lanterns on the Levee: Recollections of a Planter's Son* achieved a large readership in 1941. Zora Neale Hurston, whom Rice befriended while living in Florida, came out with *Dust Tracks on the Road* in 1942. The same year brought *Red Hills and Cotton: An Upcountry Memory,* by Ben Robertson, a title included in the Southern Classics series along with this volume. Richard Wright's semi-autobiographical *Black Boy* appeared in 1945. Soon two white women added to the impressive corpus, describing among other things how they came to reject the biological or scientific racism (as we call it today) they had absorbed in youth: Katharine DuPre Lumpkin in *The Making of a Southerner* in 1947, and Lillian Smith in *Killers of the Dream* in 1949.

Rice's autobiography fits well in this broader company. The new southern authors, both black and white, rejected the doctrine of white supremacy—Wright by direct political challenge, Hurston by thick description of African American folkways, Lumpkin and Smith by calling attention to systemic assaults by whites on the dignity of African Americans—especially women subjected to white men's sexual predation. Yet as Mark Bauerlein notes in his introduction, Rice let no party—or race—off easy. He does not elevate, at least not by much, the African American victims over their white oppressors. In *I Came Out of the Eighteenth Century* and in his later short stories, he depicted ceremonies and habits of daily life rather than titanic struggles, nonverbal communication rather than noisy confrontation, pyrrhic victories and defeats. In this he bears some resemblance to Hurston in her anthropologist's sensitivity to quotidian details, to nuances easily overlooked, as well as in the free and appreciative use of Black English Vernacular for its rich expressiveness.

It is interesting to speculate on what would have happened if Harper and Brothers had stood by *I Came Out of the Eighteenth Century* and allowed the book to earn its author a more commanding place in American letters and intellectual life. Rice already enjoyed standing as a sharp critic of American education, and his book could only have advanced that at a time when educational progressivism was consolidating its hold on the teaching profession. Because of Black Mountain and his friendship with John Dewey, Rice was widely and favorably identified as a progressive educator himself, but he had always been skeptical of the movement's scientific pretensions and bureaucratizing tendencies. With the painful dissection of the bad and heady celebration of the good in teaching in *I Came Out of the Eighteenth Century,* Rice could have challenged advocates of progressivism in the crucial 1940s and 1950s, especially since he willingly named names, as Dewey did not. And in realms of higher education and the arts, Rice's role at Black Mountain was not forgotten as the college's star continued to rise. In 1947, the faculty considered asking him to return to lead the college again, partly on the grounds of his success as a writer.

On the larger national scale, the suppression of Rice's memoir occurred just as the Civil Rights Movement was beginning. In the wake of World War II, the nation needed thoughtful presentations of social conditions in the South, not stereotypes and half-knowledge. Rice could have stood as an independent, informed observer of the troubled region, neither Democrat nor Republican, white supremacist nor black sentimentalist. He had, after all, proved a foil to his famously bigoted uncle, Senator Cotton Ed Smith, and written for *Common Ground,* a liberal political magazine that promoted racial progress. He submitted a book proposal to Harper on Pitchfork Ben

Tillman, a new breed of Southern racist politician that he savages in *I Came Out of the Eighteenth Century,* but Harper grew chary of support after the memoir's debacle.

Although some passages on African Americans in his autobiography grate on our ears today, Rice's thinking was, like his father's, in the vanguard of his time. The elder Rice crossed racial lines as early as 1907 to speak at Tuskegee, where Booker T. Washington "considered Rice among the few liberal southern clergymen on the race question." His son similarly thumbed his nose at local prejudice when he crossed racial lines and had Zora Neale Hurston to dinner at his campus home and set the table on the front porch for all his neighbors to see. (This was reported to me by Maurice O'Sullivan, a Rollins College professor, based on his work in college archives.)

What *I Came Out of the Eighteenth Century* could have offered the nation is a clear-eyed understanding of race relations and class relations up close, an understanding that Americans outside the South could not achieve on their own. Northerners, Midwesterners, and Westerners saw the South through the example of Strom Thurmond, Cotton Ed's successor, who ran for President in 1948 on an avowedly racist third-party platform, and later through images of George Wallace at the schoolhouse door. These figures were all too real as headline material but not representative of the struggles of daily life. Largely missing was a fine-grained account of the effects of slavery and Jim Crow such as Rice offered—the scornful laughter of white bill collectors preying on black households; the worn-out land, meager diet, and enduring economic depression that demoralized both races, including even the more prosperous whites; the "shiftlessness" of African Americans that Rice saw as a complex and understandable reaction to the hopelessness of any effort at self-improvement; and the tense rivalries of blacks and poor whites.

Still, Rice's views were those of a gradualist, as Bauerlein rightly notes. If he seriously considered the merits of racial integration at Black Mountain (an unusually advanced position in the 1930s), he was also mindful of Hurston's own opposition to the 1954 *Brown v. Board of Education* decision—specifically her defense of the integrity of African American culture; and by the turbulent 1960s he saw grave dangers posed alike by white reactionaries and black militants. Martin Duberman, whose treatment of Rice in *Black Mountain: An Experiment in Community* is perceptive if unsympathetic, observed of his racial views: "Perhaps what Rice said . . . about Jefferson is applicable to himself: 'Jefferson did the best he could within the thinking of his day, as you and I do within the thinking of our day.' In fact, Rice was better on the race question than the 'thinking of his day,' though that thinking did set severe boundaries—and he adhered to them."

After the suppression of *I Came Out of the Eighteenth Century*, Rice began writing fiction, mostly about black-white relations. Starting in 1943, he published a few short stories each year—first through an exclusive with *The New Yorker*, later in *Collier's*—into the mid-1950s. (Several stories were collected in *Local Color* in 1955.) These stories combine shrewd social observations and rejection of biological racism, traits found in various passages in his autobiography. His correspondence with literary agents and editors shows that he had his eye very much on the national civil rights scene and intended his stories to deepen his readers' understanding of the dynamics between the races and social classes of the South. In fact the stories increasingly allow African Americans to control the narrative and exhibit greater depth of character than the whites, over whom they quietly enjoy small triumphs. One story, "You Can Get Just So Much Justice," from *Collier's* in 1949, won the annual prize of the Bureau for Intercultural Education. The Bureau—"For Understanding, Cooperation and National Unity Among the Cultural Groups in America"—included in its masthead the anthropologist Ruth Benedict, philosopher Alain Locke (the first African American Rhodes Scholar), and "Mrs. Franklin D. Roosevelt."

As John Andrew Rice reached his seventies, he wrote less and less and mellowed greatly. He had remarried soon after the publication of *I Came Out of the Eighteenth Century* and raised a second family—a son, Peter, and a daughter, Elisabeth. His second wife, Dikka Moen Rice, like her husband an avid reader, was credited by family members with inspiring him to finish his memoir and keep up his modest output of short stories. But with the suppression of his single magnum opus and the disappointment of Black Mountain, he never again was offered, nor did he seek, a place in the limelight. Temperamentally well-suited to retirement, he planted a large vegetable garden that others, such as his grandchildren, should weed while picking raspberries, cucumbers, and cauliflower. He read voraciously, accumulating so many books that the stairs served as vertical shelves. He penned a few dozen pages of bittersweet memoirs of Black Mountain College that eventually found their way into an anthology, *Black Mountain College: Sprouted Seeds, An Anthology of Personal Accounts*, edited by Mervin Lane for the University of Tennessee Press in 1990. A neighboring virtuoso, Helen McGraw, gave piano recitals of Rice's favorites Bach and Beethoven; her husband Robert Chambers painted Rice's portrait. The Rices entertained family and friends over well-prepared dinners from the garden, the conversation enlivened by amusing oft-told stories, many of them found in the present volume. I particularly remember how in his last year he bent over a story I had written, puffing on his ever-present pipe, and encouraged me in his mellifluous South Carolina accent to keep at it. He told me to save anything I wrote for at least a few years because, no matter how bad I might later judge it to be, there was something there that I needed to write, and it was from that material that I could become an artist. The story of his later years, as of his whole life, is intelligently chronicled by Katherine Chaddock Reynolds. (Disclosure: I served on the faculty committee for her dissertation, which was an early draft of the Rice biography.)

Now, after seven decades of silence, readers may to get to know John Andrew Rice by his own account, in his cleverly crafted prose; in his liberating and painful honesty, not least about himself; in his respect for the young and suspicion of convention; in his gift for provocation and his personal warmth; and in his belief that we deserve a chance to become artists—another chance, if we have failed—as we strive to create, each of us, our own worlds. Those of us who knew him can attest, as was sometimes remarked, that John Andrew Rice was "too much Socrates, not enough Jesus." But as the Athenian said to the jury that condemned him, you will not easily find another.

SOURCES FOR FURTHER EXPLORATION

Adamic, Louis. "Education on a Mountain." In *My America* by Louis Adamic. New York: Harper & Brothers, 1938.

Duberman, Martin. *Black Mountain: An Exploration in Community*. Evanston: Northwestern University Press, 2009. First published 1972 by E. P. Dutton.

Harris, Mary Emma. *The Arts at Black Mountain College*. Cambridge: MIT Press, 1987.

Katz, Vincent, editor. *Black Mountain: Experiment in Art*. Cambridge: MIT Press, 2002.

Lane, Mervin. *Black Mountain College: Sprouted Seeds—An Anthology of Personal Accounts*. Knoxville: University of Tennessee Press, 1990.

Reynolds, Katherine Chaddock. *Visions and Vanities: John Andrew Rice of Black Mountain*. Baton Rouge: Louisiana State University Press, 1998.

Rice, John Andrew. *Local Color*. Foreword by Erskine Caldwell. New York: Dell, 1955.

Zommer, Cathryn Davis, and Neely Dawson. *Fully Awake: Black Mountain College*. Documentary Film. Ashville, N.C.: Danu Collaborative, 2007; expanded edition, 2014.